# THE OGLALA PEOPLE, 1841–1879

# The Oglala People, 1841–1879

## A Political History

CATHERINE PRICE

University of Nebraska Press

Lincoln and London

Portions of chapters 1 and 2 were
previously published as
Catherine Price, "Lakotas and
Euroamericans: Contrasted Concepts
of 'Chieftainship' and Decision-
Making Authority," *Ethnohistory*
41, no. 3 (summer 1994). Copyright American
Society for Ethnohistory, 1994.
Reprinted with permission.

⊗ The paper in this book meets
the minimum
requirements of American National
Standard for
Information Sciences—Permanence
of Paper
for Printed Library Materials,
ANSI Z39.48-1984.

First paperback printing: 1998

Library of Congress Cataloging
in Publication Data
Price, Catherine, [date]
The Oglala people, 1841–1879: a political history / Catherine Price.
p.   cm.
Includes bibliographical references and index.
ISBN 0-8032-3710-3 (cloth: alk. paper)
ISBN 0-8032-8758-5 (pa: alk. paper)
1. Oglala Indians—Politics and government.   2. Oglala Indians—History—19th
century—Sources.   3. Oglala Indians—Government relations.   4. Chiefdoms—
Great Plains—History—19th century.   5. Political leadership—Great Plains—
History—19th century.   I. Title.
E99.O3P75   1996
978'.004975—dc20
95-23153   CIP

To the memory of the Oglala elders

who honored James Walker
and Eli Ricker
with the generous gift
of their knowledge and trust

# Contents

# Illustrations

# Preface

In the latter half of the nineteenth century, the United States government, through its agents, superintendents, and commissioners, endeavored to reshape Lakota society in accordance with American ideals. Part of this policy of acculturation included periodic efforts to modify or undermine the political customs of the Lakota people and to erode the decision-making authority of tribal leaders. By synthesizing archival sources, ethnographic and historical works, and transcribed interviews conducted with Oglala Lakota elders from 1896 to the 1930s, I endeavor in this book to present the various political strategies employed by Oglala councilors as they struggled to preserve their political customs and autonomy in their ongoing relations with the United States. This study thus examines Lakota concepts of leadership and decision-making authority, highlighting the fluid political relationship among the several forms of Oglala leadership, such as the *itancan* (symbolic fathers of bands or *tiyospaye*), headmen, and warriors.

Furthermore, I demonstrate that Oglala leaders participating in *tiyospaye* and multiband councils over the years expressed numerous opinions regarding their political relations, not just with American officials but also with other Lakota bands and subtribes whose leaders, most notably Crazy Horse, resoundingly rejected diplomatic accords with the United States. From the late 1860s through the 1870s, federal emissaries frequently regarded the Oglala Bad Face leader Red Cloud as the archetypal "head chief" of the Sioux, thereby downplaying the political and diplomatic influence of other Oglala men, such as Man Afraid of His Horse, Red Dog, Blue Horse, and Little Wound. Moreover, historians George Hyde and James C. Olson in their respective works, *Red Cloud's Folk: A History of the Oglala Sioux* and *Red Cloud and the Sioux Problem,* have largely sustained this image of Red Cloud. In contrast, the current study strives to illuminate an Oglala concept of "chieftainship" by reassessing Red Cloud's political status, roles, and objectives in relation to those of his council and agency peers.

The time frame selected for this book, 1841 to 1879, reflects an Oglala perspective. The Oglalas faced a major political upheaval in 1841 when Bull Bear, a prominent *itancan* and holy man, was murdered during an intratribal quarrel. In the wake of his death, the Oglalas divided into two major sociopolitical factions—the Bear people and the Smoke people. A number of scholars, including distinguished historian Robert Utley, author of *The Last Days of the Sioux Nation,* consider the Wounded Knee Massacre of 1890 as the occasion that best symbolizes the destruction of Lakota lifeways. Yet I view the year 1877, when Crazy Horse was killed in an army prison cell at Fort Robison, as an earlier and more powerful harbinger of momentous change in the lives of the Oglala people, and specifically in their political customs. Crazy Horse and his followers chose war to counter persistent American efforts to settle all the Lakotas on the Great Sioux Reservation; and, for the most part, American officials regarded the Crazy Horse faction as a significant military force and a threat to Oglala-American diplomacy. After suffering a major defeat at the Little Bighorn in June of 1876, the United States Army launched a sustained and ultimately successful campaign against those Lakotas who had steadfastly rejected agency life. Hungry, cold, and ill-supplied, the last of the Oglala warrior camps had surrendered to American forces by the spring of 1877. Crazy Horse's murder in the fall of that year, persistent white encroachment on Lakota lands, and the perceptible loss of the buffalo herds finally forced Oglala councilors to abandon war as a viable strategy and to fully embrace diplomacy in its stead. Thus the end of the 1870s marked a major turning point in the political affairs of the Oglalas, as the Oglalas' concepts of leadership and their decision-making processes would thereafter undergo significant modifications.

The manuscript collection of James Walker, a government physician who lived with the Oglalas at Pine Ridge Reservation from 1896 to 1914, is a rich and important source for understanding the Oglalas' own views of their social and political customs.[1] Initially concerned with using his knowledge of Western medicine to combat tuberculosis at Pine Ridge, Walker developed a sincere respect for Oglala healers and holy men. Indeed, what began as a professional duty to the reservation community soon became a desire to understand and record the Oglalas' sacred ways and customs. During the 1980s, scholars Raymond DeMallie and Elaine Jahner collected, edited, and published Walker's papers in three volumes, *Lakota Belief and Ritual, Lakota Society,* and *Lakota Myth. Lakota Society,* a collection of thirty-one interviews with Oglala elders, is the single most important work for understanding the Oglalas' prereservation political customs, containing, as editor DeMallie writes, "some of the most reliable information ever recorded on the subject" and presenting "the words of Oglalas directly."[2]

Oglala elders and holy men, such as American Horse, Little Wound, Bad Wound, Bad Bear, Iron Tail, John Blunt Horn, Finger, Short Bull, Red Feather, Red Cloud, and George Sword, feared that their knowledge of traditional Lakota customs would die with them unless it was preserved "through the medium of writing."[3] Over the years, the elders came to respect and trust Walker, regarding him as a relative rather than as an outsider. Eventually, after weeks of careful deliberation and vision seeking, the elders and holy men agreed to devote many hours to Walker's instruction, honoring the doctor by entrusting him with the wealth of their knowledge and eventually inducting him into the Buffalo Society of healers.

Walker received considerable assistance in his ethnographic pursuits. As the physician was not fluent in the Lakota language, he relied upon several interpreters to overcome the language barrier: Charles and Richard Nines, licensed Indian traders at Pine Ridge who were of white and Mohawk heritage; Thomas Tyon (Gray Goose), a mixed-blood Oglala whom the elders trusted; and George Sword, the former captain of Indian police at Pine Ridge. In addition to interpreting for Walker, these associates contributed to the project by conducting fieldwork among the reservation communities, translating texts and writing their own descriptions of Lakota customs. Sword told Walker, "I have learned to write in Lakota, but I write as the old Lakota spoke when they talked in a formal manner. . . . I will write of the old customs and ceremonies for you. I will write that which all the people knew." Walker greatly appreciated Sword's efforts. In a 1910 letter to Clark Wissler, who was sponsoring the doctor's work among the Oglalas, Walker stated, "I have now, in addition to the manuscript by Sword which I showed you, about 250 pages additional, all relative to the customs and ceremonies of the Oglala Sioux, written by Sword, without suggestion by white influence."[4]

During his years of gathering information, Walker strove to be objective and "to know the Indian from the Indian point of view." More specifically, he decided to produce syntheses of Oglala political customs "as though they were written by an Oglala attempting to compile a consensus account of his people's aboriginal lifeway."[5] This point is important, as the elders at times disagreed on the finer details.

In addition to the Walker documents, I have consulted other interviews with Oglalas conducted and recorded by Judge Eli Ricker of Nebraska during the early 1900s, along with letters written by or about Oglala people to the author Stanley Vestal, the pseudonym of Professor Walter Stanley Campbell. Many of the Ricker manuscripts are available on microfilm from the Nebraska State Historical Society, in Lincoln; those of W. S. Campbell are held at the Western History Collection of the University of Oklahoma, Norman.

The Walker, Ricker, and Campbell collections all contain information provided by Oglala authorities. Also available are the numerous "sighting" reports of Europeans and Euro-Americans who contacted the Lakota and Dakota people through the centuries. The *Jesuit Relations* contain Sioux tribal names as early as the 1640s; by 1660, French explorers Pierre Esprit Radisson and Medard Chouart had encountered Dakota camps in what is now northwestern Wisconsin and eastern Minnesota. By the early eighteenth century, Pierre Gaultier de Varennes de la Verendrye and his sons had charted the Sioux tribal domain from Green Bay westward to the Mississippi River. For over two hundred years, other observers penned descriptive accounts of the Sioux, leaving for posterity a number of reports ranging from fleeting observations to detailed accounts of Sioux tribal divisions, population statistics, village leaders, tribal domains, and the occasional council. These observers included missionaries Louis Hennepin, Pierre-Jean DeSmet, and Stephen Riggs, who visited Fort Pierre in 1840 to collect information on the Lakotas; explorers, adventurers, and military men like Prince Maximilian of Weid, Meriwether Lewis, William Clark, Zebulon Pike, Stephen Long, Joseph Nicollet, and Percival Lowe; and fur traders Jean Baptiste Truteau, Pierre-Antoine Tabeau, Joshua Pilcher, and Rufus Sage.[6]

Using the Walker, Ricker, and Campbell collections as well as other published and archival ethnographic materials, I have produced my own reconstructions of Oglala political customs. Furthermore, I have tested whenever possible the efficacy of my reconstructions by examining the historical writings of those individuals, such as the ones listed above, who observed Oglala customs through the years. For instance, around 1850 Percival Lowe, an American soldier, recalled the hospitality bestowed upon him during an unplanned visit to the lodge of a Lakota "etoncha."[7] Lowe's *etoncha* is clearly an *itancan,* the Lakota word for a symbolic band father, or chief, whose duties included providing food and shelter for visitors and the needy.

Also pertinent to this study are selected records of the Office of Indian Affairs and the United States Army; these records are housed at the National Archives and Records Service in Washington DC and its regional branch in Kansas City, Missouri. These materials contain considerable information on the numerous councils held between American officials and delegated Oglala spokesmen.

The words of nineteenth-century Oglala leaders contained in the historical record have come to us through the varied skills of primarily mixed-blood interpreters, such as Joseph Bissonette. The accuracy of their translations will never be fully ascertained, of course. We cannot determine how well council interpreters understood Lakota and English, nor can we discern from council minutes the participants' vocal inflections or body language that help to project sarcasm, irony, or anger. Despite these difficulties, archival documents provide a wealth of information that serve to complement the available oral testimonies.

In his article, "Indian-White Relations: A View from the Other Side of the 'Frontier,'" Tewa anthropologist Alfonso Ortiz challenged historians to present more "balanced and honest" histories of Indian-white interactions. "The kind of history of which I speak," Ortiz writes, "is one that recognizes that Indian people have always been multidimensional and fully sentient human beings." Furthermore, he believes that "there is a special futility in trying to deal with abstract Indians or Indianness." Rather, it "makes more sense to deal with particular tribes, confederacies, and bands," to cut through "a thick tangle of particular facts about particular peoples."[8] Heeding Ortiz's advice, it is my hope that this book presents Oglala leaders as active, vital, and committed individuals—men who had their own motives, plans, and agendas designed to protect their people and to preserve their political customs.

Many people have helped to make this study possible. At Purdue University my mentor and friend Professor Emeritus Donald Berthrong enthusiastically supported this project, as did my other instructors and friends Donald Parman, Oakah Jones, and Jack Waddell. I would also like to thank Raymond DeMallie at Indiana University and Florencia Mallon at the University of Wisconsin–Madison for their helpful suggestions during the completion of the book.

I appreciate the assistance of the professionals at the National Archives and National Anthropological Archives in Washington DC, especially Robert Kvasnicka and Michael Myers, and their colleagues at the National Archives branch in Kansas City, Missouri, particularly Mark Corriston. My gratitude also extends to Jeanne Smith of Oglala Lakota College for sharing with me her photocopied collection of materials on the killing of Crazy Horse.

I am also grateful for the financial support of a 1990 National Endowment for the Humanities Fellowship for University Teachers, a grant from the American Philosophical Society's Phillips Fund for Native American Studies, a Graduate Research Committee award from the University of Wisconsin–Madison, and a David Ross Research Fellowship at Purdue University.

Many relatives, in the true Oglala sense of the word, have enriched my life over the last few years, inspiring me to reconceptualize and finish this project. The Bobs have always offered tremendous encouragement for my work. Maggie Collum, Kristy Deetz, Gertie Holder, Cheryl Kalny, Diane Legomsky, Ramona Montoya, and Victoria Tashjian also provided unlimited humor and support. Where they go, so goes the Red Room. My thanks also to the Bear.

I am grateful for the kindness and support of my friends at Madison, especially Elizabeth Arbuckle, Barbara Elgutaa, Shannon Petersen Fouts, Teresita Garza, Michelle Greendeer, Don Hamm, Jeanne Lacourt, Kristina Lee, Amy Lonetree, Denise Peltier, Janet Saiz, Angi Sauk, Darlene St. Clair, Randy Tallmadge; and also that of everyone at Wunk Sheek, the American Indian Studies Program, and MEChA.

THE OGLALA PEOPLE, 1841–1879

# CHAPTER ONE

# The Sacred Hoop

Unmounted, with only dogs to pull their travois burdened with household trappings, the Lakotas or Western Sioux had reached by the early 1700s the eastern perimeter of the Great Plains, leaving behind their woodland relatives, the Santees. Well armed and confident, these Lakota pioneers had migrated westward in search of new riches—the beavers of the rivers and streams and the bison herds that grazed upon the open prairie west of the Mississippi River. *Tatanka,* the Lakotas' buffalo relatives, were the foundation of the Western Sioux way of life, providing almost everything the people needed from food to raw materials. Buffalo horns were fashioned into spoons and ladles, skulls were used in sacred ceremonies, and sinews became bow strings. Tanned buffalo hides provided soft and warm clothing, rawhide pouches, richly decorated lodge covers, and robes the Lakotas traded at posts dotted along the Upper Missouri River. By midcentury the Lakotas had acquired horses enabling them to hunt more efficiently, travel more extensively, and wage wars for territorial dominance. After 1750 the Lakotas became embroiled in a series of intertribal conflicts. Reeling from the impact of smallpox epidemics, the agricultural Arikaras, Mandans, and Hidatsas (Gros Ventres) of the Upper Missouri River were no match for the Sioux.[1]

Almost a century later, newspaper editor John O'Sullivan would coin the term *manifest destiny* to justify white expansion across the North American continent, railroad company propagandists would lure Europeans to the "Garden of Eden," and the westward trek of hopeful gold miners, land-hungry farmers, and ranchers would disrupt tribal hunting grounds. But until then, the Lakotas would establish themselves far beyond the eastern fringe of the prairie. Driving westward from the Missouri in the latter part of the eighteenth century, Lakota groups, with the Oglalas at the helm, reached the Black Hills, and the Yellowstone and

Platte River country. By the 1840s, Crows, Cheyennes, Poncas, and Pawnees had all fallen victim to Lakota war parties. Until this time, the sacred hoop (*cangleska wakan*)—the metaphor for Lakota society—was strong and unbroken.[2]

If danger lurked outside the circle, the people sought peace, prosperity, and cooperation within. In common with other Lakota subtribes (*ospaye*),[3] the Oglalas' daily life revolved around the *tiyospaye* (band), the principal social group that, while autonomous for most of the year, remained an integral part of the Teton tribe. The *tiyospaye* was commonly composed of ten or more bilaterally extended families; larger bands were divided into several camps (*wicoti*), which bore the name of the "parent" camp. The lodges (*tiognaka*) of the camp housed families of parents with children, and occasionally unmarried siblings and cousins. Each household knew its place within the camp circle, carefully reserving for the most revered families the place of honor opposite the entrance. Holy men (*wicasa wakan*), whose dreams and visions marked them as the Great Mystery's intermediaries, understood the sacred symbolism of the circle. All in nature was round, they observed—sun, moon, stars, rocks, and Yum the Whirlwind, the younger brother of the South Wind. Even humans and animals were "round." The circular lodges were microcosms of the universe, circles within ever larger circles. Thus to dwell in the circle was to live in the cosmic center, where earth's creatures communed with the divine forces. Ostracized families were forced to move their tipis outside the circle, a punishment that most Lakotas could scarcely bear.[4]

During one of their conversations, the holy man Black Elk demonstrated to Joseph Epes Brown the importance of the circle in Lakota worldviews. Brown was particularly moved by Black Elk's ability to interact with small children; for example, the holy man was fond of getting down on his hands and knees to become a horse that his little friends could ride. For that moment, Brown marveled, there was no generation gap. As Black Elk later explained to him, "I who am an old man am about to return to the Great Mysterious and a young child is a being who has just come from the Great Mysterious; so it is that we are very close together" on the circle of life.[5]

Kinship relationships and obligations served as the ordering principles of society as embodied in the Lakota password *Mitakuye oyasin*, "We are all related." Relationships spun outward like a giant web from the extended family to the band, to the *ospaye,* to the tribe, to the land, plants, insects, animals, to the universe, and to the Great Mystery. From the moment children could comprehend it, they were instructed that it was their duty throughout their lives to be a "good relative." The people recognized private ownership of property but loathed selfish hoarding of material wealth. Good relatives honored their families by redistributing wealth to those less fortunate. A mother who desired to honor her daughter might give away in her name a beautifully quilled or beaded robe to an orphan or an old widow. A father might show his affection for a dear friend by presenting a horse to a poor family. All were thus honored—givers and recipients alike. Such acts of generosity reinforced the lesson that kinship ties were more precious than tangible goods.[6]

Communalism provided comfort and security. Only the most shameful families withheld food from the hungry or unnecessarily exposed their kin to danger. But the constant companionship of such a lifestyle could be at the same time highly stressful, especially during the winter months when people spent long hours together with relatively little privacy. Over time, the Lakotas established customs to foster harmony and cooperation and to soothe frayed tempers. Of course, these customs were never entirely successful, but in many instances they were remarkably effective.

Kinship relationships, which were universally recognized and understood, shaped attitudes and behavior. So significant were they that few individuals could interact comfortably with strangers until a kinship connection had been established. Lakota kinship terminology was complex, reflecting gender, generation, and birth order. A younger brother addressed his older brother as *ciye*, who in turn called his younger sibling *misunkala*; but a woman referred to her older brother as *tiblo*, and her older sister as *cunwe*. Grandchildren called their maternal grandmother *onci*, or *oncisi*, and their maternal grandfather *tunkansi*. They addressed their paternal grandmother as *kunsi*, and their paternal grandfather as *tunkasila*. A woman called her husband *mihingna*; he in turn addressed her as *mitawicu*. Only rude and uncouth individuals addressed their relatives by their personal names.[7]

When a man married, his wife's mother immediately became, in white usage, his mother-in-law. Henceforth they could never look at or speak to each other without appearing disrespectful and ill-mannered. The same held true for the relationship between a young woman and her father-in-law. So powerful was this mutual avoidance taboo that parents claimed they were unable to identify their children's spouses.

A certain degree of formality also marked the bond between brothers and sisters. Upon reaching puberty, a young woman declined to sit close to her brother or to look at him intently. But she would demonstrate her love and respect by lavishing attention on his children. For his part, a man showed affection and respect for his sister by caring for her welfare. The bond between siblings of the same gender was much more informal. Men publicly expressed affection for their male siblings by gently teasing them and playing practical jokes, which also helped to minimize sibling rivalry. Sisters, who typically were particularly close, engaged in similar behavior. The Lakotas recognized polygynous unions, and as sisters might share the same husband, it was imperative that they devise ways to defuse explosive situations. "In-laws" of the same generation went to greater extremes in their teasing, indulging in sexually explicit or obscene joking. The *tiyospaye* fostered the levirate and sororate, thus this "obligatory" joking prepared young women and men for the very real possibility that one day they might marry the sibling of their deceased spouse.[8]

Lakotas also drew into their circle so-called fictive kin, people who were not related along either genetic or affinal lines. Indeed James Walker, physician at the Pine Ridge Reservation from 1896 to 1914, was instructed that residence within a *tiyospaye* rested primarily on personal choice and acceptance.[9] During the reservation period, the Oglalas, in common with other Native Americans, named their agents "father," thereby defining for them a kinship relationship. As long as agents accepted and used this honorific, they were expected to behave as good Lakota fathers would: as generous providers and protectors. Unlike the few white men whose affinal ties to the Oglalas enabled them to grasp the importance of the kinship obligation, most agents failed to comprehend the true significance of their unofficial title.

Some Oglalas were bound together in a very special relationship called *hunka*. Little Wound claimed that his father, Bull Bear, a prominent holy man and *itancan* (band chief) until his death in 1841, helped to establish this unique custom during the 1830s. Older and wealthier band members often requested permission from families to adopt ceremoniously some of their children or younger adults. George Sword, a holy man and one of Walker's friends and teachers, explained that "when Indians became of kin in this way, it was like kin by birth." Thunder Bear, another tribal elder, claimed that "sometimes one would go with the Hunka, and leave the blood relations." Those united in this venerable relationship vowed to protect and support their *hunka* even in the face of danger and personal privation. An older *hunka* might be so beloved that his *tiyospaye* addressed him as *mihunka,* a title signifying great respect.[10] Little Wound proudly stated that his father had been such a man to his people.[11]

Lakota behavioral rules, therefore, were well structured so that each member of the *tiyospaye,* male or female, old or young, blood related or not, learned from earliest childhood how to conduct himself or herself within the group. This system promoted peace and harmony within the *tiyospaye,* and those who left their camp circle to join another band knew precisely how to act with their new relatives. Once individuals accepted and used kin names such as grandfather, mother, or uncle, ideally they held moral obligations to conduct themselves according to the rules and customs of the band. Knowingly or not, white men who married Lakota women, and strangers who interacted in various ways with the *tiyospaye,* were also bound to this system.[12]

It was fortunate that kinship ties kept alive the sacred hoop in the people's hearts, for they could not always predict the dissolution of their own camp circle. Prereservation Lakota society was fluid and dynamic, characterized by the recurrent fusion and fission of bands. In the late 1830s, French geographer Joseph Nicollet noted three major Oglala bands: the Onkp'hatinas (Hunkpatilas), led by Yellow Eagle, perhaps the brother or cousin of Man Afraid of His Horse; the Ku-Inyan under Mad Dog; and the Oyurpe (Oyuhpe), headed by White Earrings. All three bands, Nicollet wrote, were of equal size—about one hundred lodges strong—and occupied the territory from the Black Hills to the Platte River country. Reservation elders later claimed there were seven traditional Oglala bands. In 1879 Reverend John Robinson, a Protestant Episcopal clergyman appointed missionary at the Pine Ridge Reservation, obtained a list of these *tiyospaye*: Ite Sica (Bad Face), Kiyuksa (Breaks His Own or Cut-Off), Oyuhpe (Thrown Down or Unloads), Payabya (Pushed Aside), Tapisleca (Spleen), Wazaza (Fringed or "Osage"), and Wagluhe (Loafers).[13]

For Europeans and Americans the origins of Sioux political organization are shrouded in mystery. Over the years, they have disagreed on whether the Ocetiyotipi Sakowin, the Seven Council Fires of the Sioux (Lakota and Dakota speakers), ever existed. Pierre Charles Le Sueur, a French fur trader, recorded ethnographic data pertaining to the Sioux between 1683 and 1701. In 1680 Robert Cavelier de La Salle sponsored an exploratory expedition from the Illinois River up the Mississippi River. Led by Michel Accault, the party included Father Louis Hennepin, who published his observations on the Sioux three years later. But no mention of the Seven Council Fires was included in their reports. Years later, in

1823, Maj. Stephen Long of the U.S. Topographical Engineers led a military and scientific expedition to explore the headwaters of the Minnesota River and the Red River of the North. Serving as the expedition's geologist was William Keating, professor of natural sciences at the University of Pennsylvania. During his journey, Keating recorded, and later published, ethnographic information on the Sioux of the region including population estimates, customs, hunting territories, and also a description of the Seven Council Fires. Keating concluded that the Ocetiyotipi Sakowin (the "Ochente Shakoan") once had been a political confederacy that inexplicably collapsed at some undetermined date.[14]

Sponsored by the U.S. government in the late 1830s, Nicollet retraced the steps of Keating and Long. Gathering valuable ethnographic information on Lakota subtribes, including customs, principal leaders, and tribal domains, Nicollet suggested the existence of a confederacy such as the Seven Council Fires. So did Peter Wilson, a former army lieutenant who became the Lakotas' first official resident subagent in the fall of 1824, and Paul Wilhelm, Duke of Württemberg, who lived for a brief time in a Sioux village.[15]

From a Lakota perspective the existence of the Ocetiyotipi Sakowin is unquestioned. Even today Lakotas state that the seven stars of the Big Dipper represent the tribes of the Seven Council Fires—the Lakotas, Mdewakantonwans, Wahpekutes, Wahpetonwans, Sisitonwans, Yanktons, and Yanktonais. Establishing themselves on the headwaters of the Mississippi River as early as the sixteenth century, members of the Seven Council Fires speak essentially the same language (with dialectical differences) and share similar customs and geographic origins. The available accounts of the Ocetiyotipi Sakowin do not clearly explain, however, how and why Lakota, and specifically Oglala, political institutions came into being. Thus the dedication of James Walker, Charles and Richard Nines, Sword, and Thomas Tyon to recording Oglala customs and their attention to detail have left a legacy of valuable manuscripts whose contributions to ethnography are inestimable.

Careful and detailed analyses of these primary accounts reveal a Lakota political organization that was adaptive, organic, and pragmatic. It should be noted, moreover, that Oglala elders never drew for Walker clear-cut distinctions among "social," "religious," and "political" organization. Spirituality and ceremonialism pervade all aspects of Lakota society, and certainly the empowerment of political agents required religious sanction. The Walker collection does include detailed information on sacred beliefs and ceremonies, and undoubtedly the actions of Oglala leaders were governed at times by their personal visionary experiences. However, it is not appropriate to discuss such information in studies of this kind.

In 1912 Clark Wissler presented one model of Oglala political organization.[16] In order to demonstrate the fluid and complex nature of Oglala political customs, I have constructed three models of prereservation Oglala political organization: the *tiyospaye,* the multiband, and the ceremonial. (The *tiyospaye* system predominated, for the Oglalas lived most of their lives within the band.)

A *tiyospaye* did not recognize any centralized political body with overarching powers. It sprung to life when its member camp or camps could field enough men to establish a council (composed of several categories of leadership such as *itancan, blotahunka* (war party leaders), headmen, warriors, and holy men), and to fill the prestigious offices of *wakiconza* (camp administrator, or "one who determines") and *akicita* ("enforcer of decisions"). At least seven "husbanded" tipis were necessary to accomplish this.[17]

The Chiefs Society or Council performed the principal legislative duties in both the *tiyospaye* and multiband systems, although confusion exists regarding the actual name of the council. Wissler asserted that the Chiefs Council was also known as the Big Bellies (Tezi Tanka), whereas Walker's authorities, Thomas Tyon and John Blunt Horn, stated that the Big Bellies were actually the Silent Eaters (Ahinila Wota), a multiband feasting society for retired warriors who, after silently dining on choice cuts of buffalo and puppy, engaged in animated discussions on the political affairs of the camp. Historical documents do not help to eliminate the confusion, but they do suggest the existence of the Silent Eaters among the Sioux as early as 1669. The *Jesuit Relations* includes a brief account that the Sioux "adore the Calumet, and say not a word at their feasts."[18]

The special council lodge (*tiyotipi*) was erected close to the camp entrance within the *hocoka,* the interior space created by the circle of tipis. Anyone could speak in council, including senior women, although recognition as a council member required formal invitation, symbolized by an ash wand charred at one end. Should a councilor's peers demand the return of the wand, he was considered deposed and unwelcome in the council lodge.[19]

In accordance with protocol, the individual who convened a council meeting opened it by first offering the calumet to the six directions. George Sword, one of Walker's authorities, remarked, "When a Lakota does anything in a formal manner he should first smoke the pipe." After all the councilors had passed around the calumet, the one convoking the meeting outlined the agenda. Anyone wishing to speak called out *Itancan!* and, once recognized, addressed the council. Valentine McGillycuddy, U.S. Indian agent at the Pine Ridge Reservation between 1879 and 1886, also observed this custom of smoking the pipe before beginning a council session. Sometimes, the agent added, there was free-flowing and heated discussion "bordering on a general row," but participants normally took great pains to ensure that speakers were not interrupted.[20]

If the business under discussion was extremely important, as in treaty negotiations with whites, the councilors would "quietly among themselves, weigh it, and select" a prominent member as intermediary. Contemporary white spokesmen were often confused by the decision-making process of the Oglalas and other Plains Indian tribes. Nineteenth-century Americans were accustomed to formulating regulations according to majority rule. The Oglalas, however, decided by consensus, compromising the various viewpoints until a unanimous decision had been reached, thus enabling them to present a united front during negotiations. Evidence for this process may be found in the transcribed council proceedings and other historical documents of the nineteenth century. John Ordway, a member of the Lewis and Clark expedition, described a council held with a Brulé band on 30 August 1804. Speaking through Ordway's interpreter, Pierre Dorian, all four of the Brulé speakers presented essentially the same position in their respective council speeches to Ordway.[21] For the most part, Lakota council spokesmen adhered to several themes or issues that were acceptable to their *tiyospaye,* and whites were overwhelmingly unsuccessful in inducing them to render decisions without the general consent of their constituents.

It would be unreasonable to think, however, that consensus was always achieved in camp assemblies. On occasion, dissent within the Chiefs Council hindered the decision-making process, requiring influential leaders to attempt to sway the opposition. In a society as small as a Lakota band, and in which kinship ties and loyalty to one's extended family were paramount, dissenters were easily identified and subjected to peer pressure or humiliation in order to gain unanimity. For the most part, however, coercion was not advocated by the council. If consensus could not be achieved, the assembly adjourned and controversial issues were left unresolved, often to the dismay of Americans trying to negotiate with Oglala councilors.

The Lakotas recognized one or more band *itancan* who were expected to be "good men"—kind, generous, patient, wise, diplomatic, and brave. Indeed, most had been successful warriors. The most revered *itancan* of the oldest *tiyospaye* received a title that interpreters often translated as "head chief." Little Wound, for example, claimed in old age that he was "the head chief of the Oglalas and my father [Bull Bear] was the head chief. In a camp of all the Oglalas I am entitled to place my tipi at the chief place." As symbolic fathers, band chiefs bore the tremendous burden of caring for their people, especially the sick, orphaned, and indigent.[22]

A man was acknowledged as *itancan* when, upon entering the *tiyotipi*, he was invited by his peers to sit at the *catku*, the "chief place," opposite the entrance to the council lodge, and to speak first if he so desired. Once installed, a holy man offered him the pipe, which he smoked in communion with the other councilors. Later he selected two of his most trusted friends, often younger warriors, to serve as his assistants. These aides kept the *itancan* informed about camp matters and also served as his personal ambassadors.[23]

Band chiefs were esteemed as their people's protectors, but such status should not be equated with the American notion of decision-making authority, because often they had little or none. In his correspondence with Walter Stanley Campbell (Stanley Vestal), Robert High Eagle claimed that, customarily, true band *itancan* remained taciturn during councils unless they were requested or felt the need to speak. Consequently, the Oglalas' *itancan* could be men whom whites failed to recognize or simply ignored. On occasion, however, the *itancan* could wield considerable influence if they could induce the camp warriors to enforce their orders, but most commanded respect and loyalty from a lifelong commitment to the cardinal virtues of bravery, generosity, fortitude, and wisdom. Cowardly, selfish, or ineffectual men could not possibly hope to remain *itancan*, for their people, especially the warriors, would simply desert them.[24]

Chieftainship was somewhat hereditary. Men who were too old to fulfill their obligations to the *tiyospaye* nominated their sons, nephews, younger brothers, and, under rare circumstances, their daughters to assume the office. Although generosity was one of the Oglalas' cardinal virtues, and ideally the *itancan* accumulated possessions for the sole purpose of redistributing them, selfless acts were insufficient to sustain their influence and acquire prestige. Followers supported their *itancan* only so long as they could protect and preserve the sacred hoop. Regardless of how much an *itancan* hoped his son, nephew, or brother would assume the office upon his retirement, such transference of rank required the general endorsement of the *tiyospaye*. In July 1903 Red Cloud, then a frail elderly *itancan*, delivered a speech at the Pine Ridge Reservation "abdicating" his position to his son, Jack Red Cloud.[25] Jack, however, never enjoyed the same degree of recognition that his father had during the agency years.

If the camp refused to acknowledge a chosen heir's leadership, or wished to depose an established *itancan* for violating tribal customs, the councilors might call upon a worthier man born to a less prominent family. Avenues to success were thus open to exceptionally brave warriors, expert hunters, or gifted visionaries of modest means. Even then, dissatisfied individuals could choose to abandon their *tiyospaye* and join that of a proven leader, or to form an entirely new band. The withdrawal of support was the supreme sanction—a powerful weapon that could check a leader's behavior. This process demonstrates the fluidity of Oglala leadership as the influence of men waxed and waned according to their ability to influence followers. Without strong support, formerly respected and persuasive leaders often witnessed the rapid weakening of their political influence.[26]

Tensions often surfaced between the young men and their elders over matters pertaining to war. Time after time, the band *itancan* and headmen failed to prevent the young men from abandoning their war plans. During times of crisis, when the young men's abilities as hunters and warriors were especially vital to the camp's survival, the fighting men had a significant voice in council affairs. In the early 1840s, explorer John Frémont visited the trading post at Fort Platte. There he met several Lakota elders who warned him, through their interpreter Joseph Bissonette, not to leave the vicinity as their young men had recently assembled a war party to avenge the deaths of relatives killed by whites. Frémont wanted these older men to accompany him during part of his expedition, but they declined, adding that they preferred to remain in their lodges while the young men fought. Frémont assumed that chiefs could control their warriors and was therefore surprised to learn that the older men "had no power over the young men, and were afraid to interfere with them."[27]

Americans have long associated their notion of decision-making authority with wealth and social status. Since this does not hold true for prereservation Lakota society, what motivated a man to accept the burdensome duties of an *itancan*? Certainly not decision-making authority for its own sake, for other men might wield more; nor tangible riches, for many times the most venerable man was the poorest one of the band. Perhaps the honor and prestige accorded a popular *itancan*, coupled with the sense of accomplishment he derived from protecting the sacred hoop, brought greater psychological satisfaction. This is not to say that all *itancan* were selfless individuals immune from political machinations, but the rewards of office clearly differed from those of white politicians. A family's prestige was linked to the senior male's willingness and ability to distribute wealth or perhaps to a family member's spiritual gifts. Bull Bear, for example, was both an influential Oglala *itancan* and an esteemed *wicasa wakan* (holy man).

In addition to the band *itancan*, each extended family recognized a senior male (headman) who participated in the council, but, like the *itancan*, could be deposed for violating tribal customs or for displaying gross cowardice. According to High Eagle and George Colhoff, an interpreter at the Pine Ridge Reservation in the late nineteenth century, these headmen presided over the council meetings. The *itancan*, High Eagle added, were "supposed to listen," and only conducted the proceedings when no one else would do so. A headman's status was subject to change. If a man continued to exhibit patience, wisdom, oratorical skills, or outstanding hunting knowledge, the council might appoint him *wakiconza*. Moreover, if a headman had a sufficient following, he might attain the status of a *tiyospaye* or even a subtribal *itancan*. Conversely, prominent *itancan* who no longer inspired their people, or who had retired from official duties due to advanced age, could return to their former positions as camp patriarchs.[28]

Holy men (*wicasa wakan*) and other healers were permitted to speak at councils but were expected to limit themselves to matters of a sacred nature. Instructed by messengers from the Great Mystery, the *wicasa wakan* could prohibit the performance of established ceremonies or introduce new ones; however, deceitful actions resulted in severe punishment, sometimes even their death.[29]

*Itancan*, headmen, and holy men shared political duties with younger Lakota males, the bands' active warriors (*zuya wicasa*) and hunters. Warfare was an intrinsic part of a Lakota male's life, and warriors prepared themselves from an early age to win battle honors that elevated their status among their people. Oglala military societies—the Tokala (Kit Foxes), Kangi Yuha (Crow Owners), Ihoka (Badgers), Cante T'inza (Brave Hearts), Sotka Yuha (Plain Lance Owners), and Wicinska (Packs White), all of which cut across band lines—extended membership invitations only to the most promising young men of the *tiyospaye*.[30] Admission bestowed great honor and prestige on the chosen ones, but it also incurred heavy expenses. Aside from their military and ceremonial duties, members of the warrior societies bore numerous other responsibilities such as sponsoring giveaways for the needy and hosting camp festivities. Without strong family support, no man could hope to accumulate the material wealth required to pay his membership "dues." People gossiped that the relatives of a young man forced to decline a society's invitation were too poor, indifferent, or miserly to help him meet his obligations.[31]

The band watched closely for warriors whose abilities marked them as future leaders. A young man who aspired to positions of leadership and influence, and who had already demonstrated his talents—by counting *coup,* taking scalps, and, even more important, feeding the hungry—hosted a series of special ceremonies. When his daughter reached puberty, he honored her by sponsoring a Buffalo Sing; for either a son or daughter, he arranged the *hunka* ceremony. If the *tiyospaye* praised him, he would be expected to perform the Owns the Ghost and White Buffalo ceremonies. At each of these important rituals, the esteemed warrior and his family gave away prized possessions—horses, quilled robes, food, beadwork, lodge covers, even the clothes off their backs. The *tiyospaye* acclaimed such altruism, and the leaders endorsed his candidacy for council membership. They raised the respected warrior upon a buffalo robe and bore him to the council lodge. There he received a pipe, two eagle feathers to place in his hair, and a scalp-fringed shirt (*wicapaha ogle*), either blue and yellow (representing the sky and rock), or red and green (representing the sun and earth). The shirt's hair-lock trim symbolized the people whom the new candidate swore to defend. In unison the councilors sang, "To be a man is difficult you say, but I have looked for this. / Here with great hardship I come." The candidate was then advised of his duties: he must exercise good judgment, willpower, and patience, forever pledging himself to the people's welfare. Thus instructed, the councilors stood up and sang again: "My friends, the candidate has said it is difficult to be a man / But I looked for him." Now the honored one had "become a man," *wicasa yatapika,* the "man they praise," an "owner" (that is, caretaker) of the people.[32]

Elevation to the status of *wicasa yatapika* presents an interesting paradox. Only wealthy men from the most prominent families had the means to sponsor the four significant and expensive ceremonies. But once they became candidates (and later councilors or perhaps *itancan*), demonstrating commitment to their roles as caretakers required regular contributions to the band, particularly the orphaned, aged, widowed, poor, and, of course, their *hunka.* For some beloved leaders, sacrifice and doing without became a way of life.

Thus free-flowing and protracted discussion, disdain for coercion, and the desire for consensus characterized camp assemblies. But who made rapid decisions when time-consuming deliberation would compromise the people's immediate welfare? What Americans called executive, legislative, judicial, and police functions coalesced in the important Lakota offices of *wakiconza* and *akicita.* It was these people, approved by the council, who were temporarily empowered to supervise the daily affairs of the village. During his sojourn to the Missouri River country in 1850, Thaddeus Culbertson noted that decision-making authority among the Sioux he observed was customarily wielded not by "chiefs" but by other men whose talents for war, hunting, organization, and diplomacy enabled them to control the everyday affairs of the *tiyospaye.* Culbertson remarked that there were "a number of such men in each band."³³ Undoubtedly, he was referring to the camp *wakiconza.*

The *wakiconza* comprised an "executive committee" of two to six men appointed in the spring to organize the movement of camps and the communal buffalo hunt, to arbitrate disputes, umpire games, and supervise all wagers. *Itancan,* headmen, *wicasa wakan,* expert hunters, and famed warriors were all eligible for selection as *wakiconza,* but were obliged to set aside their former roles while in office. The *wakiconza,* whose influence did not extend outside their own *tiyospaye,* were also empowered to convene the council and even to challenge its decisions provided they had sufficient support from camp warriors. Corruption and incompetence were grounds for dismissal.³⁴

Band movements were carefully orchestrated to ensure that the people remained together on long marches and reencamped at the appropriate time. Enemies or game might appear instantaneously, so the *wakiconza* insisted that the travelers carefully obey their instructions. Merely promulgating orders did not ensure compliance, however. Thus before leaving a camp, the *wakiconza* recruited men from one of the warrior societies— usually the Kangi Yuha (Crow Owners) and the Ihoka (Badgers)—to coordinate *akicita* services, their actual number determined by the size of the camp.³⁵

Once named, the camp herald called the chosen men to the *tiyotipi* for formal notification. Any warrior could decline the invitation to serve as *akicita* ("enforcer of decisions") by paying a fine imposed by the council, but most younger men gladly accepted the appointment because a successful performance attracted the elders' attention. A *wicasa wakan* cere-moniously inducted the nominees, who were guided to sit between the *catku* and the council fire. Once installed, the younger men prayed before receiving the holy man's counsel. They were told, "You will resemble the ash. You have noticed it can not be broken. It is up to you to look after the people and take care of the laws." The *wicasa wakan* concluded the induction ceremony by painting a black stripe on the right cheek of each newly appointed *akicita,* angling it from the eye to the lower edge of the jaw. Head *akicita* received three such stripes. This badge of office was to be displayed at all times while the *akicita* remained in office.[36]

Walker's Oglala authorities stated that the term *akicita* bore other meanings in addition to "enforcer of decisions." *Akicita* may also be translated as "messenger," signifying one who had been sent by his camp's council to conduct business with, relay information, or deliver Sun Dance invitations to other bands or subtribes. Upon their return, these *akicita* reported to the councilors, who immediately terminated their appointment. In a sense, one could say that those Oglalas who visited Washington to meet the president of the United States and the secretaries of war and of the interior were *akicita* for their people—men serving in the official capacity of *tiyospaye* delegates. Furthermore, *akicita* may signify the non-human messengers, or intermediaries, of the holy beings who communicated with people during visions. In their earthly forms as animals, insects, or birds, these *akicita* enabled the Lakotas to commune with the Great Mystery.[37]

After plotting the route to the new location, the *wakiconza* assumed their positions at the head of the column, with the camp herald and the *itancan* directly behind them. The senior *itancan* brought with him precious embers from the old hearth to spark the new camp fire, the symbol of the *tiyospaye's* unity and autonomy. Like the spokes of a wheel, assistant *akicita* fanned out in all directions from the column, keeping vigil for signs of danger, while head *akicita* "policed" the people, ensuring that no one fell behind, broke from the assigned route, or violated the customs of the march. Thus we can perhaps visualize the decision-making authority exercised during a camp march as a rotating wheel. When the time arrived to break camp, the *wakiconza* commanded the people to strike their lodges and set out toward a new location, which the *wakiconza* chose. Once in transit, authority shifted to the *akicita,* who ensured that the villagers remained together on the march and encamped at the appointed destination. If the column were suddenly threatened by enemies, such as a Crow or Pawnee war party, the *wakiconza* and *akicita* immediately deferred to the *blotahunka* and their selected warriors (*zuya wicasa*). The *akicita* reminded the villagers that authority now rested with the war party leaders by washing off their black-striped badges of office.[38]

When the danger had subsided, however, decision-making authority reverted to the *wakiconza*, who directed the *akicita* to repaint their faces for the duration of the march. While the column continued to move, the wheel of decision-making authority rotated through the *wakiconza, akicita, blotahunka*, and their warriors. At each rest stop the *wakiconza* invoked the guidance of Takuskanskan, the Spirit of Movement, or Energy. When they sat down for the fourth time, the people recognized the signal to encamp either for the night or for a much longer period. Once settled in the new village, the *wakiconza* dismissed the *akicita* of the march.[39] This concept of cyclical authority during camp movements was yet another manifestation of the Lakotas' worldview that all things in their cosmos are round, that human experiences eventually come back on themselves.

Before commencing the autumn communal hunt, the *wakiconza* selected two young men noted for their hunting knowledge to search for buffalo. If the scouts located game, the *wakiconza* immediately recalled their *akicita*. Riding twenty abreast at the head of the column, the *akicita* led the hunters and their assistants to the herd, reprimanding or even beating unconscious those who would jeopardize the chase by preempting the signal to move out. An anxious hunter who repeatedly charged at the buffalo without a care for his *tiyospaye* kin returned home to find the *akicita* had killed his horses and destroyed his wife's lodge.[40]

While en route to new encampments, or during the communal hunt, the *akicita* exercised considerable, albeit temporary, authority. All—the most beloved chief, experienced *wakiconza*, powerful visionary, talented beadworker, honored mother, and prominent warrior—unfailingly obeyed the *akicita*'s orders, for defiance brought swift and harsh punishment. Yet the council and warrior societies checked any tendency for incumbent *akicita* to attain totalitarian powers by humiliating, punishing, and deposing those who dared to breach the people's trust.[41]

When winter approached, the people struck their lodges for the winter villages. At this time, several *tiyospaye* might camp fairly close together in sheltered river valleys. Women raised the tipis, driving the stakes deep into the ground. They opened their caches of jerked buffalo meat, pemmican (*wasna*), and grease; on warmer days, men and boys stepped out to hunt deer, elk, and other smaller game. Grandparents and grandchildren gathered brush and twigs to barricade the lodges against drifting snow and biting winds. As people settled in for the season they scanned the horizon daily, watching for the familiar silhouettes of horses and travois that bore their relatives to the winter villages. When all had settled, the camps anticipated weeks of feasting, renewing friendships, telling stories of Iktomi (the Trickster), playing games, and fashioning weapons, clothes, and ceremonial regalia. Multiband alliances that developed at this (or any other) time of the year were unstable, however, and could literally dissolve overnight. Agreements concluded between white representatives and Oglala delegates from one or more bands were not necessarily endorsed by others. Furthermore, such accords were certainly not binding on other *tiyospaye*. White civilian negotiators often remained ignorant of these fluid political customs, or at least preferred to ignore them.

Political organization at the multiband level closely resembled the single *tiyospaye* system. Prominent men from all the bands present in the larger encampment assembled at the *tipi iyokiheya* ("tipi thrown over together"), the grand council lodge erected from the skins of each band's *tiyotipi*. Leaders gathered to discuss myriad topics, some of extreme importance, such as upcoming war campaigns or treaty negotiations with whites. While in session, the councilors formally recognized the honorable band *itancan* and the camp *wakiconza*, whose duties shifted primarily to supervising games, settling grievances, and overseeing all wagers. The band *itancan* also appointed head *akicita*, who in turn selected assistant *akicita* from one or more of the warrior societies. These camp *akicita* (mostly men but occasionally women) assumed judicial and police authority. They enforced band customs, arbitrated personal disputes, meted out punishment to offenders of tribal laws, and occasionally prevented council meetings from degenerating into brawls. Unlike the *akicita* appointed temporarily to supervise camp movements and hunts, the camp *akicita* served for longer periods of time.[42]

Historical documents illustrate the camp *akicita*'s more extensive authority. During a visit to Sioux villages in the autumn of 1803, fur trader Pierre-Antoine Tabeau observed what must have been to him a remarkable exchange between a young Sioux male and a camp *akicita* appointed to protect the local fur trader. The former had scaled the roof of a trading post to peer between the wooden planks on the scene below. Believing such behavior could offend the trader, the *akicita* ordered the man to come down. He refused, prompting the *akicita* to fire his pistol close to the young man's face. Stunned and bleeding, he returned quietly to his lodge, but "no one murmurs; it is the [*akicita*'s] right" to punish insubordination.[43] Individuals did protest the actions of the camp *akicita*, pleading their cases before the councilors, who intervened if they agreed that the *akicita* had acted unfairly. Most plaintiffs accepted the council's decision, but even then those who rejected its judgments could leave their *tiyospaye* and raise their lodges elsewhere.[44]

The election or recognition of the head shirtwearers represented the clearest distinction between the *tiyospaye* and multiband systems. The White Horse Rider Society selected prominent warriors with impeccable reputations to serve as the head shirtwearers. Epitomizing the Lakota virtues of bravery, generosity, endurance, and wisdom, these men vowed publicly to defend the land, the sacred hoop, and to feed and clothe the poor and orphaned. American Horse, Sword, Crazy Horse, and Young Man Afraid of His Horse are believed to be the last head shirtwearers of the Oglalas.[45] True to Young Man Afraid's responsibilites as protector of the people, one of the bands at Pine Ridge later bore the name Young Man Afraid's Orphans.

Moreover, the head shirtwearers performed the role of supreme peacemakers. Bearing a pipe in their hands, the shirtwearers intervened in conflicts that threatened to tear apart the camp circle. The very sight of the pipe soothed tensions and restored the peace. The head shirtwearers enjoyed lifelong "tenure" but could be deposed by the council for major transgressions, such as murder. Eleanor Hinman, who interviewed He Dog and other Oglala elders in 1930, stated that Crazy Horse was forced to return his fringed shirt, the insignia of office, to the White Horse Rider Society after falling in love with Black Buffalo Woman, the wife of No Water.[46] Although the head shirtwearers' decision-making authority remained largely symbolic, they did command sufficient influence in multiband assemblies to oppose any *tiyospaye* chief deemed disruptive and ineffective. Young Man Afraid of His Horse, for instance, silenced Red Cloud during a multiband council in early November 1874, when the latter opposed the compilation of population data at the Red Cloud Agency.[47]

In a sense, the *blotahunka* repelled external threats to the hoop while the head shirtwearers helped to resolve internal problems and conflicts.

Political and spiritual matters at both the *tiyospaye* and multiband levels were interwoven, but there were occasions, notably during the annual Sun Dance, when heightened ceremonialism prevailed. At such times the bands united in a sacred village supervised by *wicasa wakan*.

The Sun Dance, performed each summer, sustained the sacred hoop

17

and reaffirmed the Lakotas' humble relationship with the Great Mystery. Men who successfully completed this profoundly holy rite commanded the respect of all the bands. Proudly bearing the long scars that were testimony to their public sacrifice, these men were now eligible to lead a war party or seek membership in the council. In the ceremonial camp, decision-making authority shifted from the council, *itancan,* and *wakiconza* to the holy men who assumed the former's collective roles. The *wicasa wakan* handpicked special *akicita* to keep order in the camp, and to prevent anyone from violating the customs of this sacred occasion. At the conclusion of the Sun Dance, the leaders of the various *tiyospaye* decided when and where they would reunite, recording as notches on a pipe stem the number of moons that would pass before they would reunite. Then the bands divided again, reinitiating the political system of the *tiyospaye.*[48]

The *itancan,* headmen, warriors, *wakiconza, akicita,* and *wicasa wakan* shared political duties at all levels of organization. What role, then, did women play in tribal politics? Over the years, historians, ethnographers, novelists, movie and television directors—indeed, anyone who has ever written about or portrayed Native Americans—have almost always neglected Indian women. Most of those who do include them in the story have stereotyped women as either the beautiful, pure Indian "princess," or her antithesis, the overworked, degraded "squaw."[49] Even Walker, who earned the trust of tribal elders, considered Oglala women inferior to their husbands and relegated to performing the menial chores of the camp. Despite his genuine respect for Oglala customs, Walker nevertheless remained a product of his own Anglo-American culture, which devalued domestic work and considered women innately inferior to men. Even a generation after Walker left Pine Ridge in 1914, anthropologist Royal Hassrick, conducting fieldwork among the Brulés of the Rosebud Reservation, remarked that Lakota women were tied to their camp chores, there being "no other acceptable pattern for feminine existence."[50]

This characterization of native women persists in some quarters. In his recently published book on Dakota history, Gary Clayton Anderson writes that "women had a burdensome existence, with little opportunity to accomplish much beyond preparing hides, making clothes, tending children, and preparing the camp for another move. Although statistics are unavailable, the rate of suicide was high among Sioux women."[51] Fairly recent anthropological publications such as *The Hidden Half,* a collection of essays on Plains Indian women, challenge the belief that native women were "beasts of burden." Ella Deloria, a Sioux woman trained at

Columbia University by Franz Boas in the 1920s, and Raymond De-Mallie contend that traditional Lakota society was not "male dominated" but rather was much more complementary with women and men performing quite different but equally valuable roles (*okicicupi*). Indeed, the Lakotas, like the Cheyennes, often stated that their society was no stronger than their women.[52]

Oglala women lived most of their lives within the circle, tanning hides for the fur trade and for lodge coverings, gathering roots and berries, cooking, making garments, creating elaborately beaded or quilled items, tending the very young and very old, and preparing the camp to move. Some were gifted seers and curers, others belonged to exclusive women's societies, such as the Tanners (for lodge cover manufacturers), the Praiseworthy Women (for virgins), the Owns Alone (for women over forty years of age who had known only one man), and the Medicine Society (for those who had experienced visions). Members of the latter prepared war medicine and shields for warriors. Still others, such as Crazy Horse's sister, accompanied their brothers or husbands to war.[53]

Women also held porcupine quilling contests, the winners being accorded the same high status as young men who had counted coup. Expert craftswomen and artists brought honor to their families, and warriors appreciated the talents of these women, whose beautiful handiwork embellished ceremonial and war regalia.

Lakota women honored their men by bringing food to the council lodge, but "don't assume that they were chased off," Deloria cautions. "They left because it was considered unwomanly to push one's way into a gathering of the other sex; it was unmanly for men to do so under opposite circumstances." Women did not participate directly in tribal politics. Mary Jane Sneider contends, however, that as an aspiring male leader anxious to demonstrate his altruism required quilled or beaded articles, female crafters could "control his behavior in some way suitable to them. This would give women a form of covert political [influence] which has not heretofore been acknowledged." Occasionally an old woman would speak in council and was treated respectfully, but as a rule, most women "would talk to their men in their families about [political affairs] and give their opinions as to the candidates" for leadership roles.[54] Thus in the political sphere, Oglala women served mainly as lobbyists and advisors.

It is also difficult to discern how much influence the whites who intermarried with the Lakotas and their mixed-blood offspring had on the political affairs of the Oglalas before the 1880s, and whether they held any specific political roles among the various *tiyospaye*. According to historian Brian Strayer, few fur traders "associated with the Sioux intimately learned to understand and appreciate their government and organization." Those who did, he adds, "left sparse records revealing their attitudes."[55]

Fur trader Joseph Bissonette married into the Lakotas twice. His first wife, with whom he had seven children, was Oglala; his second wife, a Brulé, bore him fourteen more. While serving as an interpreter for the Brulés and Oglalas, he won the confidence of several Lakota leaders, including Red Cloud. In 1875 Bissonette accompanied the Oglala and Brulé delegation to Washington DC, where he is said by some to have played a key role in persuading both Red Cloud and Spotted Tail to consider selling the Black Hills to the United States. James Bordeaux, called Mato (the Bear) by his Lakota family and associates, married a sister of Swift Bear, a prominent Brulé *itancan*. Also engaged in the fur trade, Bordeaux's family ties brought him enough Brulé customers during the 1840s to give his employer, the American Fur Company, the competitive edge in the Upper Platte River country. Two other fur traders forged ties to the Red Cloud family: John Richard Sr., who often transported illegal supplies of fur trade liquor; and the Swiss-born Jules Ecoffey, who operated in the Fort Laramie area after 1854.[56]

Given the importance of kinship ties, it seems quite likely that these white relatives and the mixed-blood Oglalas attended camp councils. Fur traders "could offer advice in council and use presents to gain political advantage," Gary Clayton Anderson states in his study of the eastern Dakota, but acceptance within the circle depended on whether Dakota leaders could satisfy themselves that their white kinsfolk were indeed dedicated to acting in the best interests of their Sioux families.[57] Historian Harry Anderson claims that the mixed-blood offspring of the fur traders were instrumental in persuading many Oglala and Brulé *tiyospaye* to accept agencies on the White River, away from the main white migration routes in the Platte River valley. Hoping to lure the Oglalas and Brulés away from the Fort Laramie area by courting the favor of mixed-bloods who wished to farm, federal treaty commissioners included incentives in the 1868 Treaty of Fort Laramie such as land allotments, agricultural tools, cows, and oxen.[58]

Despite their kinship ties, however, it seems unlikely that the mixed-bloods and fur traders would have enjoyed any political clout among the warrior societies or nonagency bands before the 1880s. Other than serving as interpreters, probably few, if any, became *blotahunka,* band chiefs, *akicita,* or *wakiconza.* Indeed, some sources suggest that the mixed-bloods remained somewhat separate from their full-blood relatives, either by choice or by necessity. An Oglala "winter count" (a historical record) owned by John Garnier, a son of the Fort Robinson military scout Baptiste "Little Bat" Garnier, includes an interesting entry for the year 1768: "Iyeska kecizapi [the mixed-bloods fought]." Moreover, during the early 1880s, Reverend W. J. Cleveland, a missionary at the Pine Ridge Reservation, identified a separate band there known as the Ieskacinca ("interpreters' sons," or mixed-bloods). Presumably this band had its own *itancan* and other political officers.[59]

Finally, Americans have tried to hang their own labels on the political customs of prereservation Oglala society. While obviously not monarchical, other suggestions have included oligarchical, meritocratic, and even anarchical. In the final analysis, none of these descriptions is applicable because the Oglalas adapted their political customs to serve their ever changing needs. At times—and in response to situations such as the negotiation of treaties or warfare with the United States—the *tiyospaye* council deferred to the multiband assembly, thus shifting the decision-making authority from one form of leadership to another, and making the role of the council spokesman and tribal delegate more evident. Despite these temporary modifications, however, the essential values, symbols, and beliefs underpinning Oglala concepts of leadership and decision-making authority endured. Underpinning everything was the preservation of the sacred hoop.

The North Platte River winds its way from the Rocky Mountains through the heart of Wyoming and Nebraska. By 1839 the Oglalas and Brulés had pushed southward from the Black Hills to wrest from the Skiri Pawnees the magnificent country of the Platte River valley. Here the plentiful buffalo sustained the Lakotas in their ongoing feuds with the earthlodge villagers and in their sporadic conflicts with the Crows to the north.[60] But the valley of the Platte also reminded the Oglalas of a sad and momentous event, the murder of an influential *itancan,* that would twist their sacred hoop, threatening to break it forever.

In the early 1830s, William Sublette and Robert Campbell, both experienced fur traders and former employees of the Rocky Mountain Fur Company, observed Oglala and Brulé migrations to the Platte River valley. Desiring to barter with these Lakotas, Sublette and Campbell established their own fur enterprise, and in June 1834 founded a trading post that would become Fort Laramie at the confluence of the Platte and Laramie Rivers near present-day Cheyenne, Wyoming.

Prior to 1840, trading company employees, or *engagés* (many claimed French heritage), hauled their cargoes to the annual Rocky Mountain rendezvous held in the Green River valley of southwestern Wyoming. At this great gathering, which lasted about a week, *engagés* conducted business with Native American hunters, exchanging white-manufactured goods for animals skins and food. By 1840 the nucleus of the fur trade (now largely based on buffalo robes rather than on beaver pelts) had shifted from the yearly rendezvous to trading posts like Fort Laramie.[61]

During 1830 and 1831 several bands of Oglalas and Brulés traded at Fort Tecumseh, built by the Columbia Fur Company almost a decade earlier on the Upper Missouri River near the mouth of the Teton (or Bad) River. In 1835 about two thousand Oglalas visited Fort Laramie for the first time, bringing as currency tanned buffalo robes, fresh and jerked buffalo meat, belts, and beaded moccasins. Thereafter the post became a favorite haunt for Lakotas, Northern Cheyennes, and Arapahos, all of whom traveled there at least twice a year. At this time the Oglalas knew relatively little about American society except for insights gleaned from their association with white fur traders, guides, and mountain men. What the Sioux quickly grasped, though, was that these sundry fur trade employees, several of whom later married Indian women and adopted Lakota customs, were a source of many desirable items—guns, powder, lead, beads, vermillion, mirrors, copper kettles, hatchets, steel knives, and blankets.

The *engagés* also introduced their Indian clientele to whiskey. Commenting on the quality of the liquor sold in the fur trade, Rufus Sage, a young adventurer from Connecticut, remarked that it was "generally third or fourth proof whiskey, which, after being diluted by a mixture of three parts water, is sold to the Indians at the exorbitant rate of three cups per robe—the cups usually holding about three gills each." Alcohol remained a commodity in the fur trade despite federal legislation passed in 1830 prohibiting the sale of intoxicating beverages to Indian people. In November 1843, Maj. Andrew Drips, appointed the previous year to enforce the antiliquor laws in the Upper Missouri country, identified fur trader John Richard Sr. as the principal culprit in the illegal transportation and sale of alcohol around Fort Laramie.[62]

In the fall of 1840, Lancaster Lupton, owner of Fort Lupton, the first adobe fort on the South Platte River, constructed Fort Platte just over a mile north of Fort Laramie. Within months, Lupton's operation was competing with the American Fur Company, which owned Fort Laramie. Responding to the challenge, American Fur tried to ruin its new rival by distributing free liquor to Oglala and Brulé bands camped in the vicinity, calculating that by so doing, the Oglalas, Brulés, and other Platte River Indians would favor Fort Laramie.[63]

By the fall of 1841, Bull Bear, a powerful holy man and principal *itancan* of the Oglala Bear people, had returned to Fort Laramie with his followers to barter buffalo robes for white goods. At this time the Bear group comprised four major *tiyospaye*: the True Oglala (or Oglala Proper), the Sharp Tail Grouse, the Kiyuksa (Bull Bear's own band), and an unnamed band formerly under Ghost Heart. Old Smoke, the head *itancan* of the Smoke people (notably the Hunkpatila, Bad Face, and Oyuhpe Oglalas) soon joined Bull Bear's followers on their biannual treks to the fort. While camped near the fort, a quarrel between the two groups resulted in tragedy. It is unclear how or why the altercation started, but it ended with the murder of Bull Bear. George Hyde states that white fur traders had been encouraging Old Smoke to challenge Bull Bear's influence. Enraged, Bull Bear stabbed and killed Smoke's favorite horse before returning to his own camp. Old Smoke was too cowed to oppose Bull Bear at that moment, according to Hyde, but he and his followers planned to even the score with Bull Bear at some later date.[64]

Some accounts state that around early November 1841, a young Bad Face warrior, whom Bull Bear despised, "stole" a woman from Bull Bear's camp. After receiving this news, Bull Bear led a group of warriors to Smoke's camp on Chugwater Creek, a tributary of the Laramie River, where his party found employees of the American Fur Company distributing whiskey to Smoke's people. In retaliation, Bull Bear shot the young Bad Face's father. After this incident, Bad Face warriors opened fire on Bull Bear's party, shooting the *itancan* and chasing the survivors back to their own camp. Still other accounts state that Bull Bear's warriors had also begun to imbibe, and that when a squabble subsequently erupted between the Bear and Smoke groups, Bull Bear was shot trying to stop the fight. Moreover, the 1841 entry for Iron Crow's winter count reads *"itomni kici ktepi* [while drunk, they killed each other]."[65]

William Garnett, an interpreter who lived among the Oglalas during the late 1800s, presented his version of the story in a letter to former Pine Ridge Indian agent Valentine McGillycuddy. Garnett stated that a quarrel had taken place in Smoke's camp on Chugwater Creek, resulting in a party of inebriated Bad Faces mortally wounding Bull Bear, who died of blood poisoning a month later. Moreover, all versions report that Red Cloud, a young nephew of Old Smoke who was born in 1821 in Bull Bear's *tiyospaye* on the Smoky Hill River, fired the fatal shot.[66]

If we are to believe Sage, who observed the daily life of Platte River fur traders and their Oglala and Brulé clients, tragedies such as this recurred throughout the fall and winter of 1841. Sage writes that serious accidents, numerous squabbles, fights, and the occasional murder occurred in both the Indian camps and trading posts, and, in his opinion, were directly attributable to alcohol consumption.[67]

Ideally, kinship responsibilities and political customs were supposed to protect the sacred hoop by minimizing intra- and interband rivalries and feuds. But at times nothing could prevent tragedies from taking place. A similar incident involving the families of Crazy Horse and No Water occurred almost thirty years later. Black Buffalo Woman—No Water's wife and a niece of Red Cloud—left her husband to live with Crazy Horse, who had openly courted her. In a jealous rage, No Water shot Crazy Horse point-blank in the face. This act enraged Crazy Horse's warrior friends, who intended to kill No Water and even considered waging war on his extended family. In a desperate effort to prevent more bloodshed, Crazy Horse's older male relatives—Bull Head, Ashes, and Spotted Crow—arranged for No Water to atone for his attempt on Crazy Horse's life by sending him a gift of horses. However, Crazy Horse never truly forgave No Water, who felt compelled to move his lodge permanently to another band.[68] Crazy Horse's duties as a head shirtwearer included keeping the peace, not breaking it. Moreover, the loyalty of Crazy Horse's friends, who probably belonged to his warrior society, the Kangi Yuha, exacerbated an already explosive situation. Crazy Horse's senior uncles, on the other hand, honored their kinship responsibilities by seeking peace, not promoting revenge. But when fighting broke out between the followers of Bull Bear and Old Smoke, kinship loyalties to a very influential *itancan* and holy man were probably more a hindrance to peace than a help. Furthermore, any *wakiconza* who tried at this time to restore peace by offering the pipe would face the enormous task of soothing hot tempers fueled by fur trade whiskey.

The murder of such an important man certainly generated an unprecedented schism in Oglala society. After Bull Bear's untimely death, the Oglalas divided into two major groups, southern and northern, eventually dominated by the Kiyuksas (Bear people) and Bad Faces (Smoke people), respectively. Old Smoke remained head *itancan* of his group until the mid-1850s, when his age prompted him to retire from his position and spend his remaining years near Fort Laramie. Hyde writes that Smoke's son succeeded him as band chief. He bore the nickname Bad Face, an appellation also claimed by the *tiyospaye* to which Red Cloud, Smoke's nephew, belonged.[69]

Historian James C. Olson claims that after Bull Bear died, the Kiyuksas recognized as *itancan* his son, Bull Bear the Younger, although Hyde states that it was Whirlwind who attained the status of principal chief of that band. Bull Bear the Younger and Whirlwind were conceivably the same man, as it was customary for many Native Americans to use several names. In his conversations with James Walker, resident physician among the Oglalas at the turn of the twentieth century, Little Wound, another of Bull Bear's sons, stated that the Kiyuksas honored him as head *itancan* of the band. He must have won this recognition in later years, however, for in 1841 Little Wound would have been a boy of thirteen still preparing to fight in his first war party. Philip Wells, a mixed-blood district farmer on the Pine Ridge Reservation in the late 1800s, informed Judge Eli Ricker that Little Wound accompanied his father on an expedition against the Shoshones in 1844.[70] This father obviously could not have been Bull Bear, who perished in 1841. In Lakota society, a man's brother is also a "father" to his children. Thus the father of whom Wells spoke was probably a brother of Bull Bear, or perhaps Little Wound's *hunka* (adoptive parent).

After 1841 the southern Oglalas (the old Bear faction now comprising mainly the Kiyuksa, Two Crow, and Gopher *tiyospaye*) hunted more frequently to the south of Fort Laramie on the Republican and Smoky Hill Rivers in present-day Kansas, eventually forging alliances with the Southern Cheyennes. The northern Oglalas (the Smoke people now including the True Oglala, Oyuhpe, Bad Face, and Hunkpatila [later Payabya] bands) frequently wintered north of the Upper Platte River in the Yellowstone and Powder River country, where they associated with the Miniconjous and Northern Cheyennes. Although the rift between southern and northern Oglalas in time became less noticeable, it did not disappear entirely, as tensions between the two continued well into the reservation era. During the Sun Dance of 1883, the old rivalries resurfaced when the Bad Faces usurped the place of honor that the followers of Little Wound, Bull Bear's son, had traditionally claimed.[71]

As for Red Cloud's leadership aspirations, Olson contends that Bull

Bear's murder "perhaps did the most to establish young Red Cloud's position among his people." (Presumably Olson is referring here to the Bad Face *tiyospaye* to which Red Cloud belonged.) Red Cloud had been born in Bull Bear's camp, but he had moved to his uncle Smoke's *tiyospaye* long before 1841. Author Mari Sandoz states that the Kiyuksas, Bull Bear's band, later dubbed Red Cloud a "chief killer," a reputation she implies adversely affected Red Cloud's leadership ambitions outside his own *tiyospaye*.[72]

According to William Girton, a Carlisle-educated Oglala who in the early 1900s worked as an assistant farmer at the Pine Ridge Reservation, Red Cloud "plotted the whole affair in the belief that with Bull Bear out of the way he might be in a position to assume the old chief's position of leadership."[73] At the time of Bull Bear's death, Red Cloud would have been twenty years of age, hardly old enough to win widespread recognition as an *itancan*. Moreover, the premise that Red Cloud schemed to usurp Bull Bear is plausible only if one accepts that the Oglalas lived in a society in which people followed without question the commands of a small governing elite and its heirs. Other sources strongly indicate that Bull Bear indeed led a sizable constituency, but his supporters remained with him only as long as he promoted their best interests. Any man claiming to replace Bull Bear as principal *itancan* must first have demonstrated his ability and commitment to provide for the band's welfare. At the tender age of twenty, did Red Cloud have the necessary ability, experience, and respect?

Red Cloud did not premeditate the murder of Bull Bear; however, the political factionalism that became evident after the *itancan*'s death would place an additional burden on Oglala councilors as they faced a new series of challenges. For within a few years after Bull Bear's murder, Oglala leaders witnessed the migration of Americans through their Platte River valley homelands—a harbinger of a much graver external threat to the preservation of the sacred hoop and Oglala political customs.

# CHAPTER TWO

# American Emissaries among the Lakotas: Federal Endeavors to Modify Lakota Political Customs, 1851–1857

While the Oglalas scattered after Bull Bear's murder, American politicians were reevaluating their official policy of removing tribes whose lands lay east of the Mississippi River to Indian Territory, the country west of Missouri and Arkansas (present-day Oklahoma). In his annual message to Congress in December 1835, President Andrew Jackson had announced that the trans-Mississippi West would be forever "secured and guaranteed" to displaced tribes. Moreover, Congress pledged to protect the Indians' new homelands from future white encroachment.[1] The concept of a permanent Indian frontier—an impenetrable barrier separating Indians and whites enunciated during the Monroe administration—was hardly new, of course. As early as 1763 the English Crown took action to prevent its colonists from invading Native American lands west of the Appalachians, and twenty years later the Continental Congress of the infant United States issued a similar decree to its citizens. However, just as the proclamations of 1763 and 1783 fell on deaf ears, so too did the nineteenth-century policy of separating white settlers and Native Americans.

Bull Bear's death had shaken Oglala society, but for thousands of Americans the 1840s were exciting years. By mid-decade, for instance, the United States had resolved its Oregon boundary dispute with Great Britain, thereby claiming the Pacific Northwest territories for the public domain. As early as 1841, the very year that Bull Bear fell, the United States embarked on a new phase of westward expansion with the first wagon trains rumbling slowly toward California and Oregon along the Platte River road, the principal white migration route of the 1840s. Although these emigrants became the first Americanss to build settlements in Oregon and California, they were not the first whites to travel along the Platte River road. In the summer of 1834 Jason Lee had led a missionary party to Oregon. Other clergy and their spouses soon followed, including Reverend Samuel Parker, Marcus Whitman, and Mr. and Mrs. A. B. Smith.[2] But after 1841 this migratory scene would repeat itself annually as American pioneers and their livestock trampled through Oglala buffalo grounds in their quest to tap the agricultural and mineral wealth of what would become the states of California, Oregon, Utah, Montana, Idaho, and Colorado.

The first white emigrants passed through the Platte valley without fanfare. To the Oglalas and their relatives, the Brulés, these white travelers journeying through their country seemed harmless enough. Additional wagon routes and later railroads would be built, however, not merely through the Platte River valley but deep into the heart of the Yellowstone and Powder River hunting grounds. Telegraph poles with miles of wire would sprout out of the ground, and more dauntingly for the Oglala people, Americans would come in numbers that now cast them as invaders rather than as fleeting visitors.

In 1844 Capt. James Allen led Company I of the First Dragoons on a brief exploratory tour from Fort Des Moines to the Missouri River. The few Lakotas Allen and his men met, although described as "timid," instructed the soldiers to leave their country at once. During the summer of the following year, Col. Stephen Kearny with five companies of fully equipped and mounted dragoons left Fort Leavenworth on a two-thousand-mile round trip to the Rocky Mountains. Kearny later blustered that the sight of his well-armed dragoons had left an indelible impression on the Indian people he encountered and to whom he gave gifts, but to the Lakotas of the Platte River valley the colonel's offerings seemed to indicate the high esteem in which Kearny and his troops held them. Kearny neglected to identify all the Sioux leaders at their council, but he did list Bull Tail, an elderly Brulé *itancan* who died in 1854, as the principal spokesman present. In his official report of the mission the colonel noted that over two thousand white emigrants driving seven thousand head of cattle and four hundred mules and horses had passed along the Platte River road that summer en route to the Willamette River valley. W. B. Ide, an emigrant of 1845 who met the Kearny expedition, estimated that the total number of travelers for that year was closer to six or seven thousand, and that the number of wagons was approximately five hundred. Joining them on the Oregon Trail by 1847, moreover, were parties of Mormons fleeing religious persecution in Missouri and Illinois.[3]

In 1848 the Treaty of Guadalupe Hidalgo transferred to the United States vast tracts of land from Mexico, and five years later the Gadsden

Purchase added southern Arizona and New Mexico to American land reserves. The year 1848 proved momentous for another reason than the conclusion of war with Mexico. In January gold was discovered on the American River in California, and this strike lured many hopeful prospectors from the states and territories. By the following year, twenty-five thousand miners had trudged through the Platte River valley seeking prosperity in California. As the decade drew to a close, the United States considered itself a continental nation, even though the Great Plains were still uninhabitable in the minds of many Americans. In 1850 white migration exceeded 55,000, double that of the forty-niner rush, and the passage of the Kansas-Nebraska Act in 1854, which opened two additional western territories to American settlement, swept away any lingering hopes that a permanent barrier separating whites and Native Americans would stand.[4]

The collision of these two very different peoples—Oglala and American—highlighted and exacerbated the internal tensions that invariably exist in all human societies, prompting Oglala and American leaders to cope as effectively as possible with changing circumstances. After 1841 all Oglala *tiyospaye,* independently or in unison, Bear people or Smoke people, faced numerous uncertainties. How would bands sustain their war parties against the Pawnees and Crows while simultaneously contending with Americans who brought desirable trade goods and sometimes acted as kin but who also spread life-threatening diseases, attacked their villages, disturbed or killed the buffalo, and eventually coveted their lands? Furthermore, how should Oglala leaders deal with these strange people whose urges to alter and control tribal lifeways, especially their political customs, were threatening and barely comprehensible?

Oglala councilors formulated various and often conflicting strategies to answer these difficult questions. For instance, some leaders, such as Holy Bald Eagle (Black Twin) and Crazy Horse, steadfastly refused to negotiate and sign treaties. Favoring war to drive whites from their lands, they preferred to die rather than give up their political autonomy. Other spokesmen, such as Man Afraid of His Horse, Young Man Afraid, Little Wound, Red Dog, Red Cloud, Blue Horse, and Bad Wound eventually advocated peace, using the agency system to preserve their people by wringing concessions from American officials.

While Sioux leaders attended to *tiyospaye* affairs, American politicians drew up lengthy agendas for their nation's future. Leaders wondered if they should even attempt to regulate the migratory impulse of the settlers who continued to stream into Indian lands. Moreover, Congress debated which arm of the government should control American relations with the Oglalas and other Lakotas—the U.S. Army or the Office of Indian Affairs? Although simple responses to these questions also evaded American politicians, one thing stood abundantly clear to them by midcentury: no adequate force existed to prevent Americans from entering Lakota and other Indian lands east of the Rocky Mountains and west of the Mississippi River.

By the early 1850s the annual hegira of whites through the Platte valley had begun to transform the Oregon Trail into a swath of stinking refuse. Half-buried corpses of humans stricken with Asiatic cholera, and rotting carcasses of worn-out horses, mules, oxen, and sheep putrified the air and water of the valley. Broken-down wagons, old shoes, clothes, papers, cans, and other effects littered the road. Living beings inflicted further ecological damage. Emigrants chopped down cottonwood trees for fires in a land where vegetation was already scarce, and the beasts they drove— over one hundred thousand cattle and fifty thousand sheep in 1853 alone—competed for water and nutrients with indigenous buffalo herds.[5]

Throughout most of the 1840s the Platte River Oglalas and Brulés devoted more of their time to fighting the Pawnees and Crows than they did the white settlers. The fur traders, who often reached for the whiskey bottle to drive hard bargains with Indian customers, were also tolerated despite (or perhaps because of) their business practices. As the years wore on, however, violent outbreaks between emigrants and Lakotas became more commonplace. Western newspapers were partially to blame for the intensification of hostilities, as several sensationalized or completely fabricated Indian "massacres" of whites along the Overland Trail. These reports influenced the writing of emigrant handbooks that counseled pioneers to threaten Native Americans with physical violence if they deemed them unruly. Such advice predisposed some whites toward distrusting all Indians.[6] Thus as long as the prairie schooners continued to roll by in the summer months, driving herds of domestic animals and spreading terrifying sicknesses, the Oglalas continued to reassess their relationship with Americans, and with other Lakota subtribes hunting in the Platte valley.

Field agents and superintendents notified the commissioner of Indian affairs that the Native Americans were complaining bitterly to them about the disruptive presence of emigrants in the valley. In 1846 the federal government had established the Upper Platte and Arkansas Indian Agency, one of the largest agencies in the western plains, covering an estimated

122,500 square miles, to facilitate communications with the Lakotas, Cheyennes, and Arapahos. Thomas Fitzpatrick, agent for the Upper Platte; Thomas Harvey, of the St. Louis superintendency; Harvey's successor, Col. David Dawson Mitchell; and Thomas Moore, of the Upper Missouri Agency, had repeatedly requested their superiors to intervene before war broke out between Indians and overlanders. Federal officials finally took note in 1850 and turned their attention to drafting a viable policy for improving Indian-white relations on the plains. They had grown concerned about pervasive intertribal warfare because the sight of war parties terrified pioneers. Furthermore, in an attempt to stave off hostilities between Lakotas and emigrants, the U.S. government planned to compensate Lakotas and other Indian tribes for the loss of game in their hunting grounds. Thus the Office of Indian Affairs summoned Fitzpatrick to Washington, where he was given the primary responsibility of informing the plains Indians of a grand peace council scheduled to convene the following year.[7]

In mid-September 1851 agent Fitzpatrick and superintendent Mitchell concluded a treaty between the United States and representatives of the Sioux, Cheyennes, Arapahos, Crows, Assiniboines, Gros Ventres, Mandans, and Arikaras.[8] Fitzpatrick, known to the native people as Broken Hand, was very familiar with the Great Plains, having previously guided expeditions of Cols. John Frémont and Stephen Kearny. Formerly a trader, Fitzpatrick and his business partners had purchased the old Rocky Mountain Fur enterprise from William Sublette in 1835, before being bought out themselves the following year by the American Fur Company.[9]

Assembled at the council site on Horse Creek thirty-five miles southeast of Fort Laramie, the tribes of the northern and central plains, the most militarily powerful of whom were the Lakotas and their Northern Cheyenne and Arapaho allies, agreed to cease intertribal hostilities, to permit the United States to construct roads and military posts within their territories, to allow limited white emigration through their hunting grounds to the far west, to make restitution for any depredations committed against white travelers and their property, and to accept some notion of a definable tribal domain. According to article 5 of the treaty, Sioux territory commenced at the mouth of the White Earth River, proceeded southwest to the forks of the Platte River, up the south fork of the Platte River to Red Butte (where the overland road left the river), along the Black Hills range to the headwaters of the Heart River, down the Heart

River to its mouth, and down the Missouri River back to the mouth of the White Earth River. In consideration for signing the treaty, the United States would provide the tribes combined annuities of fifty thousand dollars for fifty years, which was later reduced by the Senate to fifteen years.[10]

Numerous accounts describing the grand council at Horse Creek have appeared over the years. Several of the most interesting were compiled by B. Gratz Brown, a former attorney who provided his newspaper, the *Missouri Republican,* with eyewitness accounts of the council. On 4 September 1855 Colonel Mitchell began preparations for the council that was anticipated to be attended by over ten thousand Native Americans and U.S. citizens and to last at least two weeks. The proceedings opened on an ominous note, Brown reported, when the colonel learned that the twenty-seven wagons bearing provisions and gifts for the Indians had been delayed indefinitely. Brown astutely observed that important occasions warranted spectacular gifts, and that tobacco, blankets, knives, beads, vermillion, and especially food would be distributed to honor the assembled Indians. Without these gifts, he remarked, "no man living—not even the President of the United States—would have any influence with them, nor could he get them into council, or keep them together a day."[11] Presents symbolized friendship and served to create temporary kinship bonds among all the people. Without such symbolic ties, peace could not prevail among current enemies. Mitchell respected the custom and took great pains to procure as many items as possible from the sutler's stores at Fort Laramie, now owned by the U.S. Army. Much to the relief of the treaty commissioners, the wagon train finally arrived at Fort Laramie on 20 September, merely four days before the official adjournment of the grand assembly.

Reporters, interpreters, treaty commissioners, and their military escorts reached Horse Creek in the afternoon of the fifth. The following day, about one thousand mounted Sioux men, mostly Oglalas and Brulés, trotted slowly along the Upper Platte River from their encampment north of the council site. Riding four abreast, singing, and with their principal men in the center carrying an old American flag, the column entered the council ground. Mitchell stood waiting to honor them with tobacco and vermillion. Several hundred Northern Cheyenne men rode after them in similar fashion, and were also greeted by Mitchell. On the seventh, Lakota and Northern Cheyenne women erected the *tipi iyokiheya* ("tipi thrown over together"), the formal council lodge. In the center there was constructed an arbor for the tribal delegates, commissioners, interpreters, and other officials. Once completed, the Americans raised Old Glory and rolled out the cannon that they would fire to signal the start of each day of negotiations. While the council preparations continued, various bands of the other tribes assembled. Although there were some tense moments as the tribes, presently in a state of truce, debated who should take precedence in the camping order, peace descended over the council site. The Sioux, it seems, had claimed the place of honor, as Brown wrote in his field notes that they had gathered north and west of the entrance to the circular council arena. Each night the tribes honored one another with dog feasts and dance invitations.

During the Fort Laramie peace talks, the commissioners refused to recognize the political customs of the attending tribes. For instance, Colonel Mitchell warned tribal delegates that the United States would not negotiate with their respective bands independently. He thus directed each group to select a "suitable man" to serve as "chief of the whole nation . . . through whom your Great Father will transact all Government business." This supreme executive would be empowered as both leading spokesman and final arbitrator for his tribe. As long as he acted in a manner deemed proper by Americans, the president of the United States would "support and sustain him in his place as Head Chief of the nation." Henceforth, all tribal members would be required to respect, obey, and uphold him in his new political office.

Colonel Mitchell's request illuminates three general misconceptions he harbored. First, he believed that the political systems of all the gathered tribes were identical. Although the institution of a council of honorable men existed in both Lakota and Cheyenne society, for instance, membership in the Cheyenne assembly, the Council of Forty-four, was much more formal and restrictive than in the Sioux Chiefs Society. Second, Mitchell presumed that Native American delegates embraced the American definitions of *nation* and *nationalism,* which, certainly in the case of the Lakotas, divided as they were into autonomous subtribes and bands, seems highly improbable.

Finally, Colonel Mitchell's conception of a head chief's status and role differed markedly from that of the Lakotas. To Mitchell, a head chief was a man at the apex of a hierarchical political system that granted him sweeping decision-making powers over all bands and considerable wealth and prestige. Indeed, the colonel's notion of a "head chief of the nation," with his supreme authority to represent and direct all Sioux, more closely resembled a European absolute monarch than it did even the president of the United States. To the Lakotas the head chief was the first *itancan,* or the most beloved leader of the oldest band. Although such a man might enjoy considerable influence depending on his ability to provide for his *tiyospaye*, a head *itancan*'s decision-making authority was circumscribed. Like other members of the band, a head *itancan* was expected when necessary to defer to the *wakiconza* (camp administrators), the camp *akicita* (enforcers of decisions), or the war party leaders (*blotahunka*), especially in times of crisis. An elderly head *itancan* enjoyed high status, but more often than not his political contributions diminished as he approached his twilight years. Old Smoke, for example, retired from the chieftainship in the 1850s to spend his remaining years around Fort Laramie.

After requesting nominations for the office of head chief, Mitchell directed the Indian spokesmen to convene private councils at which they would select their principal candidates. Two days later, on the tenth, negotiations resumed. Before commencing, however, word arrived that the Crows were coming in. Mitchell greeted them, and the other Indian representatives, some of whom had recently sent war parties against the Crows, approached the newcomers to smoke for peace. Once the Crows had taken their place under the council arbor, the Sioux presented their position. They did not approve of the boundaries established for their tribal domain. "You have split the country and I don't like it," Black Hawk of the Oglalas told Mitchell. "What we live upon we hunt for, and we hunt from the Platte to the Arkansas, and from here up to the Red Butte and the Sweet Water." This area had once been claimed by the Kiowas and Crows, but, Black Hawk continued, the Oglalas "whipped these nations out of them, and in this we do what the white men do when they want the lands of the Indian." Furthermore, Blue Earth, an elderly Brulé spokesman, tactfully explained to Mitchell that his delegation considered absurd the directive to select a supreme executive. "We have decided differently from you, Father, about this chief for the nation." Instead, his people wanted a principal spokesman for each band, a proposition more in tune with their own political customs. If Mitchell would "make one or two chiefs [spokesmen] for each band, it will be much better for you and the whites. But, Father," Blue Earth continued, "we can't make one chief."[12] Unfortunately, we do not know which Lakota leadership term Blue Earth used in his speech. Perhaps he said *wakiconza*, but the interpreter Colin Campbell translated it as "chief," a term whites frequently used when referring to an Indian leader.[13]

Painted Bear, a Yankton, also commented on the commissioners' strange request. "Father, this is the third time I have met with the whites," he began, rather sarcastically in B. Gratz Brown's opinion. "We don't understand their manners, nor their words. We know it is all very good, and for our good, but we don't understand it all."

Mitchell had more success with the Northern Cheyenne and Arapaho delegations who apparently had selected as head chiefs Walks with His Toes Turned Out and Little Owl, respectively. The commissioners duly acknowledged them before adjourning the meeting. However, Mitchell continued to press the Sioux delegation until twenty-four band representatives nominally approved the colonel's selection: Conquering Bear (Frightening Bear, or Scattering Bear), a Wazaza Brulé, whom Mitchell dubbed "head chief" of the Sioux. Conquering Bear did not relish the opportunity to wield what even the whites would deem such enormous decision-making authority. "Father, I am a young man and have no experience," he implored. "I do not desire to be chief of the Dahcotahs." But, if Mitchell insisted, he would oblige.

On 17 September the treaty was finally ready for signatures. The Brulé spokesmen—Conquering Bear, Blue Earth, Yellow Ears, Standing Bear, Burnt Man, and Eagle Body—and the Oglala delegates—Smoke, Bad Wound, Medicine Eagle, Man Afraid of His Horse, and Big Crane— "touched the pen," thereby endorsing the treaty. Six days later the commissioners distributed treaty gifts, and the great encampment of people and animals, which had long worn down the grass at dusty Horse Creek, dispersed happily.[14]

The Oglalas and Brulés were experienced negotiators, having bartered with whites since the establishment of trading posts in the 1820s, but the Lakotas' business transactions with fur traders and mountain men did not require them to adopt radical and permanent changes in their political customs. The 1851 Horse Creek council, however, marked Congress's first major attempt, through its official appointees, to interfere directly in native political affairs. Conquering Bear was a respected *itancan* among his own *tiyospaye*, but his authority did not extend to other Brulé bands and certainly not to the other subtribes and bands of the Sioux. Not only was the Wazaza chief expected to represent all the Sioux encamped at Horse Creek, but he was also required to accept responsibility for all depredations committed by individual tribal members, regardless of band or subtribal affiliation. The Lakotas at the council, including Conquering Bear himself, undoubtedly dismissed the appointment of a supreme executive for all the bands as yet another unfathomable white custom. Surely few, if any, among them seriously considered embracing it.

After the parties dispersed, the white emissaries carefully stored the treaty for the president's signature and Senate ratification.[15] If ratified and proclaimed, each word of the treaty would bear legal significance and in theory was to be strictly followed. Native Americans did not place the same degree of importance on written treaties as legal documents, however. That is not to say that they refused to honor them, but to Indian spokesmen it was the words *spoken* at the council that were important, not the words *written* in the treaty. Indeed, even if the Senate refused to ratify a specific treaty, Native American negotiators still considered it binding on both parties. (This distinction reflects the differences between the native people, whose cultural matrix was transmitted orally, and Americans, whose culture was passed down primarily in written form.) By placing their marks on the treaty, Indian spokesmen were essentially attesting to what they had said at the council, not what was necessarily written in the document. In 1805, for example, Zebulon Pike held a council with several bands of Sioux in which he requested the right of passage through their country as well as a small grant of land. After presenting a copy of the agreement to the councilors, Pike noted that it was "somewhat difficult to get them to sign the grant, as they conceived the word of honor should be taken for the Grant, without any Mark." However, Pike "convinced them, that not on their account but my own I wanted them to sign."[16]

Indian representatives often did not fully realize that whites deemed their signatures or marks as committing them only to those statements actually set down in the treaty. Muddied translations also marred efforts to obtain mutually satisfying agreements. Undoubtedly there were occasions when white commissioners deliberately deceived Indian councilors, or at least concealed some of the terms written in the document, in order to force settlements; and for their part Native American negotiators, in excusing their own treaty violations, could later pretend they had misunderstood the facts.[17]

If Native Americans placed little significance on written documents, why then did they endorse them? Raymond DeMallie argues that some Indian councilors signed treaties out of fear that if they did not, Americans would shift their allegiance to other Indian groups, possibly depriving the councilors' people of popular trade goods such as powder, lead, guns, steel knives, copper kettles, and calico. Perhaps Indian spokesmen also "touched the pen" in order to acquire the gifts whites had promised them in exchange.[18] The Indians at the Horse Creek council site knew that the U.S. government had promised them twenty-seven wagonloads of presents. Did their delegates sign the treaty merely to obtain them? Certainly they did not understand or accept the article of the treaty prohibiting intertribal war, for the Sioux resumed their campaigns against the Pawnees and Crows after the council adjourned.

In the summer of 1854 several Brulé and Oglala bands returned to the general vicinity of Fort Laramie. The Brulés were located on the North Fork of the Platte River near the independent trading post of James Bordeaux, approximately ten miles from Fort Laramie, whereas the Oglalas were situated near the American Fur Company warehouse, about five miles south of the fort. These Lakotas had come to trade buffalo skins and to collect from John Whitfield, Thomas Fitzpatrick's successor as agent for the tribes of the Upper Platte, the annuity goods provided by the 1851 Fort Laramie treaty. On 17 August a Mormon wagon train driving a small herd of cattle passed the Indian villages en route to the Salt Lake valley. As the Saints trundled by, a young Miniconjou warrior named Straight Foretop, or High Forehead, killed and butchered a straggling, half-dead cow from the Mormon herd that had wandered into the Wazaza Brulé village. The beast's owner reported the incident to Lt. Hugh Fleming, commander of Fort Laramie who had already locked horns with a band of Miniconjous over a separate incident during the summer of 1853. On the same day the Wazaza Brulé leader, Conquering Bear, appointed "head chief" of the Sioux at the Horse Creek council three years earlier, and whose *tiyospaye* was located in the area, arrived at the fort to discuss the incident.[19]

According to white authorities later investigating the complaint and the tragedy that would stem from it, the young Miniconjou lived around the Missouri River agencies but had come down to the Platte intending "to do something bad" before returning to his own *tiyospaye*. (His actions, the post officers concurred at the time, violated article 4 of the 1851 treaty, which required Indians to make restitution for any wrongs committed against American citizens or their property.) Resenting the damage inflicted annually by the tide of white emigrants, several Miniconjou warriors had seized the North Platte River ferry boat docked near Fort Laramie. A sergeant successfully recaptured the vessel but was fired on by the Miniconjous as he made his escape. This incident was brought to the attention of Lt. Richard Garnett, then commanding the post, who dispatched Fleming with twenty-three men and an interpreter to the Miniconjou village with orders to arrest the warriors responsible for shooting at the sergeant. If the Miniconjous refused to cooperate, the officer was directed "to take two or three prisoners, by force, if necessary." Fleming marched his detachment into the village where it was met with force. Three Indian men were wounded, three were killed, and two were seized as prisoners. After Straight Foretop butchered the Mormons' cow, Fleming ordered Lt. John Grattan of the Sixth Infantry to lead a detachment of twenty-nine men armed with two cannons and a mountain howitzer into the Wazaza Brulé village in order to seize the young Miniconjou temporarily lodged there.[20]

A Major E. Johnson later remarked that Lieutenant Grattan had left Fort Laramie "unusually excited." Fearing trouble, Conquering Bear sought the assistance of Man Afraid of His Horse, the Oglalas' principal *itancan*. Upon hearing of the gathering storm in the Brulé village, the Oglalas, who were encamped nearby, began heading toward it. In accordance with Lakota customs, Conquering Bear tried to compensate for the butchered cow by offering the Mormon the pick of his own herd of sixty horses, a a peacemaking gesture that would have yielded a beast undoubtedly more valuable than the lame cow. Grattan rejected this settlement, continuing instead to demand the surrender of the Miniconjou warrior. Conquering Bear warned the lieutenant that the young man was headstrong; besides, he was a Miniconjou, and no one among the Brulés could influence him.

Having failed to placate the lieutenant, both Man Afraid of His Horse and Conquering Bear went twice to the Miniconjou's lodge pleading with him to emerge, but the young man steadfastly refused, preferring to die rather than submit to a white soldier. The drunken demeanor of the post interpreter, Auguste Lucien, a mixed-blood Iowa intermarried with the Lakotas, only aggravated the already tense situation. Lucien hurled insults at the Brulés, taunting them that they were no match for Grattan's men, and that he would "eat their hearts raw." Man Afraid of His Horse tried to rectify the matter by begging James Bordeaux, the husband of a Brulé woman, to assume translation duties, for Lucien "did not talk straight" and "all his talk was about fighting." Lucien would have his wish. Unable to resolve the matter, a frustrated Lieutenant Grattan commanded his men to commence firing upon the Brulé encampment. When the hostilities ceased, Conquering Bear, the American government's "head chief," lay mortally wounded, and Grattan and his entire detail had been killed.[21]

Bearing the seriously wounded *itancan* on a travois, the Brulés and

Oglalas immediately struck their lodges, crossed the North Platte River, and headed to Rawhide Creek, eight miles from their former camp. The next morning a party of Oglala and Brulé warriors descended on the American Fur Company warehouse, where their annuities had been stored. After taking some goods they hastened back to their village where they made further plans to return to the warehouse to strip it bare. Even Bordeaux was threatened, his life spared only by the intervention of his Brulé relatives. On the third day after the incident, a large throng of Oglalas and Brulés assembled outside the American Fur Company store, where they discovered that the employees had fled in terror. Red Leaf brought a message from his brother Conquering Bear, who, although wounded nine times, was still alive. Red Leaf harangued the warriors that Conquering Bear had worked tirelessly for peace, that the American Fur Company and other traders had shown kindness to the people over the years, and that they should leave the warehouse—but his efforts proved futile. Ignoring the advice of their *itancan,* the warriors stormed the door and removed everything except for provisions and a keg of whiskey.[22]

Conquering Bear died nine days after the Grattan incident, his decision to intercede having cost him his life. The *itancan* had known from the beginning that he could not coerce the young Miniconjou in his camp; perhaps he had also anticipated that whites would consider the loss of one cow a violation of the 1851 treaty, and that if steps were not taken to settle the matter, his followers would lose their annuities. When Conquering Bear discussed the Mormon's complaint with post officers, was he fulfilling his role as Colonel Mitchell's head chief of the Sioux, or did he intervene merely because it was his *tiyospaye* to which Straight Foretop had come? If Conquering Bear felt comfortable in his new role as supreme executive, why did he immediately seek the advice of Man Afraid of His Horse, the Hunkpatila Oglalas' principal and most respected *itancan*? It is conceivable that Brulé and Oglala councilors temporarily accepted Conquering Bear's new role as the Americans' head chief because these Lakotas believed he was the only man to whom the white soldiers would listen.

Army brass investigating the affair released several reports, some of them highly critical of Lieutenant Grattan's actions. Maj. O. F. Winship, who arrived at Fort Laramie shortly after the incident, blamed the young lieutenant's inexperience and the irresponsible actions of the drunken interpreter for the sad event. Winship believed that Indians abhorred confinement, preferring to die rather than suffer the humiliation of arrest and imprisonment. If Grattan had known this, the major doubted he would have taken the steps he did. Major Johnson also considered the lieutenant, a recent graduate of West Point, ignorant of Lakota customs and consequently ill prepared to handle negotiations. Commenting on Conquering Bear's inability to deliver the young Miniconjou warrior, Johnson remarked that while the Wazaza Brulé leader's influence was notable among his own *tiyospaye,* "mainly attributable to his great personal courage," his failure to order the youth to surrender was "nothing more than might be expected, for we all know how feeble the authority of a single chief is over the individuals of other bands."[23] Indeed, Major Johnson might have added that even if the young warrior had been a Brulé, chances are that Conquering Bear would have failed to seize the youth without the cooperation of the camp *akicita.*

Despite criticism leveled at Grattan by some of his colleagues, the army retaliated the following year for what it had dubbed the Grattan Massacre, and for the raids by the Wazazas and other Brulés along the emigrant road to avenge Conquering Bear's death. Shortly after the *itancan* died, Red Leaf, Spotted Tail, Young Conquering Bear, and Long Chin attacked a mail stagecoach at Cold Spring, thirty-five miles south of Fort Laramie, killing the driver and his assistant. The only passenger sustained a leg wound but managed to escape while the Brulés looted the stage. This deed done, the Brulés and Oglalas temporarily left the Platte River, dispersing northward to the Missouri River, the Black Hills, and the Powder River country.[24]

In August 1855 Thomas Twiss, the new agent for the Upper Platte and Arkansas, attempted to forestall further conflicts by presenting his own recommendations for securing peace. He believed most Lakotas within his jurisdiction desired peace, and that only a few Brulé bands, most notably the Wazazas, advocated war. The agent thus informed Oglala and Brulé leaders in the area that if they wished to be considered friendly by his government, they should move their bands to the south side of the Platte River. Those who opted to remain on the north bank surely would be deemed hostile. By early September, Little Thunder's Wazaza people were still north of the Platte, and on the third, Brig. Gen. William Harney (whom the Sioux named the Hornet) subdued them at Ash Hollow, several miles north of the Upper Platte River near present Lewellen, Nebraska. Before firing on the camp, Harney personally contacted Little Thunder, who, in the words of Capt. John Todd, a member of the general's command, told Harney that "he could not control his young men, that he himself was friendly," and that "he did not want to fight." After this exchange, according to Todd, the general refused to shake hands with Little Thunder. Instead, Harney ordered the Brulé *itancan* to tell his warriors to come out and fight, for only with a battle could they "settle their differences." After Little Thunder had returned to his village, Harney ordered his men to fire. The general later reported eighty-six Wazazas killed (none of them warriors), five wounded, and seventy women and children taken in chains to Fort Laramie.[25]

Highlighting the factionalism that was unfolding between the Departments of the Interior and War over the regulation of Indian-white affairs, Interior commissioner George Manypenny criticized Harney for ravaging Little Thunder's band of forty-one lodges. But his subordinate, Thomas Twiss, reported that many of the Oglalas and Brulés who had moved south of the Platte River on his orders did not sympathize with the plight of Little Thunder's people. They argued that Little Thunder had only himself to blame for the loss of life and property, for Twiss had warned him of the army's intentions weeks in advance. Harney dismissed the various opinions emanating from the Office of Indian Affairs, believing that only military intervention could avert widespread conflicts with the Sioux. The general had recently received orders from Secretary of War Jefferson Davis to negotiate a peace treaty between the army and the Sioux. After delivering his Brulé prisoners to Fort Laramie, Harney went on to Fort Pierre, where he had asked representatives of the Lakotas and Yanktons to meet him in late October, at which time he notified them of a formal peace council slated to convene at Fort Pierre the following spring.[26]

In the first week of March 1856, leaders of the Two Kettles, Yanktons, Hunkpapas, Blackfeet Sioux, Sans Arcs, Miniconjous, Platte River Brulés, and Yanktonais gathered for talks with Harney.[27] He ordered them to return all stolen property seized from the wagon trains in recent months, to surrender those responsible for killing white emigrants, to settle their differences with the Pawnees once and for all, and to avoid henceforth the Overland Trail and the road linking Forts Pierre and Laramie. During the proceedings, the Miniconjou delegates agreed to surrender Straight Foretop. (He was immediately placed into custody at the fort.) In return, the assembled representatives were promised presents and the reinstatement of their treaty annuities.[28]

Whereas the Horse Creek council of 1851 had marked Congress's first endeavor to modify Lakota political customs, the 1856 Fort Pierre proceedings symbolized the U.S. Army's attempt to interfere with Sioux political affairs. Harney directed the Sioux delegations to select and appoint once again a predetermined number of "head chiefs" and "subchiefs" to govern themselves and to maintain peaceful relations with whites. Those chosen, he cautioned, "would be the only chiefs recognized by the President, myself, or their Indian agent." Harney believed that since confusion reigned, what with the president appointing some men "chiefs," military officers recognizing others, and *tiyospaye* and traders acknowledging altogether different men, only chaos could thrive in this situation. So "to correct this evil," Harney hoped the president would hereafter consider as head chiefs only the principal men nominated and appointed at the Fort Pierre council. Once chosen, only presidential consent could remove them from office.[29]

The general directed the head chiefs to handpick a number of men from each band, mostly younger warriors, to serve as subchiefs and "marshalls" that would assist them in implementing the new plan. Harney insisted that these men always obey the chiefs, for he had grown weary of the Lakota elders' usual plea that they could not control the young men. The Hornet predicted that as long as the appointed chiefs, subchiefs, and warriors—who would receive official uniforms in accordance with their designated "ranks"—were compelled to depend on the federal government to sustain them in office, their extended families would be "easily controlled."[30]

On the advice of Thomas Twiss, agent for the Upper Platte and Arkansas tribes, the Oglalas in his vicinity did not attend the March sessions at Fort Pierre despite Harney's repeated demands for an Oglala delegation. As a civilian Indian agent, Twiss answered not to the War Department but to the Department of the Interior, whose superintendent, Alfred Cumming, and commissioner, George Manypenny, had not sanctioned Harney's campaign and had openly criticized the Fort Pierre proceedings. Twiss himself complained that it would be inappropriate for the military to dominate peace talks. Twiss therefore notified Oglala leaders around Fort Laramie that they were under no obligation to attend the Fort Pierre assembly. Harney reacted to this news by ordering Col. William Hoffman to restrict Twiss's communications with the Lakotas at the fort, and by dispatching messages to the Oglalas and other Sioux bands that if they did not appear at Fort Pierre, the army would consider them enemies. By the following month several Oglala bands had reached the fort, where the general discussed with them the treaty and his proposal for modifying Sioux government. According to official reports, Harney selected Mischief Maker as the Oglalas' primary chief. Secondary sources, however, list Bad Wound, a prominent southern Oglala *itancan,* as the general's head chief.[31]

General Harney predicted that his modified political system for the Lakotas would ameliorate Indian-white relations by improving the channels of communication between the two peoples. Much to his dismay, President Franklin Pierce reacted unfavorably to the Fort Pierre treaty. The president did not regard the general's stipulations drafted at the councils as a suitable basis for such an important legal document. He therefore refused to submit the treaty to the Senate for its consideration. As Pierce considered the Fort Pierre plan a "mere administrative regulation" that required only funding, not ratification, he sent it to the House of Representatives for its approval. The representatives failed to respond to the president's request for immediate appropriations "on account of a misconception of facts." The House resented the Senate's ratification powers, and sometimes stubbornly refused to allocate funds for Indian treaties over which they had little control. Even though the House by 1858 had appropriated monies to implement Harney's proposed modifications, the impending secession crisis and the outbreak of the Civil War placed enormous drains on congressmen's energies and treasury funds.[32]

Consequently, Harney's plan died a slow death, but there is no evidence to suggest that most of the Sioux would have at that juncture entertained such blatant interference with their own political customs. Nowhere in the general's report does he explain how the United States intended to enforce his proposals. Harney's plan for a head chief with life tenure, removable only with the president's permission, was so absurdly rigid that even American citizens would have balked at the concept if it had been applied to them. The plan ran counter to the exceptional fluidity of Lakota political customs. How did Harney expect young warriors to obey unfailingly the word of a supreme leader over extended periods of time? Not even a *blotahunka* or camp *akicita* wielded that much decision-making authority, as dissenting Lakotas were free to leave their *tiyospaye* at will to join others. Providing limited annuities in the form of food, agricultural implements, and seeds, and doling out cast-off military uniforms to selected men hardly seemed effective tools for drastically and permanently redefining the roles and statuses of the *wakiconza, blotahunka, itancan,* headmen, and camp *akicita.*

The Hornet failed to create a new political order for the Sioux. Indeed, American policymakers as a whole would discover through the years that converting the Oglala Lakotas into docile, pliable people with dependent leaders would prove more difficult than they could possibly have imagined. Still, Harney's military campaign against Little Thunder's people had stung sufficiently to induce the Oglalas and Brulés to abandon temporarily the Oregon Trail. The Bear people—many of them Kiyuksas and True Oglalas whose influential leaders were Bad Wound, Little Wound, and Whistler—moved southward to hunt on the Republican River, from which they sent out war parties against the Pawnees. The Smoke people, Bad Faces, Oyuhpes, and Hunkpatilas, whose most prominent *itancan* by this time was Man Afraid of His Horse, headed north to the Cheyenne River and Powder River country to barter with Americans. There, they took advantage of the fur trade to obtain weapons for their fights with the Crows. Lakotas had already pushed the Crows from the Laramie Plains, and now continued to drive them deeper into the Yellowstone River country.[33]

Not all Oglalas and Brulés left the Platte River valley, however. A new band became more prominent by the mid-1850s comprised of both Oglalas and Brulés, many of whom had intermarried with white traders and soldiers. Some of their kin scornfully dubbed them Wagluhe, or Loafers, as they preferred to remain around Fort Laramie and other trading posts.[34]

# Various Strategies of the Oglala Leaders, 1859–1868

While the Oglalas and Brulés periodically harrassed the Pawnees and Crows, American prospectors moved eastward from depleted California strikes into the Rocky Mountains, searching once more for gold and silver. Just two years after the Fort Pierre peace talks, miners discovered precious metals at Cherry Creek on the South Platte River, in the Colorado Territory. News of this and additional strikes in Idaho and Montana triggered other waves of white emigration across the Great Plains. Although few panhandlers struck it rich, the lure of gold and silver proved far too strong for the thousands who streamed steadily into the new federal territories. Furthermore, eastern and European capital poured in to construct transcontinental railroads, thereby facilitating movement to and from the east, Rocky Mountains, and the Pacific coast. Responding to recent developments in the West, the federal government turned its attention to the Bighorn and Yellowstone River country, the lands claimed by northern Oglalas and their relatives, the Miniconjous, Hunkpapas, Two Kettles, and Sans Arcs.

By 1860 Capt. William Reynolds had put together the Yellowstone expedition whose objectives included determining the region's climate, topography, flora, fauna, and suitability for military bases. In addition, Reynolds received orders from his superiors to mark out a wagon route connecting the Oregon Trail and the Yellowstone-Missouri Basin. The route followed by the expedition from the Bighorn River to the Platte River approximated the future Bozeman Road to Montana.[1]

The Oregon Trail through the Platte valley had generated new problems for the Oglalas and other Lakotas, but the construction of the Bozeman Road in the 1860s ushered in a new era in Oglala-American relations, eventually prompting the United States to develop further its western Indian policy. While American civilian and military leaders hotly debated the best method of regulating Lakota-white affairs on the plains, Oglala councilors adopted various strategies in response to the challenge of incessant encroachment on their lands, including outright warfare, treaty diplomacy, or merely leading their bands away from American settlements.

After the Oglalas emerged from their winter villages in early 1861, heeding the commands of their *wakiconza* and *akicita* as they busily directed movement to the spring encampments, far to the east gunshots fired at Fort Sumter, South Carolina, signaled the beginning of the bloody and protracted Civil War, a conflict that mirrored on a much larger and more violent scale the feud that had splintered the Oglalas into northern and southern divisions twenty years earlier. On 12 April 1861 American Northerners and Southerners launched their own violent campaigns to settle grievances. This war between the states pitted Unionists against Confederates, but it hindered neither the predictable hegira of American emigrants nor their nation's territorial designs. By the time the Confederacy surrendered at Appomattox on 9 April 1865, the territories of Dakota, Montana, and Nebraska had already been carved out of American land claims.

During the Civil War years, and especially in the immediate postbellum period, new transportation routes—such as the Bozeman Road, a major artery branching from the old Overland Trail west of Fort Laramie, surveyed and constructed between 1863 and 1864 by John Bozeman—proliferated in the West. In January 1865 Congressman Asahel Hubbard of Iowa introduced a bill to cut a wagon trail from the Missouri River to Virginia City, Montana Territory. Congress approved his recommendation, and the act of 3 March 1865 authorized the Department of the Interior to supervise, with army assistance, not one but four new wagon roads. The first would originate at the mouth of the Niobrara River, snaking northwest to Virginia City, with an eastern branch linking the city of Omaha, Nebraska Territory; the second would begin at the mouth of the Cheyenne River, Dakota Territory, weaving southward to intersect the Niobrara River; the third would run from the western boundary of Minnesota to the Cheyenne River, and the fourth would start at Virginia City, heading further west to Lewiston, Idaho. On Hubbard's advice, Secretary of the Interior John Usher awarded a lucrative surveying and construction contract for the Niobrara-Bozeman trails to Col. James Sawyer of Sioux City, Iowa. Officials anticipated that by the late 1860s the Bozeman Road and the interconnecting Sawyer Road would provide transportation networks linking northeastern merchants to the mining settlements of Montana and Idaho.[2]

Despite federal funding for additional wagon roads, this mode of transportation was rapidly becoming obsolete. American entrepreneurs clamored to construct transcontinental railroads before the Civil War erupted, and in the postbellum period they poured capital into revamped railroad projects. Such schemes delighted western travelers, but each new railroad section jeopardized Native American lifeways. By 1867 the westward progress of the Union Pacific railroad had driven a wedge through the great bison herds of the plains. By 1878 commerical and sports hunters had slaughtered so many beasts that the southern bison herd had been seriously depleted. Five years later a scientific expedition to the Great Plains found only two hundred bison during its sojourn. Moreover, the survival of the northern herd also had been in jeopardy for some time. Buffalo hides were shipped eastward to tanneries that accepted them as alternative sources of commercial leather, whereas buffalo tongues, a delicacy for both Plains Indians and whites, were hauled to pickling and canning factories. Many buffalo carcasses, however, were simply left to rot on the dry prairie.[3]

By August 1859, Lakota, Northern Cheyenne, and Arapaho spokesmen had complained repeatedly to Thomas Twiss, agent for the Upper Platte tribes, regarding the perceived loss of buffalo in their hunting grounds. In a special report to Commissioner of Indian Affairs A. B. Greenwood, Twiss remarked that Oglala and Brulé bands in the Platte valley had prevented parties of white travelers from entering their hunting territories, "pretty roughly too, for fear that the buffalo would be destroyed or scared away, and never return again." Twiss added that the Indians "entertain a superstitious belief that the buffalo will not return to the same place again where he may have scented the white man." Twiss had tried to allay the Lakotas' rising concerns in a council the previous September, but he had been "put down and most effectually silenced" by one of the band *itancan*.[4]

From July to late September 1859 Twiss convened several councils with the Upper Platte Oglalas, Brulés, Northern Cheyennes, and Arapahos near his agency at Deer Creek to discuss the issue. The most prominent Lakotas in attendance at the session were Man Afraid of His Horse (the northern Oglala head *itancan*), Stabber, Bold Bear, Sitting Bear, and Standing Elk. Joining them were the Northern Cheyennes White Crow, Big Wolf, and White Cow; and the Arapahoes Little Owl, Friday, Cut

Nose, Black Bear, and Medicine Man, the latter appointed primary council spokesman by the allied tribes.[5]

The shortage of the buffalo in the Platte River valley at this time, Medicine Man opened, had forced their young men to hunt in Crow country along the Yellowstone River—a ten-day trip that wearied their ponies. So they had agreed to try a more sedentary lifestyle near the agencies if the president of the United States would promise to supplement their needs. Indeed, as long as the president accepted the position of Great Father, thereby forging a kinship tie with the Lakotas, his role as the bands' symbolic father required him to respond positively to any favors asked of him, including providing supplies and protection when necessary.[6]

The Oglalas at the council chose Horse Creek and Deer Creek for their reserve, the Brulés selected a White River location, and their Northern Cheyenne and Arapaho friends agreed to settle along the Laramie and the Cache la Poudre Rivers, respectively. But the Great Father might as well take the rest of their land in the valley, Medicine Man concluded, for it was "no longer of any use to us, as nearly all the game has disappeared."[7]

To what extent were the Lakotas in need of buffalo meat and other supplies? Peter Wilson, the first official resident agent for the Lakotas of the Upper Missouri wrote in April 1825 that the "Indians are starving" because they had found few buffalo. Around this time, Paul Wilhelm, Duke of Württemberg, visited Fort Recovery on the Upper Missouri River. There he met fur trader Joshua Pilcher of the Missouri Fur Company and several bands of hungry Lakotas, Yanktons, and Sissetons camped in the vicinity. According to the duke, because so many people were traveling along the banks of the Missouri, "the bison had withdrawn, and the hunt was very sparse for the needs" of the Sioux. The "lack of food is at times so great among the Indians," he added, "that they consume all sorts of things that would seem most unwholesome to other human beings."

When missionary Stephan Riggs left Lac qui Parle in the fall of 1840 to visit Fort Pierre, on the west bank of the Missouri River, he saw relatively few buffalo on his journey, but had been told that great numbers had passed north of his course just a few weeks earlier. Still, Riggs mentioned that when he spoke to trader Robert Campbell at Fort Pierre, a man who had lived in the region for twenty-five years, Campbell claimed that the bison population was steadily decreasing. And explorer John Frémont remarked in July 1842 that a grasshopper plague had forced the bison herds to move away from the Platte River valley in search of grass. Consequently, the Oglalas he met "had been nearly starved to death," and forced to consume their horses. After encountering several other Lakota *tiyospaye* between 1842 and 1843, Frémont continued, "I found the Sioux Indians of the Upper Platte *demontés*, as their French traders expressed it, with the failure of the buffalo; and in [1843], large villages from the Upper Missouri came over to the mountains at the heads of the Platte, in search of them. The rapidly progressive failure of their principal and almost their only means of subsistence has created great alarm among them." Just over a decade later, fur trader Edwin Denig also remarked that the bison herds had dwindled in the Upper Missouri River country, leaving the Oglalas short of buffalo meat and hides. However, Capt. John Todd, who traveled from Fort Laramie to Fort Pierre in June of 1855, noted in his journal that the buffalo were "very numerous" and that "the eye grew heavy with the countless thousands that covered the plains on both sides of the road and [North Platte] River." Still, historian John McDermott claims that the buffalo had virtually disappeared in the Fort Laramie area by the mid-1860s.[8]

The Lakotas could certainly hunt antelope, deer, elk, and other small game instead of buffalo, but whether they chose to do so is not the crucial issue from a Lakota perspective. More important is the belief that the Lakotas' ancestors were born from the Pte Oyate (the Buffalo Cow Nation); that White Buffalo Cow Woman brought the sacred pipe to the people; and that they, *tatanka* (the male buffalo relatives), and Maka Ina (Mother Earth) are united in a sacred, harmonious relationship. One cannot exist without the other. Should the buffalo disappear entirely, the tightly woven threads that bind together the Lakotas, the land, and buffalo in this sacred relationship would begin to unravel.[9] Thus, it is understandable why even the perceived loss of buffalo would cause concern among the *tiyospaye*.

Some of the Oglalas' relatives encamped in the Upper Missouri River valley likewise expressed frustration over the disturbance of the buffalo herds. Rather than appealing to the president for aid, however, several *tiyospaye* advocated severing diplomatic ties formed a decade earlier with Americans at the great Horse Creek council. In May 1862, Samuel Latta, federal Indian agent for the Upper Missouri Lakotas and Dakotas, boarded the steamer *Spread Eagle* bound for Fort Pierre, Dakota Territory. He brought with him the 1851 treaty annuity goods designated for the Sioux people. When Latta disembarked on 27 May he found waiting for him two to three thousand Sioux—mostly Blackfeet, Sans Arcs, Miniconjous, Two Kettles, Hunkpapas, Brulés, Yanktonais, and a few Oglalas.

The following day he reread the 1851 Fort Laramie treaty to tribal spokesmen before delivering the annuities, but later reminded the commissioner of Indian affairs that these people at Fort Pierre did not share the sentiments of the majority of the Sioux.[10]

Bear's Rib, a Hunkpapa appointed "head chief" by Gen. William Harney six years earlier, and eleven other spokesmen representing the Sioux gathered at Fort Pierre. Each year since the great council at Horse Creek it had been the same old story, Bear's Rib told Latta. The president had not kept his word; no agreement had been made to allow the right of passage for white emigrants who brought disease into their country and disturbed their buffalo relatives who sustained them. Traders and teamsters hauling annuities were welcome but only if they came via the Missouri River. He warned that many Sioux *tiyospaye* now harbored grudges against the United States, and wished to dissolve all social bonds with Americans. Indeed, some Lakotas had grown so angry that they had even threatened to punish their own relatives—the bands now assembled before the agent—if they accepted the annuities.[11]

Latta remarked that Bear's Rib, "a brave and good man" in his opinion, hesitated when the treaty goods were offered him. The Hunkpapa instructed the agent not to distribute the items, the quality and quantity of which, he added, brought little satisfaction and only "created discord rather than harmony." His followers had honored the 1851 treaty and heeded Harney's words at the 1856 council. They longed for peace but the Great Father must also do his part to assist them. When Bear's Rib concluded his speech, Latta finally convinced him to take the treaty supplies with the understanding that none would be sent the following year. This act sealed the Hunkpapa's fate. Bear's Rib had already been ostracized by most of his subtribe for steadfastly supporting the Great Father's people, and his latest act proved too much for a small party of militant Sans Arcs camped near the fort. A few days later several Sans Arcs warriors entered the gates of Fort Pierre, killing Bear's Rib and others for accepting annuity payments. Feather Tied to His Hair, Bald Eagle, Red Hair, One That Shouts, Little Bear, Crow That Looks, Bear Heart, Little Knife, and White at Both Ends, all of whom were Hunkpapa spokesmen, later dispatched a foreboding message to their agent at Fort Berthold, Dakota Territory. Bear's Rib had been warned repeatedly not to take annuities. "He had no ears," the Hunkpapas stated, so Sans Arcs warriors "gave him ears by killing him. . . . We acknowledge no agent, and we notify you for the last time to bring us no more goods." The murdered Hunkpapa's two hundred and fifty followers, Latta continued, were now "wandering outcasts in the country," for few bands dared or desired to shelter them. After observing these events, Latta quickly concluded that white emigrants could no longer expect safe passage anywhere on the western trails or up the Missouri River.[12]

Although the United States in subsequent years continued to send annuities by Missouri River steamer, Samuel Latta had witnessed enough to fear the Sioux people camped near his agency. Newton Edmunds, governor of the Dakota Territory, discovered in the summer of 1865 that Latta had completed his assignment to distribute annuity goods to the bands along the river but had failed to submit his annual report, instead returning immediately, without gubernatorial permission, to his home in Leavenworth, Kansas.[13]

Reports such as the ones filed periodically by Twiss, Latta, and other Sioux agents further dampened the morale of the Indian Office, already publicly maligned for alleged corruption and inefficiency. Prior to the Civil War, government officials generally neglected Indian affairs until news of interracial violence spurred civilian and military policymakers into action. Moreover, after 1861 the slavery issue, the secession crisis, and later the impeachment trial of President Andrew Johnson largely overshadowed in Americans' minds the tensions between Indian and whites. All too often employees of the Indian Office did little while Congress delayed or ignored Indian appropriation bills and administrative reforms. Furthermore, successive American presidents tended to follow the established custom of staffing the Indian Office with men who were popular with western politicians. Appointments were frequently rewards for loyal party service—qualifications for posts being considered inconsequential or minor hindrances at best—and little coordination existed between the staff in the office's Washington headquarters and Indian agents in the field.[14]

Henry Whipple, bishop of the Minnesota Protestant Episcopal Church and missionary to the Santee Sioux, often denounced the inexperience and dishonesty of Indian Office party hacks. In one of his frequent diatribes, Whipple charged that inefficiency and fraud characterized the entire U.S. Indian Office. Senator James Nesmith of Oregon echoed the bishop's sentiments. "If there is any one department of our Government worse managed than another," he remarked, "it is that which relates to our Indian affairs." In the senator's opinion, "mismanagement, bad faith, fraud, speculation, and downright robbery have been its great distinguishing features."[15]

Both Whipple and Nesmith probably overstated their case, although documentation does exist to support numerous allegations of fraud and poor judgment on the part of Indian Office personnel. The office hired private contractors to provide Indian tribes with goods and services such as food, transportation, clothing, and agency buildings. Local legislators or territorial officials, often friends of the contractors, kept themselves informed of funds allocated to Native Americans in their region and encouraged their acquaintances to submit high contract bids to the Indian Service. Furthermore, government traders, who relied on the patronage of agents and local politicians to obtain their licenses, were not averse to dipping their fingers into tribal annuity pots. Some traders gained notoriety for overcharging Indian clients, deliberately maintaining incomplete or inaccurate records in order to convince government superintendents that their Native American customers were forever in debt and to support reimbursement requests directly from annuity funds. Governor Edmunds learned that some Lakotas believed licensed traders schemed with their agents to obtain treaty items that were subsequently sold, not distributed, to band chiefs and headmen. Sioux leaders accused a few of their agents of profiting handsomely by turning over only half of the annuity goods—while requiring the chiefs and headmen to sign receipts for a full issue—and then selling the remaining goods to traders, military posts, and white settlers.[16]

On the eve of the Civil War, philanthropists who advocated sweeping reform in the Indian Service were few in number but nevertheless vociferous. In 1858 John Beeson of Illinois privately published *A Plea for the Indians,* in which he argued that "highly energized savageism" characterized Plains Indian cultures. In a petition to President Abraham Lincoln, Beeson suggested that only formal education, private ownership of property, Christian instruction, and democratic representation could "civilize" all Native Americans and prepare them for assimilation into American society. Several illuminaries supported and extended Beeson's version of Indian reform: Bishop Henry Whipple, who would later dominate the reform movement; Senator Henry Rice; Philadelphia merchant and benefactor William Welsh; and abolitionists Henry Ward Beecher, Samuel Tappan, and Wendell Phillips. Rather than deploying troops to engage Native Americans in endless skirmishes throughout the trans-Mississippi West, these self-appointed "Friends of the Indians" argued that it was morally correct (and more economically expedient) to settle Indians on reservations, where honest traders and agents could instill in them the true spirit of evangelical Protestantism. The crusaders lobbied Congress to act on behalf of the Indians, and by 1863 their efforts had convinced a number of congressmen to develop fully the reservation system as the best method of controlling the tribes of this vast region. By the end of the 1850s eight reservations had been established in the far West, inaugurating the reservation system as standard U.S. Indian policy.[17] Major problems persisted, however. How would American politicians persuade or otherwise compel the plains tribes, including the Lakota people, to accept reservation life?

In 1851 and 1858 the Dakotas negotiated treaties with the United States by which they ceded over twenty-eight million acres of land in exchange for annual payments and supplies, along with a reservation beside the Minnesota River. Congressional indifference and the callous attitude of the Dakotas' agent, who did little to ensure that the Indians received adequate food, money, and supplies guaranteed by treaty, infuriated Dakota leaders. By 1862 the pent-up anger and frustration led the Dakotas into war against the whites surrounding their reservation. Gen. Henry Sibley was dispatched into the field to subdue the Sioux, ending the Dakota-U.S. conflict within weeks. By December President Lincoln had condemned thirty-eight Dakotas to death on the gallows and later approved the westward removal of the Sioux from Minnesota into the Dakota Territory.

Similarly, in 1861 several bands of Southern Cheyennes and Arapahos relinquished to the United States all of their people's lands in the Colorado Territory except for a small reservation along the Arkansas River named Sand Creek. By the following year the shortage of food at the reservation forced the young men to hunt outside its boundaries where clashes with local white farmers, ranchers, and militia soon escalated into war. In November 1864 Col. John Chivington's volunteers, in a brutal dawn raid at Sand Creek, slaughtered almost all of Black Kettle's and White Antelope's peaceful band of two hundred Southern Cheyennes and Arapahos, two-thirds of them unarmed elders, women, and children. Telegraph wires hummed as news of the atrocities reverberated throughout the United States. The Friends of the Indians publicly denounced the tragedy, and with renewed zeal challenged the Indian Office to weed out its corrupt and incompetent appointees. While Washington bureaucrats

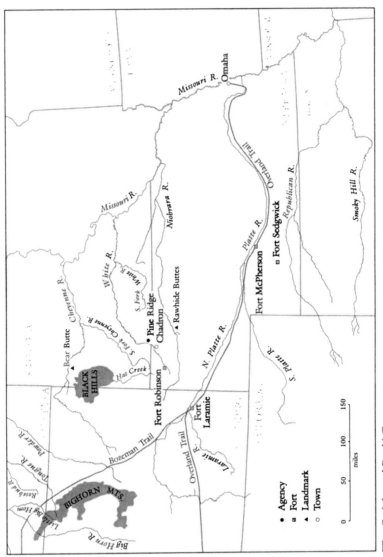

The Oglala and Brulé Country

continued to champion the reservation system, survivors of Sand Creek bore the news of the brutal assault to their relatives and Lakota allies. War erupted throughout the plains in the wake of the massacre, as predicted by army officers. While U.S. congressmen hastened to conclude the Civil War and make preparations for reconstructing the Southern states, Lakota, Cheyenne, and Arapaho war parties coordinated retaliatory strikes against the emigrant trails, torching ranches and stage stations along the South Platte River, sacking the town of Julesburg, Colorado, seizing livestock, destroying miles of telegraph wires, and virtually severing Denver from the rest of the United States.

Incapable of immediately restoring peace in the West, Congress and the president permitted military forces to take the upper hand in Indian-white affairs. Under the direction of Maj. Gen. John Pope, commander of the Division of the Missouri and a strong advocate of using military force against Lakotas and their Cheyenne and Arapaho allies, the U.S. army sent thousands of men into the field, many of them volunteers, to defend the overland routes. In the summer of 1865, however, troops discovered war parties suddenly heading north from the central plains to confront Americans steaming up the Missouri River and passing over the Bozeman Road. Ironically, even while the army continued its campaign against the allied tribes, federal legislators were hastily assembling a new policy toward Native Americans—one that stressed peace and patient diplomacy rather than military force, and one they deemed more appropriate for inaugurating the plains reservation system. Thus, prior to adjourning, Congress established a joint committee—the Doolittle committee—the first of many official investigations into Indian-white affairs in the West, and also authorized treaty commissioners to initiate talks with as many Sioux, Cheyenne, and Arapaho bands as possible.[18]

The Doolittle committee included two members of the Senate Committee on Indian Affairs, chairman James Doolittle of Wisconsin and James Nesmith of Oregon. LaFayette Foster of Connecticut was the third senator. U.S. representatives included William Windom of Minnesota, chairman of the House Committee on Indian Affairs; William Higby of California; Asahel Hubbard of Iowa; and Lewis Ross of Illinois. Hubbard proved an interesting selection for the committee. While he publicly worked for peace, he also praised Pope's intentions to continue the 1865 campaign against intertribal war parties on the northern plains. Dividing into small groups, Doolittle, Foster, and Ross agreed to visit the state of Kansas, the territories of Colorado, New Mexico, and Utah, and the Indian Territory; Nesmith and Higby were assigned the Pacific coast, the state of Nevada, and the territories of Idaho and western Montana; and Windom and Hubbard were given the state of Minnesota and the territories of Nebraska, Dakota, and eastern Montana.[19]

During the summer Senators Doolittle and Foster and Representative Ross visited Colorado Territory as part of their lengthy fact-finding tour. When they reached Denver, Governor John Evans greeted them with a grand reception at the opera house, where only a few months previously Col. John Chivington had displayed to a standing-room-only crowd the bloody scalps of Southern Cheyennes and Arapahos slaughtered at Sand Creek. Doolittle discussed federal Indian policy with the audience. During open debate, the question arose as to whether Native Americans should be placed on reservations or exterminated in a sustained genocidal campaign. Doolittle was shaken and appalled by the audience's response, which, he remarked, was "almost loud enough to raise the roof of the Opera House—'Exterminate them! Exterminate them!'"[20]

The chilling emotions expressed in the Denver Opera House symbolized the degree to which American citizens themselves had become polarized over current Indian-white relations. Lakotas, including the Oglalas, were also dividing again, this time into two other major factions—war and peace—as the U.S. commissioners would soon discover when they tried to secure and maintain peace on the plains. In a similar vein, the deepening animosity between the military and civilian wings of the federal government reflected the broad dichotomy between western and eastern Americans, between those who advocated a policy of genocide and those who crusaded for paternalistic but peaceful reforms. A number of army officers, including General Pope, argued that they understood Native American customs far better than civilian bureaucrats, and that relations with Lakotas and other Indian people could be improved considerably if only Congress would transfer the Indian Office back to the War Department where it had originated, and where the generals believed it rightfully belonged. Broadly speaking, westerners supported military control of official Indian policy, dismissing eastern politicians and philanthropists like Bishop Whipple and Senator James Doolittle as do-gooders who were too far removed both geographically and emotionally from the plains to grasp fully the nature and scope of Indian-white conflicts.

After long months of fieldwork and analyzing the responses of a twenty-three-question circular previously mailed to army officers, Indian agents, superintendents, and other field employees, the Doolittle committee returned to Washington in the fall of 1865 to commence writing its final report to Congress. In January 1867, almost two years after the committee's creation, the members submitted their exhaustive findings. The five-hundred-page document, entitled *The Condition of the Indian Tribes,* painted pictures of Indian disease, decimation, and poverty. But aside from recommending a system of five inspection districts—each served by a triumvirate composed of the assistant commissioner of Indian affairs, an officer of the regular U.S. Army, and a third person nominated by religious groups and selected by the president, all of whom would pay annual visits to tribes, investigate complaints against army and civilian personnel, and preserve the peace—the Doolittle report failed to provide a lasting solution to interracial strife.

On the heels of the Doolittle committee, Congress appropriated twenty thousand dollars to appoint yet another special commission to negotiate with the Sioux. During late October 1865, Governor Edmunds of the Dakota Territory, ex-officio superintendent of Indian affairs for the Northern Territory, Maj. Gen. Samuel Curtis, Brigadier General Sibley, Henry Reed, and Orrin Guernsey met Lakota and Dakota representatives at Fort Sully, near the mouth of the Cheyenne River. Governor Edmunds's official report suggested that the desire to hold autumn peace talks rested in part on regional self-interest rather than on a strictly concerted effort to conclude the northern plains war. Edmunds feared that Dakota territory had gained a reputation in the states of being war-torn and unsafe for white settlement. Indeed emigrants had ceased relocating there, jeopardizing the territory's chances for future statehood. Thus the sooner peace could be publicly proclaimed with the Sioux, the better.[21]

By the twenty-eighth, several *tiyospaye* of the southern Oglalas, Lower Brulés, Blackfeet, Hunkpapas, Sans Arcs, Two Kettles, Yanktons, and Yanktonais had successfully concluded, in separate assemblies, a peace treaty with the Edmunds commission, thereby permitting the United States to establish roads through their hunting grounds and to assist those among the Sioux who wished to farm. In return the various bands were promised ten thousand dollars per annum for twenty years. Long Bull, Charging Bear, and Man Who Stands On the Hill represented approximately two thousand southern Oglalas at the Fort Sully council. These men had adopted their own strategies to protect their extended families and certainly could not speak for other southern Oglala *tiyospaye* nor for the great body of northern Oglalas camped in the Black Hills and Powder

River country, many of whom had opted to prolong the war with the United States. But the commissioners claimed that their nation had made peace with all the Sioux, prompting newspaper editors to declare the Bozeman Road to Montana safe for westbound whites. General Pope refused to participate in the celebration. Scoffing at the Fort Sully treaty, he countered that only sustained military engagements would convince the Lakotas to abandon war as a viable means of expelling Americans from their homelands.[22]

After the treaty had been signed, a copy was forwarded to Maj. Gen. Frank Wheaton, commandant of the District of Nebraska who assumed the task of contacting and persuading other Lakota leaders to add their marks to the document that had been drafted to replace the Horse Creek treaty, due to expire in 1866. General Wheaton ordered Col. Henry Maynadier, commanding officer at Fort Laramie and of the West Subdistrict of Nebraska, to send runners to the war villages "to inform them that other tribes were making peace and an opportunity would be offered them to do the same." White emissaries considered the mission so dangerous that no one would volunteer, but Maynadier (or Many Deer, as the Lakotas called him) persuaded members of the Loafer band—Big Ribs, Big Mouth, Eagle Foot, Whirlwind, and Little Crow, an elderly man of seventy-five—to transmit the message.[23]

Despite fears that the Lakota war faction would murder the party led by Big Ribs, the Loafers returned three months later, starving and frostbitten, with good tidings that the followers of Red Cloud, a Bad Face Oglala war leader, or *blotahunka* (and perhaps also a *wakiconza*), were coming in. The information proved inaccurate, however. Congress had earlier awarded a construction contract for a wagon road north of the Upper Platte River to Colonel Sawyer, and Red Cloud had quickly attracted the attention of the Indian Office by strongly warning Sawyer in the summer of 1865 not to enter the Powder River hunting grounds.[24]

Accompanying the Loafer party were Swift Bear, the brother-in-law of trader James Bordeaux, and his Corn band of Brulés. They had lost many horses during the bitter winter and desperately needed food and clothing. Swift Bear told Maynadier that his followers desired peace but had been afraid they would be killed by white soldiers if they ventured to Fort Laramie. The post commander treated Swift Bear's people kindly, and the *itancan* agreed to bring a tobacco offering to the nontreaty bands in the hope that they might consent to negotiations.

Swift Bear reached Red Cloud on 3 March 1866; the Bad Faces accepted the commandant's gift, and *akicita* were dispatched to Fort Laramie with news that Red Cloud would come in within nine days. On 10 March, Spotted Tail of the Brulés and his followers were seen making their way to the post in great sorrow, for his daughter had died en route to the fort. She had asked to be buried there, and Maynadier's cooperation had touched the grieving father. Hervey Johnson, a corporal stationed at the fort, described their arrival in a letter to his sister Abigail. "At twelve o'clock today," he wrote, "the Indians could be seen crossing the river about a mile and a half from the fort, and forming a line along the bank." As the officers went out to greet them, the Lakotas separated into three divisions, later forming one line as they passed through the gates onto the parade ground. When Red Cloud, the aging but still prominent warrior, reached the post on the twelfth, Maynadier set up a telegraph conversation between him and E. B. Taylor, head of the northern superintendency who had been appointed chair of the newly created peace commission authorized to hold talks with the Lakota war faction at Fort Laramie. After the conversation Red Cloud agreed to coax other councilors of his band to attend a grand assembly at the fort.[25]

Federal commissioners gathered on 1 June at Fort Laramie to obtain the official consent of northern and southern Oglala and Brulé bands to the construction of emigrant trails through the Lakotas' hunting territory in the Powder and Yellowstone River country. Assisting chairman Taylor were Colonel Maynadier, Col. R. N. McLaren of Minnesota, and Thomas Wistar of Pennsylvania. When the council convened on the fifth, the Oglalas sensed that the white envoys had now singled out Red Cloud as the "head chief of the Sioux," ignoring the fact that their principal *itancan*, Man Afraid of His Horse, was present. Indeed, that the treaty commissioners considered the Bad Face *blotahunka* a man with considerable political power was supported "by the pains taken to procure his attendance at the [council], and the distinguished consideration shown him more than to any other" Lakota present.[26]

Americans expected varying degrees of symbolic or actual decision-making authority to reside in a number of rigidly structured hierarchical offices with fixed terms and clearly defined roles. Moreover, incumbents were expected to be "in charge," empowered to make decisions that often affected their entire citizenry. Thus when federal commissioners participated in councils with the Oglalas and other Native Americans, they were culturally predisposed to seek out, or in some cases to appoint, a very small number of men they called head chiefs or chiefs. Moreover, the visitors assumed that these chiefs exercised political power as Americans defined it, including the ability to dictate or control the behavior of others through the implementation of written laws, by threatening to use physical force against perceived offenders, and otherwise imposing culturally acceptable sanctions. In contrast, Oglala concepts of political power and chieftainship were much more fluid. From an Oglala perspective, chieftainship, as reflected in the title of *itancan,* represented merely one of several forms of Lakota leadership.

Perhaps the simplest way to understand this mutual misconception of political authority is to consider the subtle but crucial distinctions between status and role in Lakota society.[27] In the context of a council meeting, the American designation *chief* merely signified to the Lakotas present a special *role* that their spokesmen had agreed to accept, namely, as intermediaries for their respective social units. It did not necessarily indicate the spokesmen's actual *status* within their own *tiyospaye,* which could be headman, *itancan,* holy man, war leader, and so on, or the true extent of their decision-making authority.

Very little was accomplished during the first meeting at Fort Laramie as most of the other Oglala and Brulé councilors were still located on the White River northeast of the fort. Man Afraid, Red Cloud, and the Brulés Iron Shell and Red Leaf refused to comment until they had discussed the pertinent issues with their peers in private assemblies, so Maynadier issued supplies from the quartermaster's stores to be sent as peace offerings to these other bands and arranged to reopen negotiations on the thirteenth.[28]

During the interim the Oglalas conferred with the Northern Cheyenne councilors also in attendance at the post. Man Afraid of His Horse and Red Cloud informed them that they thought the Great Father wanted only one emigrant road that would not disturb their buffalo grounds north of the Big Horn Mountains. After formal talks resumed on 13 June, Col. Henry Carrington arrived at the fort and was presented to the assembly. The Lakota and Northern Cheyenne councilors quickly learned that Carrington's seven hundred officers and men of the 18th Infantry were marching toward Fort Laramie en route to the disputed territory. Presuming that Carrington's detail had entered Lakota land to build roads and garrisons without tribal permission, the northern Oglala-Brulé war faction became enraged. Man Afraid of His Horse, Iron Shell, Red Cloud, and his friend Red Leaf of the Wazazas rejected the whites' peace overtures by refusing treaty gifts and withdrew immediately from the council arena. By shunning Maynadier's offering they destroyed the symbolic kinship relationship formed between the two sides for the purpose of negotiation. Maynadier and the commissioners were now strangers and could be treated as enemies. Striking out at once for the Powder River country, the militant Oglalas and Brulés chose the strategy of war, renewing their alliances with bands of Miniconjous and Northern Cheyennes for this purpose.[29]

After the war faction departed, the commissioners resumed dialogues with the remaining Oglalas and Brulés as if nothing had happened. These people were at the time impoverished and gladly accepted the gifts proffered by the treaty commissioners. Besides, these Lakotas, who camped often in the White River valley and the Sand Hills south of the river, did not claim the Powder River hunting grounds and saw no reason why they should not sign the peace accord authorizing the U.S. Army Corps of Engineers to construct two new posts along the Bozeman Road (Fort Philip Kearny, Mountain District Headquarters, established 15 July about eighty miles south of Fort Reno, and Fort C. F. Smith, erected 3 August at the crossing of the Bighorn River, seventy miles beyond Fort Philip Kearny). Colonel Carrington, commanding the district, had moved old Fort Connor to the Powder River, renaming it Fort Reno in honor of Maj. Jesse Reno, who was killed in action during the Civil War. These Powder River garrisons continued the cordon of posts erected on the northern plains to guard white emigrants and miners. In return for endorsing the treaty the commissioners granted the Oglala and Brulé peace faction annuities for twenty-five years and encouraged the bands to move south of the North Platte River, away from the nontreaty Sioux.[30]

In his official account of the 1866 Fort Laramie proceedings Commissioner Taylor claimed that the peace faction at the post represented the vast majority of the Oglalas and Brulés, and that "from what we saw and heard the treaty gave as much satisfaction to the parties concerned as under existing circumstances could have been expected."[31]

By September, the Spotted Tail, Swift Bear, Man That Walks under the Ground, and Standing Elk *tiyospaye* (about 850 people total, most of them old men, women, and children) had moved south of the Upper Platte to hunt along the Republican River, later establishing their winter villages near Fort Sedgwick, in the Colorado Territory. An additional three to four hundred peaceful Oglalas and Brulés, comprising a number of smaller, unnamed bands, also chose peace with the United States. They refused to follow their relatives to the southern hunting country for fear that white *akicita* stationed at Forts Riley, Hays, and Wallace would mistake them for the northern intertribal war faction. Blue Horse, Big Mouth, and three hundred Loafers preferred to camp near Horse Creek and instructed about 150 women and children to remain at Fort Laramie. M. T. Patrick, who succeeded Vital Jarrot as Upper Platte Indian agent, soon discovered that these dependents were starving. By leaving the women and children in camp at the post, their relatives undoubtedly hoped the army would feed them until hunters could bring fresh meat. Patrick remarked that some of the peaceable faction were again "anxious to go on the reserves they were promised" years before, and the agent hoped that if these Indians settled down they would eventually succeed in restraining and controlling the militant northern bands.[32]

Southern Oglalas Little Wound, Bad Wound, and Pawnee Killer, a prominent warrior of Bad Wound's *tiyospaye*, also rejected the war plans of their northern Oglala kin, reflecting the old division between the Bull Bear and Smoke groups. After the war faction bolted the council arena, Little Wound, the Kiyuksa head *itancan* and son of Bull Bear, informed the Hunkpatila northern Oglala headmen, Worm (Crazy Horse's father) and Long Face, that his *tiyospaye* "had lived up here [in the Fort Laramie area] around the big-talking Bad Faces for two years." They would now strike their lodges and return to the South Platte and Smoky Hill Rivers, where they would renew their friendship with the Southern Cheyennes.[33]

The stance of the Oglala-Brulé peace faction demonstrates how American concepts of Lakota government and the roles of Indian leaders contrasted with the way the Oglalas and Brulés themselves viewed their political process. Commissioner Taylor assumed, perhaps for the sake of convenience, that the Sioux comprised a *nation* in the whites' sense of the word, with Lakota "citizens" pledging their primary allegiance to protecting the "state" rather than to defending their extended families. Lakota *tiyospaye* leaders, however, looked after their own people first and foremost, demonstrating their primary loyalty to their own bands of extended families. To them, the American concept of "nationalism" was unworkable. Thus, the Oglala and Brulé spokesmen who "touched the pen" at Fort Laramie were ultimately adhering to their own agendas, not necessarily to those of other Lakota bands and subtribes.

When special agent E. B. Chandler recalled the recent peace talks at Fort Laramie in his January 1867 statement to Superintendent H. B. Denman, he concluded that the Taylor Commission had been determined to draft "a treaty upon some terms, either with or without the consent" of all

Lakotas. Numerous officers and employees at the garrison supposedly overhead Taylor remark that the government had authorized him to make a treaty, and he would do so "if made with but two Indians." On a more ominous note for the United States, Chandler had received information from a scout belonging to one of the Republican River Oglala or Brulé *ti-yospaye* stating that after the Fort Laramie council adjourned, many of the young warriors from these and the Platte River bands, seizing the opportunity to win military honors, had temporarily rejected their elders' peace strategy and followed the Oglala and Brulé war faction to the Powder River country.

The messenger estimated (perhaps exaggerated) the strength of the intertribal war faction (Lakota, Northern Cheyenne, and Arapaho) to be over 11,000 warriors, and thought more would soon join. With this information in mind, the special agent, fearing a protracted war was now inevitable, dismissed the 1866 treaty proceedings as "little better than a farce." Unknown to the Oglala and Brulé signers, the U.S. Senate agreed, quickly rejecting the document. But the army continued to adhere to its terms in the form of military orders from the Department of the Missouri, and certainly the Lakotas who had touched the pen at Fort Laramie still considered the treaty binding on all parties.

Chandler believed that the federal government's only hope of defusing this explosive situation lay in establishing reservations for those Indian people who opposed war. If they were treated well, the agent hoped, the war faction could be convinced of the Great Father's peaceful intentions. At least for the time being, the Indian Office should create a makeshift reserve near a military post where all the protreaty Indians could settle.[34]

For almost two years after the tumultuous Fort Laramie assembly of 1866, bands of Oglalas, Brulés, Hunkpapas, Miniconjous, Sans Arcs, Two Kettles, Yanktonais, Santees, Northern Cheyennes, and Arapahos waged what historians have termed Red Cloud's War. By the end of 1866 many American settlers, miners, U.S. Army regulars, and volunteers believed that the united tribes had virtually closed the Bozeman Road to western travel. Gold miners were afraid to venture along the route; army officers and their troops considered themselves prisoners in their own forts while Indian warriors drove off their stock, and supply teamsters believed they risked their lives every time they set out for the Powder River posts. On 21 December 1866, warriors killed Capt. William J. Fetterman and every member of his eighty-man force dispatched from Fort Philip Kearny to relieve a woodcutting party under attack.[35]

This incident shocked the United States and put fear in the heart of every soldier stationed on the northern plains. C. M. Hines, acting assistant surgeon at Fort Philip Kearny, writing to his brother John Hines on New Year's Day 1867, remarked ruefully that the recent Fort Laramie treaty had not amounted to much. The three Bozeman posts authorized in the document, he wrote, were "really in a state of siege." Fort Reno had just one piece of artillery and three companies of infantry; his own post was better armed but had only four hundred effective men including garrison employees. Communications with Fort C. F. Smith, commanded by Lt. Col. Nathaniel Kenney, had been completely severed, but the last communiqué from the post mentioned it could field only two undermanned companies of infantry, two pieces of artillery, and twenty-eight cavalrymen. Hines believed that most of the militant bands were located about fifty miles away, on the Tongue River. He estimated the strength of the intertribal war faction at four to five thousand men—all, he feared, well armed and mounted. Warriors taunted the troops daily, Hines lamented, and had attacked the wood trains on numerous occasions.[36]

Other army personnel at Fort Philip Kearny, headquarters of the Mountain District, blamed the recent peace commission for their predicament. A sergeant writing from the fort to a clerk at the Division of the Missouri headquarters in St. Louis just a few days after the Fetterman disaster railed that a Chicago newspaper had just published a story, based on the commissioners' testimony, stating that the army had exaggerated Indian hostilities along the Bozeman Road. The sergeant excoriated the commissioners for providing weapons and ammunition to the Indians, who, he believed, used them not to hunt game but "to murder white men." In the sergeant's opinion, federal envoys were "a nuisance to the government." Instead of sending negotiators to the plains, he felt, the Indian Office would be wise to dispatch men prepared "to exterminate this accursed race of savages."[37]

Sensitive to criticism from both the War Department and the nation at large, the Office of Indian Affairs appointed a special commissioner in July to investigate conditions at the garrison. In his preliminary report, remarkable for its obsession with statistical details, the inspector noted that between 26 July and 21 December 1866 Lakotas and their allies had killed ninety-one enlisted men, five officers, and fifty-eight civilians. In addition, they had wounded twenty more, driven off 360 oxen and cows, 304 mules, and 161 horses. In sum, warriors had attacked Fort Philip Kearny on fifty-one separate occasions and besieged every wagon train and white emigrant attempting to pass over the Bozeman Road, compelling the investigator to conclude that the war for the Lakotas had been thus far "very successful."[38]

The following month Congress, also concerned about the apparent state of affairs on the northern plains, created the Department of Dakota, a component of a grandiose plan to reorganize military affairs in the West. Incorporating the state of Minnesota and the territories of Dakota and Montana, the new department spanned almost four hundred thousand square miles. Lt. Gen. William Sherman's strategy to counter Native American advances hinged on his proposal to restrict the intertribal war faction to the country north of the Platte River, ranging from the Upper Missouri River as far west as the Bozeman Trail. Lakota *tiyospaye* discovered outside these limits without the army's permission would be dealt with harshly.[39]

The Department of the Interior responded promptly and angrily to Sherman's scheme. Commissioner of Indian Affairs Lewis Bogy fumed to Interior secretary Orville Browning that the actions of the general and other high-ranking officers were exacerbating an already precarious situation. In the commissioner's opinion, the current northern plains war had been sparked by Brig. Gen. Philip St. Cooke's persistent endeavors to curtail the Indian trade in guns and ammunition, and the issue of such items during formal councils. Sherman informed Gen. William Hancock, commander of the Division of the Missouri, that he had in his possession a letter from ranking Interior Department officials, including Commissioner Bogy himself, granting trader D. A. Butterfield permission to barter with Lakota *tiyospaye*. "We, the military, are held responsible for the peace of the frontier," Sherman stormed, "and it is an absurdity to attempt it if Indian agents and traders can legalize and encourage so dangerous a traffic." The general insisted that the sale of firearms to various Sioux bands be rigidly controlled, but if the Office of Indian Affairs continued to permit, or even promote, the distribution of weapons to Indians, then the army should withdraw its troops from the Bozeman Road, for they already had a "herculean task on their hands."[40]

Bogy reacted angrily to Sherman's comments, a stance that seemed particularly strange considering that an Interior Department circular, issued in 1865 to all agents and superintendents, specifically instructed them to ensure that traders did not deliver firearms and ammunition to Indian bands deemed hostile. But this time Bogy had retorted that Lakota hunters needed rifles simply to hunt buffalo, not to wage war upon the United States, as Sherman insisted. Gold and silver miners were swarming into the Powder River valley, their campsites and livestock destroying the prairie where Indian ponies grazed. Consequently the Sioux had fewer horses, rendering it difficult for them to hunt successfully with bows and arrows. A steady trade in guns would at least enable them to take enough meat to feed their families through the winter months. The rumors of three to five thousand intertribal warriors milling around Fort Philip Kearny, Bogy claimed, had been fabricated by army officers who failed to admit that the Fetterman tragedy had been brought about by the "foolish and rash manner" of Colonel Carrington, Fort Philip Kearny's commandant. The Lakotas and their allies had come in peace to request that Carrington rescind the military order banning the sale of weapons and ammunition. Army officers, Bogy added, should understand that their primary role was not to interfere in the affairs of the Indian Office but to serve merely as policemen in support of authorized Indian agents.[41]

Despite the dire predictions cast by Sherman and his colleagues in the War Department, Commissioner Bogy remained optimistic that a mutually satisfactory settlement to Red Cloud's War could soon be reached. "These chiefs control their different tribes, with the exception of a few bad men found among them, as among us," he wrote, obviously ignorant of Lakota political customs. However, "with proper means, I am satisfied that these chiefs can all be made to see and fully understand their position, and the necessity imposed upon the government of securing this belt of country to the whites." Bogy viewed the forthcoming peace talks, uncomplicated by army interference, as the best vehicle for inducing militant bands to accept reservation life. Preserving peace, he was certain, entailed simply increasing the Indians' annuities until they had learned the art of subsistence agriculture.[42]

General Sibley, a member of the 1865 Edmunds commission, seriously doubted that the Lakota war faction would readily acquiesce to reservation status, particularly in light of their recent military victories. Confiding in Major General Curtis, Sibley concluded that federal commissioners had simply wasted their time trying to establish diplomatic ties with a limited number of Lakota "chiefs." True chiefs, even those recognized in multiband assemblies, Sibley claimed, were "without any authority except as they reflect the wishes" of the warrior societies, which he rightly believed now held the upper hand in the band councils. Indeed "nothing permanent in the way of negotiation can be expected" without the general approval of the active warriors.[43]

The protracted nature of the war, with its unsettling effects on the bands, generated perceptible but neither radical nor permanent changes in the political affairs of the militant Oglalas. The *blotahunka* and the warriors, whose duties to protect their families often bore them away from the villages, persuaded the older men of the council, the *itancan* and headmen, whose primary concerns often focused more on the inner workings of the camp circle, to support their war plans. Furthermore, the *wakiconza* (camp administrators) and their *akicita* (the enforcers of decisions), representing two other forms of Oglala leadership, moved the camps more often during wartime to keep them out of harm's way. Under these circumstances, decision-making achieved through council consensus, a deliberate and formal process sometimes requiring days or even weeks to achieve, temporarily gave way to the quick commands of the war leaders, the *wakiconza*, and the *akicita*. Empowered by Oglala customs, all members of the band, regardless of status, were expected in times of crisis to obey the *blotahunka*, *wakiconza*, and their *akicita*.[44]

Although special federal agent Chandler in official communiqués had referred to Man Afraid of His Horse and Red Cloud of the Oglalas and the Wazaza Brulé Red Leaf as "the principal instigators and leaders" of the war,[45] many extant primary documents and secondary sources concentrate on the role of Red Cloud while neglecting the authority wielded by other headmen, *itancan*, and prominent warriors, whom the Oglalas and other Lakotas themselves recognized. Consequently it is difficult to ascertain Red Cloud's role, status, or the extent of his decision-making authority among all the Oglalas at this time.

Although appoaching his midforties, a time when most distinguished *blotahunka* had made the transition to council elder, Red Cloud was still recognized among the northern Oglalas for his commitment to removing the American presence from the Powder River hunting grounds, his ability to maintain the support of the warrior societies, and for his superb war strategy. Furthermore, it is possible that his *tiyospaye* also recognized him as a *wakiconza* of the camp during wartime. Red Cloud was not a band chief, however. Bad Face, son of Old Smoke and father of Woman's Dress, still held the status of the most prominent *itancan* among the Bad Faces, even if his own following had dwindled during the war years.

Deriving information from Red Cloud's nephew, He Dog, historian George Hyde writes that Red Cloud was born into a prominent family and most probably was eligible for selection as *itancan*. He Dog recalled that Red Cloud's mother was Walks as She Thinks, a sister of Smoke, and his father, Lone Man or Only Man, an *itancan* of a Brulé band that had merged with the Oglalas in the early 1800s. Hyde claims that Man Afraid's father had been an *itancan* in Lone Man's Brulé band, whereas Robert Ruby states that it was Man Afraid of His Horse who had ceremoniously acknowledged Lone Man's status as *itancan* during a multiband assembly.[46]

The Oglalas and Brulés often camped together and intermarried, and sometimes even entire *tiyospaye* changed their subtribal identity. For instance, Lone Man's band—and later, in 1854, Lip's band of Brulés—eventually united with the Oglalas.[47] If Lone Man, Red Cloud's father, had indeed been an influential Brulé leader who resided after marriage with the Oglala Bad Faces, conceivably he received an invitation to participate in the *tiyospaye* council. Given the importance of kinship, it seems unlikely that the Bad Faces and other Oglala councilors would have excluded Lone Man from their assemblies—unless, of course, he was deemed unworthy of council membership. At the very least, Lone Man probably attained the status of headman, but this alone would not guarantee his son's eventual acceptance as a Bad Face band chief.

Doane Robinson, former state historian for South Dakota, contends that Red Cloud was never eligible for Oglala chieftainship precisely because his father was a Brulé. Moreover, Pine Ridge interpreter George Colhoff (deriving his information from Clarence Three Stars in the late nineteenth century) informed Judge Eli Ricker that, although Red Cloud's reputation as a fearless warrior was unparalleled, his social status never equalled that of Man Afraid of His Horse, a "chief of great worth." Three Stars claims that Red Cloud was a headman, but while he was never formally invited to become a *tiyospaye itancan* in the preagency years, eventually "his bravery, promptness, and efficiency . . . led his people to trust him at length as a chief" during the later reservation years. Red Cloud lacked a gift for oratory, Three Stars continued, but he was "emphatically a man of action," and the great care that he showed for the agency Oglalas' welfare eventually "endeared him to them."[48]

But while Red Cloud was not yet recognized as a band *itancan*, he nevertheless claimed by 1867 an estimated following of 250 lodges, mostly young warriors and their families, representing a constituency as large as that of the Oglala head *itancan*, Man Afraid of His Horse. These fighting men, many of whom belonged to powerful military societies, served to augment, at least temporarily, Red Cloud's influence during the war, in contrast to that of the hereditary band *itancan*.[49]

Furthermore, Congress continued to believe that Red Cloud wielded the political authority to make binding decisions for all the Sioux people. He was the man, many civilian officials presumed, with whom they must negotiate if peace were to be achieved. Their endeavors to court his favor during the postwar peace councils—and, as they had done with Conquering Bear in the 1850s, to regard Red Cloud as the "head chief"—strengthened (at least temporarily) whatever influence he had already mustered among his own people.[50]

In February 1867 the president established the Sully commission, six persons (two selected by the secretary of the interior, and four chosen by the commanding general of the army) to proceed to Fort Philip Kearny and examine the factors precipitating the Fetterman tragedy, take steps to separate the peaceful bands from the war faction, and attempt to prevent the escalation of hostilities. The emissaries were not authorized, however, to make treaties with the Lakotas. Assisting chairman Alfred Sully were his military colleagues John Sanborn, Napoleon Buford, and Ely Parker (a Seneca sachem, former aide-de-camp of Gen. Ulysses Grant, and future commissioner of Indian affairs). Representing the Office of Indian Affairs were the old Indian trader and ranchowner G. P. Beauvais and Jefferson Kinney. While the committee completed preparations to visit Fort McPherson, where they intended to interview Colonel Carrington (whom Parker had already judged "not fit to be in this Indian country"), runners were dispatched to the winter villages of the southern Oglalas and Brulés dotted along the Republican and Niobrara Rivers. The scouts delivered messages that the Great Father's *akicita* (envoys) wished to "hold friendly talks" with band representatives at the fort by the end of the month, and that presents would be distributed as evidence of the government's good faith.[51]

Lakota runners in the Black Hills relayed word to the commissioners that three of the key instigators of the Fetterman tragedy had perished in that fight. The Oglalas' most distinguished warriors had earlier selected their four head shirtwearers: Sword, American Horse, Young Man Afraid of His Horse, and Crazy Horse—all except Crazy Horse sons of prominent *itancan*. Despite his military contributions, Red Cloud had been passed over. Disappointed and "dissatisfied," he had temporarily left his own *tiyospaye*, moving his household to a Miniconjou band.[52]

In April, Lakota *akicita* found the Spotted Tail, Swift Bear, Two Strike, Big Mouth, Blue Horse, and Man Who Walks under the Ground bands camped along the Niobrara River. Oglala and Brulé councilors agreed to meet Commissioners Parker and Beauvais, both of whom owned ranches in western Nebraska and had been sent ahead to schedule a meeting with the Indians at California Crossing, near Fort Sedgwick. The assembly convened on the twenty-second, continuing throughout the night to enable the representatives to return to their camps the next day, for they were afraid of their northern relatives, some of whom were still fighting along the Laramie Road to within sixty-five miles of the post.[53]

During the proceedings Oglala and Brulé spokesmen complained that the Great Father had not sent them their promised annuities. Although the Senate rejected ratification of the 1866 treaty, Sioux delegates still considered it binding, and the U.S. Army itself continued to adhere to its terms in the form of military orders from the Department of Missouri. After the council adjourned, the Sully commission distributed gifts, greatly pleasing the Indians and prompting the chairman to conclude that such action had induced over seven hundred young Lakota men to cancel their plans to join the militant bands that spring. Before departing, the commissioners requested the councilors to separate their people—including the young men, if possible—from the intertribal war faction by confining their camps to the territory between the North and South Platte River, and to the country between Pole Creek and Plum Creek. In addition, they gave each councilor who came forward "papers of protection" and the services of special interpreters who would speak for the bands should they encounter white troops. Even though buffalo and small game were scarce in the southern country at that time, Sully and his colleagues assured the Oglala and Brulé delegates that the food supply was sufficient to feed their bands, at least for the time being.[54]

Writing from Fort Sedgwick on 28 April, chairman Sully mentioned an encounter with a reconnaisance party of twenty Brulés from Iron Shell's band, including the *itancan's* brother. The scouts had struggled through deep snow from their spring encampment on the White River to glean information about the white soldiers in their country. On their journey they met a Miniconjou war party returning from the Upper Platte. The war faction was disintegrating, the Miniconjous told Iron Shell's *akicita*. Too many Platte River Brulés and Oglalas had perished fighting American troops, and forty lodges of these Lakotas were heading for Iron Shell's *tiyospaye*. All the remaining Brulés of the war faction had splintered into small parties and were presently heading south. They desired peace and "would have all come in," the scouts later told Sully, but they had camp *akicita* and *blotahunka* among them "who would not let them," opting instead to prolong the war. Some *wakiconza* of the war faction had moved their villages to the mouth of the Tongue and Yellowstone Rivers. Red Cloud's Bad Faces were camped along the Rosebud Creek, and Man Afraid's people were believed to be with them. Even the Bad Faces, usually strong advocates of war, were quickly losing supporters to other *tiyospaye*. By late spring Man Afraid and Red Cloud claimed merely fifty lodges each out of a previous combined constituency of five hundred. Only Red Dog of the northern Oglala Oyuhpes still had a following of over one hundred tipis. Rumors circulated that soldiers intended to hound Lakotas indefinitely, so "they kept moving" to avoid them. Some Brulé and northern Oglala leaders decided the time had come to meet the commissioners. Red Leaf's Wazaza Brulés, Conquering Bear's old band, then located west of the Black Hills, had already departed for Fort Laramie.[55]

By July an estimated twenty-five hundred Oglalas and Brulés had ventured south from the militant camps to swell the ranks of the peace party. Band councilors sent word to the commissioners that they would assemble all their *itancan*, headmen, and *blotahunka* to decide whether to forgo war. Sully sensed that the Indians had grown weary of conflict and thought the United States should abandon the Bozeman Road soon, deeming it unnecessary for the defense or economic well-being of the nation. Moreover, the general proposed reserving eight thousand square miles of the Missouri and Yellowstone basins for the Lakotas, elevating the Indian Office to a separate cabinet-level department, and limiting American military presence merely to the protection of whites in the Upper Platte valley.[56]

Special Commissioner N. B. Buford also recommended a revised federal Indian policy based on peaceful negotiation with the northern plains tribes. Buford suggested to Edward Stanton, secretary of war, that unless the army wished to retaliate for the loss of Fetterman and his men, war should cease north of the Platte River. "Peace," he wrote, "can be obtained by a more humane and cheaper means than by an invading army, who never can bring the Indians to battle unless they can surprise them in their villages."[57]

Reflecting the opinions of both Sully and Buford, Congress approved on 20 July 1867 Senate Resolution 136, creating the Indian Peace Commission. This new committee comprised four civilians, named in the bill, and three military officers nominated by President Andrew Johnson. On 6 August the federal envoys assembled in St. Louis, selecting as chairman Commissioner of Indian Affairs Nathaniel Taylor, a Tennesseean and former Methodist clergyman. Other members of the commission's civilian wing included Senator John Henderson, chair of the Senate Committee on Indian Affairs; Samuel Tappan, a reform advocate; and John Sanborn, who had also served on the Sully commission. Representing the military position were Lt. Gen. William Sherman, commanding the Military Division of the Missouri and an opponent of closing the Bozeman Road; Maj. Gen. Alfred Terry, commanding officer of the Department of Dakota; and retired Gen. William Harney, who had treated with the Sioux at the Fort Pierre assemblies of 1856. Maj. Gen. Christopher Augur would later replace Sherman, who was occasionally called to Washington on official business. The Taylor commission's duties were similar to the preceding ones: to arrange a general truce on the Great Plains, to acquire unanimous intertribal consent for the construction of railroads and posts in Indian country, to suggest or inaugurate a plan for acculturating Native Americans by concentrating them on reservations east of the Rockies, and to formulate an effective and lasting peace policy. However, the act of Congress authorizing the peace commission also implied that if diplomacy should fail, the U.S. Army would be given free rein to conquer a peace.[58]

From the outset there were signs that the Indian Peace Commission itself was as factionalized as the Lakotas. Espousing the views of Indian reformers, Commissioner Taylor insisted that reservations would protect Native Americans from further decimation by white troops while facilitating the acculturation process. Removed from the corrupting influence of whiskey peddlers, Indians could be educated "intellectually and morally" and trained "in the arts of civilization" by dedicated government employees. Once stripped of their cultural heritage, the optimistic Taylor predicted the plains people would cast aside tribalism, embrace in its stead the ideals of white America, and assume the rights and responsibilities of U.S. citizenship. The commission's military wing, however, remained skeptical of the new peace policy, believing that only a resounding military defeat could bring the militant Lakotas and their allies to their knees.[59]

Despite differences of opinion voiced within the peace commission, the members continued with their preparations to contact the war faction by fall, a daunting task since the bands could strike their lodges within fifteen minutes and slip quietly into the night as they had done so many times before when danger threatened. Sending messengers to locate the villages, the commissioners requested the northern tribes, including the Oglalas, Brulés, Miniconjous, and Northern Cheyennes and Arapahos, to proceed to Fort Laramie by the end of September. (The southern tribes— Kiowas, Comanches, Apaches, Southern Cheyennes and Arapahos— were to appear at Fort Larned by late October.) In the meantime the envoys chartered the steamboat *St. John's* to explore the Upper Missouri River. Along the way they purchased food supplies and sundry gifts to honor the northern tribal delegates they hoped would soon gather at Fort Laramie. During their sojourn the commissioners convened councils with several Lakota and Dakota bands at Forts Sully and Thompson before proceeding to the Ponca, Santee, and Yankton reserves bordering the river. These meetings were called primarily to inquire about the welfare of the "friendly" Missouri River Indians, and to determine the suitability of the Upper Missouri country for an immense reservation for all the Sioux. Returning down river to Omaha on 11 September, the federal emissaries boarded a Union Pacific train bound for the Platte valley.[60]

By mid-September several southern Oglala, Loafer, and Brulé *tiyospaye* had consented to meet the Indian Peace Commission at North Platte, Nebraska. During the first council with the bands on the nineteenth, Commissioner Taylor and his colleagues introduced a revised treaty they hoped would inaugurate a new era of unbroken peace between the northern plains tribes and the Great Father's people.[61]

Swift Bear and Spotted Tail of the Brulés spoke first. They were unconcerned about the transportation routes already established between the Missouri River and the North Platte and Arkansas Rivers. They did object, however, to the Union Pacific railroad near the Smoky Hill River and the Powder River wagon trail, both of which disturbed the buffalo. That these *tiyospaye* should now oppose the Bozeman Road is interesting, given the fact that they had raised no objections to it during the chaotic Fort Laramie council of the previous year. Perhaps the bands' current misgivings reflected their rising concern that the Powder River country did indeed contain the last of the Lakotas' reliable buffalo hunting grounds.

The commission's tentative suggestion that the Indians abandon the chase and adopt agriculture in its stead encountered quiet resistance. Spotted Tail and Swift Bear thought the idea ludicrous as long as game of any sort still migrated through their homelands. Instead, they hoped fur traders would live among them again, and expected presents, predictably guns and ammunition, as signs of the president's friendship and integrity.

Without such gifts, Swift Bear reminded the visitors, it would be difficult to induce the bands to trust the Great Father, as firearms had long been promised but seldom given.

Man Who Walks under the Ground spoke next for the Oglalas, and he appeared decidedly more defiant than the Brulé *itancan*. He reminded the commission that the Great Father had still not fulfilled his promises to the Oglala and Brulé peace faction as stipulated in the council of 1866, unaware that Americans placed no legal significance on an unratified treaty. But Man Who Walks under the Ground believed that the document he signed with federal commissioners had made him a "chief" among the Oglalas. Lately it had caused him "to be very poor," as no treaty goods had been forthcoming; consequently, his "children [*tiyospaye*] have suffered by reason of my [endorsing] it." The president should simply abandon the disputed roads and furnish guns and ammunition for the chase. After all, his people had fulfilled their promises by remaining apart from the intertribal war faction.

Big Mouth, a Loafer *itancan*, realistically surmised the strength of the whites. He warned his followers not to kill them, for "they are as thick as the grass." He was not conciliatory, however, for he ordered the Great Father's *akicita* to relay his band's displeasure about the Powder River and Smoky Hill routes to the president. If this were not done, no *itancan*, headman, *wakiconza*, or even camp *akicita* could control the warrior societies, whose members slipped back and forth to the northern war faction. After Big Mouth concluded his remarks, the meeting adjourned until the following day.

The next day at noon the commissioners and the Oglala and Brulé councilors gathered at Spotted Tail's camp. Internal conflicts within the commission resurfaced when both Taylor and Sherman independently prepared papers outlining the commission's public response to the Indians' requests and grievances. Taylor, speaking for the civilian side, continued to advocate diplomacy and negotiation, whereas the general, espousing the opinions of his army colleagues, believed the threat of military force against Lakota villages should not be entirely abandoned during their mission.

On this occasion Sherman's views prevailed, and Taylor introduced him at the council as the commission's principal spokesman for that day. The general announced that the Great Father thought the Southern Cheyennes and Arapahos had consented to the Smoky Hill railroad, as mail stations and military posts had been built along its path more than two years ago without generating opposition. He bluntly informed the Oglalas and Brulés that the commission intended to meet the Southern Cheyennes next month on the Arkansas River, and if they had suffered damages from the railroad passing through their country, they would receive compensation. But "the road must be built," he warned the Lakotas, "and you must not interfere with it."

As for the Powder River road, Sherman continued, it was a vital artery, furnishing supplies to the gold miners and white settlers of the Montana Territory. He dismissed the delegates' contention that the roads disturbed the bison herds, and stated that as long as the war raged on, the Great Father would never abandon the Bozeman trail, nor the posts along it. The commissioners would carefully weigh the Lakotas' grievances at Fort Laramie, however, and if "we find the Indian right to be good, we will give it up, or pay you for it, if you keep the peace." For the present time, the envoys agreed to issue powder and lead to the Spotted Tail, Swift Bear, Standing Elk, and Big Mouth bands, which had lived peacefully throughout the summer. But the remaining bands were to do without, as the general believed some of their warriors had recently murdered several parties of white emigrants.

Sherman paused briefly before introducing the major purpose of the commission's visit. The Great Father desired the Sioux to select land bordering the Missouri River and including the White Earth and Cheyennne Rivers, which they would hold forever. There, shielded from unauthorized white intruders, Sioux families would learn to cultivate the soil, tend herds of sheep, ponies, and cattle, and settle in log cabins. The Lakota delegates gathered around him should consider these provisions carefully, Sherman warned, for the commission represented war as well as peace. Senator Henderson of Missouri added that once the conflict ended, the Sioux could expect all the powder and lead they required, along with presents and annuities stipulated in the new peace treaty. The commission was scheduled to resume its mission among the Lakotas in November, so they had only two months to "appoint chiefs" with full decision-making authority, not merely mouthpieces of the multiband council, to consider the proposal.

The Oglala and Brulé spokesmen relayed the consensus of the *tipi iyoki-heya*, the multiband council lodge. They professed friendship but remained adamant about the promised rifles and ammunition. After all, they had postponed their hunt to hear the commissioners' words. Who among their people would respect their oratorical and diplomatic abilities

if they could not acquire what the president's *akicita* had previously offered? Big Mouth reminded the commission that he, along with Spotted
Tail and Swift Bear, had been the first "who tried to get the bad Indians
[war faction] in to make peace." The visitors' refusal to honor all the *tiyospaye* with gifts only made the people question their true motives and
honesty.

Pawnee Killer, a *blotahunka* of Bad Wound's band, voiced the Lakota
warriors' suspicions concerning the president's message, and his defiance
certainly hints at the influential role played by the young fighting men in
the council. "My Grandfather," he stated, "may have some mighty good
ideas and notions in his head. I have some very good ones also." His people would decide nothing until all the northern and southern Lakota *tiyospaye* and their allies had united in a grand multiband assembly to debate
the whites' new peace treaty. After Pawnee Killer's comments, Commissioner Taylor yielded and distributed small quantities of ammunition to
all bands present. "We think we have made peace with you," he ventured,
but the commission would continue its plans to conclude a treaty with
other Lakotas in November.

After the September preliminary meeting, the commissioners proceeded
to Medicine Lodge Creek where delegates of the southern tribes signed
the Treaty of Medicine Lodge, the first major result of the United States'
renewed public commitment to diplomacy. After the formalities, Taylor,
Tappan, Sanborn, Terry, and Harney left to greet the northern tribes at
Fort Laramie. General Sherman departed for Washington on official business and was temporarily replaced by Major General Augur, who joined
the commission at Fort Larned.

By late November only the Crows had reached Fort Laramie. Spotted
Tail's Brulés and Blue Horse's Loafers were on the North Platte and arranged separate talks with Tappan, the only commissioner present among
them at that time. The other officials were still fretting that Red Cloud, in
their words "the formidable chief of the Sioux," had not yet arrived. They
greatly regretted not meeting the Bad Face war leader, for they insisted
that if they had done so, a "just and honorable peace" could have been
readily obtained. Why Red Cloud failed to appear at the post remained a
mystery to them. Did he question the sincerity of their motives, Taylor
wondered, or was he delayed by his band's decision to procure the winter
meat supplies? Fatigued and exasperated, the commissioners decided they
could wait no longer. As they packed their belongings at the fort, they

agreed to reconvene in their nation's capital on the ninth of December. In their absence, the emissaries ordered A. T. Chamblin and H. M. Mathews, special agents of the Indian Office, and government interpreter Charles Garrou, to remain at Fort Laramie, where they would persevere with their plans to contact the intertribal war faction. The commission also left instructions with the post commander, Brig. Gen. A. J. Slemmer, to persuade as many of the northern councilors as possible to congregate either at Fort Philip Kearny or Fort Rice by the following spring, when negotiations were scheduled to resume.[62]

In March 1868 the Indian Peace Commission battled deep snow and freezing temperatures to continue its peace mission among the Lakotas and their friends. When the weather moderated, a number of Brulé bands with a few Oglalas set out once more to greet the Great Father's *akicita*. Between 4 and 29 April, they attended several councils at Fort Laramie and along the banks of the North Platte River. During the sessions commissioners Sanborn, Tappan, Harney, Terry, and Augur received a telegram, dated 4 April, from special agent Chamblin, then in camp on the Big Laramie River. Lakota runners had come in from the Powder River country with information that many villages of the northern war faction were located on the headwaters of the Little Powder, and that they had consented to speak with commissioners Harney and Sanborn.[63]

The latter waited patiently until the end of the month, but there was no sign of Red Cloud, the man they hoped would appear. Cook, a Fort Laramie Loafer, had spent much of the previous winter in the Bad Face *tiyospaye*. When the blizzards abated, Cook, a companion named Tongue, and several other Bad Faces journeyed to Fort Laramie, where they received a box of crackers and a sack of flour from the sutler. Cook informed the commanding officer that many of the bands of Red Cloud and Man Afraid of His Horse were short of food. The weather had made the winter hunt difficult, so Cook, Tongue, and the other Indians brought many beautiful tanned buffalo robes to exchange for army provisions. On the return journey to the winter camps, Cook, now alone, encountered Man Afraid of His Horse and a hundred men hastening to Fort Laramie to see the commissioners. The Loafer opted to accompany the Hunkpatila *itancan* to the garrison rather than continue on to the Bad Face village.

When Man Afraid of His Horse reached the fort, he inquired as to why scouts had summoned him. He understood that the Great Father's *akicita* earlier had visited the fort, leaving with the commandant gifts to be distributed, presumably when Red Cloud arrived for negotiations. But Man

Afraid of His Horse believed that the goods were for all the Oglalas. "Why do you not give [them] to us?" the *itancan* asked agent Chamblin. "We have come a long way to receive these provisions but I see we do not get anything." Man Afraid and Cook then departed. Soon after, thirty young men from Man Afraid's *tiyospaye* reappeared at the fort, also hauling buffalo robes to trade for food and blankets. They complained bitterly when W. G. Bullock, the resident post trader, took advantage of their needy condition by demanding more buffalo robes than was customary in exchange for essential supplies. The warriors summoned the post interpreter to relay their displeasure to Chamblin, but the translator refused to talk to anyone other than the band chiefs. When the Hunkpatilas insisted that the interpreter ask agent Chamblin, their "father," to issue cloth and other essentials, they were refused.

In times of privation, Lakotas often demanded food or clothing from their own kinsfolk with the unspoken assumption that at some future date they would reciprocate. It was the height of bad manners to reject such requests, so when the interpreter ordered the men to depart empty-handed, they became enraged. Cook avoided a debacle by obtaining some food from the agent. Before leaving the post, the young men remarked to Chamblin that the Great Father's messengers always sent for their people in a hurry, but the next time the Hunkpatilas were summoned, their councilors would wait until the commissioners actually arrived before setting out for the post.[64]

After this incident it was uncertain if and when the Hunkpatila Oglalas would consent to a formal meeting, but the commissioners decided to commence discussions with those Oglala and Brulé delegations now gathered at the fort.[65] Big Mouth, who had conversed with them the previous fall, still expected the envoys to recognize his efforts to persuade the war faction to consider peace. He reminded the Americans that his band wished to remain in the vicinity of Fort Laramie where they had always felt welcome. American Horse, an Oglala head shirtwearer, attended this council, but not even his high status entitled him to sign the peace treaty on behalf of all the Oglalas. "You know very well that if the treaty is signed by only a portion of our people," American Horse cautioned, "it is not likely to stand good." He would wait for Man Afraid of His Horse and Red Cloud, and remarked in the spirit of consensus that "whatever they do, I am willing to do the same."[66]

By early May, Lieutenant General Sherman had grown uneasy about the enormous responsibilities thrust upon the Indian Peace commissioners by American leaders. The committee had labored unremittingly over the last ten months, but Congress had not even appropriated funds to implement the new peace treaties. Writing from Fort Laramie, Sherman praised those Oglalas and Brulés who supported peace but failed to gauge the temperament of the northern Oglalas and Miniconjous, who were still patrolling the Bozeman Road. He sensed that some of the militant bands supported diplomacy, although he had heard that many war leaders and their fighting men were waiting to see if the commissioners were "honest in our resolve to withdraw those [Powder River] posts, which they assert were the cause" of the conflict. Actually, the Department of War had already authorized the abandonment of Forts C. F. Smith, Reno, and Philip Kearny, but intended to postpone withdrawing the garrisons until the summer.[67]

On 24 May, Man Afraid of His Horse returned to the fort to learn what the envoys of the Great Father desired. Exercising his right as an *itancan* to address the council first, Man Afraid broached the subject of how difficult it was to persuade all the autonomous *tiyospaye* to accept peace. Sanborn and Harney listened politely, perhaps respecting the head chief's high status, and then explained the Missouri River plan to all the assembled Indians. The Great Father had consented to abandon the Bozeman Road, withdraw the garrisons stationed there, and to exclude whites from Sioux land, which was defined in the treaty as north of the Niobrara River, west of the Missouri River as far north as the mouth of the Grand River, and including the Black Hills. Although the Sioux might continue to hunt north of the Upper Platte River, and on the Republican Fork of the Smoky Hill River, as long as the presence of buffalo justified the chase, the president expected them henceforth to live within their reservation boundaries. Those who wished to farm would receive cattle, sheep, seeds, and agricultural tools. Other treaty goods would be issued near Fort Randall, at the mouth of the White River. In addition, the president would send farmers, schoolteachers, missionaries, and physicians to help the Lakotas learn white customs. All the Great Father asked in return was peace between the two peoples, and the cession of those tribal lands now devoid of game. But if the Lakotas rejected his peace overtures, the United States would continue the war until their bands had been destroyed. Man Afraid of His Horse responded that his followers intended to remain in their present homelands where they might resume trading at Fort Laramie.

The following day Harney and Sanborn smoked the pipe again with the Oglala councilors before rehashing the terms of the treaty. Conversation flowed freely. In this session Man Afraid of His Horse and Little Wound expressed pleasure that the president intended to abandon the Powder River posts, but some of the other *itancan* and active warriors in council remained skeptical of the government's motives. Black Hawk and High Wolf reasoned that if the Great Father now promised to withdraw the posts and order whites from their country, why would he then interfere with trade and request them to settle on a reservation near the Missouri River, a site they now avoided on account of the thriving but illegal whiskey business? American Horse, tentatively approved of the treaty but warned the visitors that should the Great Father again break his promises to the bands, he himself would find the commissioners, and "they will be the first ones I will whip." Kills the Bear, a prominent warrior, also threatened dire consequences: "I am a rascal," he boasted, "and if the whites don't fulfill this treaty, I will show myself [to be] one."[68]

On 25 May 1868 a number of Oglala councilors—mostly southern Oglalas and Loafers—signed the Fort Laramie treaty, which, among many things, established peace, created the Great Sioux Reservation, and granted to the Lakotas the services of farmers, Christian missionaries, teachers, and a government agent.[69] But the Oyuhpes and Bad Faces present at the fort refused to sign the treaty until they had evidence that the Powder River posts would indeed be removed. By early June, however, twenty-six lodges of these bands under Tall Wolf, Sitting Bear, and Mad Elk had apparently changed their minds. Charles Garrou, the special Sioux interpreter, remarked that these men touched the pen "with great willingness, and expressed much satisfaction with the prospects of being once more at peace with the whites," although their names are not listed on the official copy of the treaty. After receiving presents from the post commandant, the followers of Mad Elk, Tall Wolf, and Sitting Bear set off to hunt along the Tongue River. Red Leaf's Wazazas and Iron Shell's *tiyospaye* also departed, heading south toward their favorite haunts along the Republican River, and then on to the headwaters of the Niobrara River.[70]

When the May council adjourned, the commission divided as previously arranged. Sherman and Tappan made plans to visit the Navajos at Bosque Redondo; Christopher Augur, Sherman's erstwhile alternate on the commission, headed to Fort Bridger to conclude a treaty with the Shoshones; and Terry set out for Forts Randall and Sully to prepare to settle the Sioux on the Missouri River reservation. Generals Harney and Sanborn were scheduled to hold talks with bands of Missouri River Sioux at Fort Rice, but Sanborn lingered briefly at Fort Laramie in the hope that

Red Cloud might suddenly appear. He did not, and the general finally left the post on the twenty-eighth.[71]

On his way out, Sanborn encountered forty-five lodges under Yellow Eagle (Man Afraid's brother) and Little Hawk (Crazy Horse's uncle), who had taken his nephew's name after the younger died in combat. Yellow Eagle and Crazy Hawk stated they had come many miles to sign the treaty. The commandant immediately issued provisions from the sutler's store, and interpreter Garrou gifted the bands with blankets, calico, cooking utensils, knives, and some firearms. After camping near Fort Laramie for three days these Oglalas suddenly struck their lodges and departed, supposedly intending to inform their kinsfolk of the kind treatment they had received at the fort. Sanborn rejoiced at the news, for he believed Little Hawk belonged to one of the most militant Oglala camps. Man Afraid of His Horse left the fort on the twenty-ninth. The Hunkpatila *itancan* made arrangements to visit his old friend, Col. William Dye, stationed at Fort Fetterman, before the *wakiconza* moved the village to the mountains overlooking the headwaters of the Powder River's main fork. Fort Fetterman, established in July 1867 and named for Capt. William Fetterman, was located at the point where the Bozeman Road veered northward from the Upper Platte River. By midsummer Red Leaf, Iron Shell, and other Brulés, along with a few Southern Cheyenne and Arapaho friends, had traveled south to the Republican River and to the headwaters of the Niobrara. The Oyuhpes and Bad Faces recently at the fort were encamped somewhere on the Tongue River.[72]

On 28 July 1868, troops filed out of Fort C. F. Smith as the intertribal war faction watched from the Bighorn Mountains overlooking the fort. At dawn the following day, after the last white soldier had left the area, warriors swept down and burned the fort. A few days later, as soon as the garrison departed, Fort Philip Kearny also succumbed to the flames, and Fort Reno was later abandoned.[73]

In September, ten Northern Cheyenne scouts notified Lieutenant Colonel Slemmer, commanding Fort Laramie, that the Lakotas, Northern Cheyennes, and Arapahos were forming a grand intertribal circle near the sacred Bear Butte in the Black Hills. Man Afraid's band had already arrived, and Red Cloud's *tiyospaye* was at the mouth of Rosebud Creek. The Bad Faces had sent word to their relatives that they were looking for buffalo, and if successful they would be the last to arrive at Bear Butte. The minutes of this important multiband council are obviously not available, and Slemmer was unable to ascertain its purpose from the Northern Cheyenne messengers. Mari Sandoz contends that the Oglalas, especially the Bad Faces, had raised some concerns about Red Cloud's mounting fame among the whites. Why did American citizens deem his signature on the treaty imperative for maintaining a firm peace? During the council Black Twin (Holy Bald Eagle), a distinguished Bad Face *blotahunka*, was selected as a head shirt wearer. Red Cloud failed once more to attain this honor. Instead, he was selected as a "treaty chief," or, from an Oglala perspective, a prominent council spokesman whose role was limited to discussing the peace treaty for the Bad Faces.[74]

Fragmentary evidence exists to suggest that the Oglalas quarreled bitterly during this sacred assembly, not just over Red Cloud's role in the peace talks but also over whether the bands should even consider abandoning the war effort. But by 1868 the Union Pacific railroad was approaching the Salt Lake City and Virginia City links, making the Powder River route obsolete for Montana-bound emigrants. Lakota warriors believed, however, that the Great Father's soldiers feared them and had finally withdrawn from Forts C. F. Smith, Reno, and Philip Kearny at their insistence.

In early October the Indian Peace commissioners convened their last meeting in Chicago, still hopeful that Red Cloud, their "head chief of the Sioux," would endorse the Fort Laramie peace treaty. On 4 November 1868, while the former commissioners resumed their professional duties, the Oglalas Man Afraid of His Horse, Red Cloud, Iron Crane, and High Eagle, along with an impressive entourage of prominent councilors of the Hunkpapas, Blackfeet, Brulés, and Sans Arcs, some of whom had already signed the document, were meeting Fort Laramie's new commandant, Col. William Dye. Also assembled were the interpreters Antoine LeDuc and Louis Richard.

Dye reported that Red Cloud "affected a great deal of dignity and disinterestedness" while the other Lakota delegates rose to speak. When it was Red Cloud's turn to address the council, he remarked that nothing satisfactory could be accomplished because neither the official Peace Commission nor any other high-ranking white dignitaries were present. Red Cloud feared that if he touched the pen, the Great Father's people would expect peace to prevail; that was something he alone could not guarantee. Furthermore, he had not come to the council because military officers had summoned him, but because he wished to hear news of recent developments at the fort, and to obtain powder and lead to fight the Crows.[75]

The following day Colonel Dye explained the treaty's provisions. The Great Father especially desired peace with Red Cloud, the colonel added, as he considered him a "Big Chief." Despite such flattery, Red Cloud made "but few advances." Returning on the sixth, the Lakota councilors renewed their requests for firearms and ammunition. Then, after posing numerous questions about the treaty's provisions, a "cautious" Red Cloud, "with a show of reluctance and tremulousness," finally signed the document. Following him in this act were Man Afraid of His Horse, Iron Crane, High Eagle, and the Brulés Thunder Man and Thunder Flying Running. Red Cloud also asked all the whites present "to touch the pen," after which he cordially shook hands with everyone. But he also warned Dye that while he personally intended to honor the treaty, he did not possess the authority to control the warrior societies. He trusted that the officers at Fort Laramie would treat the Sioux kindly, as they had done in former years, and that their favorite traders would be permitted to return to their lodges. The Bad Face mentioned that he, Man Afraid of His Horse, and Brave Bear, were presently in camp at Bear Lodge, on the north fork of the Cheyenne River, but that *wakiconza* would soon establish the winter villages along the Powder River, where their young men would organize war parties against the Crows. Transforming themselves into farmers on the Great Sioux Reservation appealed to very few at this time.[76]

When the council broke up, the post trader, by previous authority of the commission, distributed gifts such as shirts, blankets, kettles, and vermillion. Fort Laramie's sutler also issued some rations, including sugar, flour, coffee, crackers, beans, and tea. After the giveaway, the *tiyospaye*, "apparently well pleased," left to prepare their winter meat supplies.[77]

While Fort Laramie's officers celebrated what they hoped signaled the conclusion of the northern plains conflict, a group of warriors, previously loyal to Red Cloud, left his *tiyospaye* to join the Bad Face head shirtwearer, Black Twin; his brother No Water, a headman and future *itancan*; and the Hunkpatila war advocates Big Road, Long Face, and Crazy Horse.[78] The 1868 treaty with the Oglalas bore the marks of mostly southern Oglala and Loafer councilors—most of whom had earlier rejected a protracted war with the Great Father's people. But many of the northern Oglalas and their allies had never seen a peace treaty, and the militant postcouncil demonstrations of Bad Face warriors signaled that peace between all the Lakotas and the United States might prove to be a most fragile concept.

# CHAPTER FOUR

# The Struggle to
# Establish an Oglala Agency

In the opening months of 1869, United States senators debated the recently concluded treaties of Fort Laramie and Medicine Lodge Creek, the tangible results of the Indian Peace Commission's negotiations with the northern and southern plains tribes. The decades of the 1850s and 1860s represented a protracted period of treaty signing between numerous Native American communities and the United States. The formal ratification process was the constitutional province of the Senate, and members of the House became weary of playing a relatively insignificant role in establishing diplomatic alliances with sovereign Indian nations other than to appropriate monies to carry out ratified treaties. Thus when the Senate first approved the Fort Laramie and Medicine Lodge Creek treaties, members of the House rejected a Senate amendment appropriating over two million dollars to fulfill their terms.[1]

The representatives yielded, however, when the Fortieth Congress convened in the spring of 1869. They approved the appropriation but also claimed some control over Indian affairs by allocating an additional $25,000 for the appointment of ten commissioners, "eminent for their intelligence and philanthropy," who would exercise joint control with the secretary of the interior over the disbursement of funds for Indian people. Among its intended duties, this Board of Indian Commissioners would examine the records and activities of the Indian Office, inspect agencies, supervise the purchase of Indian goods, witness annuity distributions, confer with field employees, and advise the secretary of the interior and the commissioner of Indian affairs on future personnel appointments. The first nine appointees to the Board of Indian Commissioners were William Welsh (chairman), John Farwell, George Stuart, Robert Campbell, William Dodge, E. S. Toby, Nathan Bishop, Henry Lane, and Felix Brunot, the Pittsburgh steel magnate who soon replaced Welsh as chair. The board became embroiled in disputes with the Interior Department within weeks of its creation, however. Welsh resigned after serving only one month, highly critical of the commissioners' limited supervisory role in Indian-white relations. As Congress had failed to clarify the board's status, the commissioners possessed limited authority to influence departmental decisions.[2]

While the treaties of Fort Laramie and Medicine Lodge Creek reignited power struggles between the U.S. Senate and the House, president-elect Ulysses Grant came to view these documents, along with the Doolittle report of 1867, as the foundation of a new American approach to Indian-white relations. During the 1860s, civilian and military leaders debated whether the Department of the Interior or the Department of War should govern the formulation of federal Indian policy. By the end of the decade the United States had waged several unsuccessful wars against the Lakotas and their allies. Furthermore, the vocal campaigns of the Indian reform movement, widely condemning the continued use of force advocated by army generals, had reached critical mass and were beginning to sway public opinion. The Sand Creek massacre occurred in November 1864, and tragedy struck again four years later when a band of Southern Cheyennes under Black Kettle, who had narrowly escaped death at Sand Creek, were killed at the Washita River during a raid by Lt. Col. George Custer. Such actions prompted many Americans, especially those residing in eastern cities, to demand an end to the bloodshed on the plains.[3]

Believing that veterans were better acquainted with tribal customs than civilian agents, president-elect Grant initially sympathized with those army commanders who sought greater control over federal Indian policy and the military administration of reservations. After the Civil War, Congress considerably reduced the size of its standing army, leaving hundreds of officers without posts. Many had opted for service in the Indian Office, supervising the settlement of tribes, constructing agency buildings, and inspecting and distributing rations. Despite storms brewing in Congress over recent military conduct on the plains, by the end of 1869, forty-nine of the seventy Indian agents still held army commissions. The following summer, however, Congress passed the Army Appropriations Act, prohibiting the employment of army veterans as Indian agents because of their perceived inability to "civilize" Native Americans.[4]

But despite Grant's illustrious military career and his loyalty to army colleagues, his inauguration as president of the United States signaled a public commitment to a change in federal Indian policy—one predicated on peace rather than force. A few weeks prior to taking the oath of office,

Grant entertained in his Washington office a delegation of Quakers who had just attended the national convention of the Society of Friends, in Baltimore. Quaker delegates had adopted resolutions at the conference calling for the incorporation of Christian teachings into future Indian policy, and Grant's guests were anxious to discuss these ideas with him. They hoped the president would consider appointing Quaker missionaries, subject to Senate confirmation, to serve as reservation agents. Church men, the Friends argued, would be immune to the political graft and nepotism that allegedly characterized the Office of Indian Affairs; once the tribes were settled on reservations, the visitors added, they would soon abandon warfare.[5]

Grant and his handpicked commissioner of Indian affairs, Ely Parker, a Seneca of the Iroquois Confederacy and the general's former aide-de-camp, showed interest in the Quaker plan, requesting that the Friends submit a list of nominees for the Indian Office. By December the president was ready to announce the official implementation of the newly designed peace policy. In his first annual message to Congress, Grant expressed the hope that the plan "will in a few years bring all the Indians upon reservations," where they would build houses, attend Christian churches, and pursue "peaceful and self-sustaining avocations." The following year, in the wake of the statute prohibiting the appointment of military agents, Grant proclaimed that he intended to place all the agencies under the auspices of those religious denominations prepared to follow the Quakers' lead. Immediately, the Methodist, Presbyterian, Protestant Episcopalian, and Catholic churches began to establish their programs and nominate men for reservation service.[6]

Article 2 of the 1868 Treaty of Fort Laramie provided for the formal recognition of the Great Sioux Reservation, including the lands spanning the present state of South Dakota west of the Missouri River. Lakotas who signed the treaty also reserved the right to dwell and hunt in the Black Hills and Powder River country. American policymakers, however, wanted all the Sioux to relocate at once to the reservation and to accept the assimilationist programs later outlined in Grant's peace policy. But coaxing or compelling the Oglalas to accept agency life, and destroying the political influence of recognized tribal leaders, would quickly test the mettle of federal agents who took up those tasks.

Lakota *tiyospaye* scattered in all directions after the November 1868 treaty councils closed at Fort Laramie. Camp *wakiconza* had directed the villages to set out for their favorite winter camps away from the Great Sioux Reservation, while the younger war leaders, the *blotahunka*, reminded the fighting men not to abandon their plans for spring forays against the Crows and Pawnees. Federal officials remained optimistic, however, that all the Sioux would soon relocate to reservation lands east of the Upper Platte valley and north of Nebraska. Indian commissioners had already selected the Whetstone Agency, located on the right bank of the Missouri River about eighteen miles by wagon road from Fort Randall, as the first federal headquarters for Oglala and Brulé bands. Now that a number of Lakotas had "touched the pen," thereby accepting the terms of the treaty, at least from the Americans' point of view, Brig. Gen. William Harney commenced preparations to escort the bands to the Missouri River site.[7]

Many U.S. congressmen and members of the executive branch still regarded Red Cloud of the Bad Face Oglalas as the "head chief" of all the Lakotas. He was the man, they believed, who could persuade the Sioux to settle on the reservation. But Red Cloud had already stated that his relatives, and other Oglala kinsfolk, would never live near the Missouri River agency as long as hunting was so poor there, and as long as traders offered expensive whiskey to those willing to barter. Convinced that alcohol invariably corrupted Indian people, William Welsh tried to thwart the whiskey trade during a visit to the Whetstone Agency in the summer of 1870.[8]

American settlers termed the left bank of the river "ceded land," and rushed to claim homesteads in the area, with or without legal title to the land. One squatter seized three "forties" (120 acres) opposite the Whetstone Agency, on which he proceeded to construct a whiskey still to furnish the illegal traffic in liquor. Welsh attempted to halt the production of alcohol by purchasing the squatter's tenuous title to his acreage and arranging for him to leave the vicinity. But as soon as Welsh had departed, the squatter returned, only to claim another three forties adjacent to the very land he had sold to Welsh. The unlicensed trader soon reconstructed his still, and whiskey, "put up in tin cans, labelled and purporting to be peaches [and] tomatoes," once again flowed freely to the Whetstone Agency. Liquor traders did not face arrest unless caught red-handed, and as it was virtually impossible for officials to watch their every move, the act of 1832 prohibiting the sale of alcohol to Indian people remained largely unenforceable.[9]

The Oglala head *itancan*, Man Afraid of His Horse, and Red Leaf of the Wazazas also supported Red Cloud's steadfast rejection of the Whetstone Agency. Moreover, the Loafer leaders Big Mouth and Blue Horse, who often appeared conciliatory in their dealings with Americans, accused federal officials of duplicity when the latter ordered Lakota *tiyospaye* to abandon the Upper Platte River and Republican River valleys. The Loafers reminded them that the 1868 treaty guaranteed Lakota rights to dwell in the Powder River country and to hunt north of the Upper Platte River and south along the Republican Fork of the Smoky Hill River as long as there was sufficient game to sustain the bands. According to the Loafers' interpretation of the 1868 document, removal east was optional; on the other hand, actually compelling the Lakotas to move to the Missouri River constituted a violation of the treaty. Rather than relocate there, the protreaty Oglalas hoped the Americans would resume trading operations at Fort Laramie, a practice the Indian Office had curtailed in preparation for moving the Lakotas onto reservation lands.[10]

In the late spring of 1869, Capt. DeWitt Clinton Poole was appointed federal agent for the Spotted Tail, Swift Bear, Fire Thunder, Big Mouth, and Blue Horse bands, which, despite previous objections, had finally consented to live in the vicinity of the Whetstone Agency. In early 1870 Congress authorized an expedition into the Black Hills and Bighorn Mountains to prospect for gold, a decision that risked precipitating yet another northern plains war. On 4 March, Poole informed John Burbank, ex officio superintendent of Indian affairs, that rumors of the proposed expedition had angered the Oglalas and Brulés camped at the agency, many of whom, Poole reported, "affiliate more or less" with Man Afraid of His Horse and Red Cloud, key participants in the conflicts of the 1860s. The agent feared that if the gold seekers proceeded, "a war upon the expedition will commence—the results of which will be difficult to foretell."[11]

Indian Department officials disregarded Poole's warning, however, when they received news that Man Afraid of His Horse, Red Cloud, Brave Bear, and Red Horse (Dog),[12] along with fifty prominent warriors, wished to visit President Grant to discuss the 1868 treaty directly with him. Red Cloud requested rations, guns, and ammunition for the Oglalas, especially the younger warriors, as evidence of the president's goodwill. Honoring the Bad Face's kinsfolk with such a grand gift would help to influence them toward peace, Red Cloud had suggested, for surely gifts would show how much the Great Father valued his leadership skills. Cheered by the possibility of moving all the Oglalas onto the reservation, and averting another war, President Grant forbade the gold prospectors from leaving Cheyenne, Wyoming Territory. In late spring Grant's cabinet approved the Oglala delegation's visit to the American capital, also inviting Spotted Tail and other Brulés.[13]

Lt. Gen. William Sherman frowned on the executive decision to invite Lakota spokesmen to the White House. Sherman wrote Lt. Gen. Philip Sheridan in late April that federal officials should dictate terms to the Oglalas rather than bargain with them. "They should be told plainly and emphatically," Sherman began, "that they are expected to occupy the reservation north of Nebraska and to trade down the Missouri River." Indian delegations would only do "more harm than good," he felt. But with the next breath he conceded that the Office of Indian Affairs "might as well deal with them now" rather than allow the matter to "drag on indefinitely." He supported on humanitarian grounds the distribution of food to hungry Oglalas and Brulés at Fort Fetterman, but certainly not the weapons and ammunition that Red Cloud expected.[14]

Maj. Gen. Christopher Augur concurred with Sherman. He doubted that Lakota delegations to Washington would prevent future Indian-white conflicts on the northern plains. Furthermore, Augur predicted dire consequences if the Interior Department continued to consider Red Cloud "the head and front of all the hostile bands." It was not solely Bad Face Oglalas who had participated in recent skirmishes, the general believed, but also numerous bands of Miniconjous, Hunkpapas, Northern Cheyennes and Northern Arapahos, and Republican River southern Oglalas under Whistler and the war leader Pawnee Killer. "Red Cloud cannot control any of these bands," Augur cautioned, "and his influence will be no greater than that of Spotted Tail." Moreover, the general sensed that any Lakota leader "who becomes friendly to the whites will cease to exert any influence over the hostiles, unless of his immediate family."[15]

Top military brass could sound the alarm as loudly as they wished, but the president, the secretary of the interior, and the commissioner of Indian affairs continued to place their faith in Red Cloud to secure a binding peace. On 16 May hundreds of Oglalas gathered near Fort Fetterman to bid farewell to their delegates embarking on their journey to the Great Father.[16]

It is difficult to ascertain definitively the status of each of the Oglala spokesmen, most of whom had signed the 1868 treaty. For example, Red Dog, Brave Bear, High Wolf, and Yellow Bear were band *itancan*; Sword held the prestigious title of head shirtwearer but was not yet recognized as a band *itancan*; Red Cloud could claim the status of headman and former *blotahunka* while the other men probably represented the warrior societies. Long Wolf would later become a reservation chief; Black Hawk was a headman or prominent warrior in Yellow Bear's *tiyospaye* (later called the Melt band); during the agency years, Red Fly and Sitting Bear chose to reside in the bands of the head shirtwearers Young Man Afraid of His Horse and American Horse, respectively, while Rocky Bear would associate first with Red Cloud's band and then with Red Dog's.[17] American dignitaries may refer to Red Cloud as "head chief," but in the eyes of the Oglala people, many of Red Cloud's fellow delegates, such as Red Dog, Brave Bear, and High Wolf, were at least as influential among their own band councils.

Two days later the Oglalas arrived at Fort Laramie, where they met former commanding officer Col. John Smith, who had returned from Washington to escort them to the American capital. Accompanying the party were the Lakotas' interpreters—John Richard Jr., the "son-in-law" of Yellow Bear; W. G. Bullock; James McCloskey; and Jules Ecoffey. Richard was the oldest son of the French trader John Richard Sr. (also known as John Resha, Reschaw, Rishan, and Richau), who had married one of Red Cloud's sisters. Man Afraid of His Horse, senior *itancan* of the Hunkpatilas, had elected to remain at Fort Fetterman. Historians James C. Olson and Peter Powell state that the old man had intended to join the party but had taken ill while at the post, although Man Afraid's absence might also signal his tacit disapproval of the attention lavished on Red Cloud, the Great Father's "head chief."[18]

The Oglala delegation finally left Fort Laramie on 26 May, arriving safely in Washington on the first of June. The *New York Times* published several detailed accounts of the delegates' visit.[19] With hyperbolic flourishes, editors portrayed Red Cloud as "the most celebrated warrior on the Plains," with a following of ten thousand people including two thousand warriors. Indeed, the *Times* continued, the Bad Face's friendship "is of more importance to whites than that of any other chief." Furthermore, as Red Cloud was such "a powerful and wise man," federal officials must take great pains, the paper wrote, to win his friendship and to "create in his mind a favorable impression" of American people.[20]

Secretary of the Interior Jacob Cox and Commissioner Ely Parker were in no hurry to meet their Oglala guests, however, keeping the Lakota delegates waiting for two days before finally greeting them on 7 June for the first of several discussions. For over a week the Oglala and Brulé visitors were honored with lavish displays of diplomatic hospitality—city tours, grand feasts, and weapons demonstrations. Although the Lakotas must have felt unnerved by the cultural differences, rounds of formal introductions, and the close scrutiny they endured from curious onlookers, they remained dignified and businesslike, as the role of a Lakota delegate required. Oglala councilors had previously selected Red Cloud to serve as their primary spokesman, empowered to relay the consensus of the multiband Oglala council. As Red Cloud later explained to Commissioner Parker, "the demands I have made upon you from the [councilors] I left behind me are all alike." During the delegation's public audience with President Grant, Red Cloud reiterated that most Oglala bands would never relocate to the Missouri River agency. In addition, he reissued his request for guns, ammunition, and provisions, and asked the president to ban American settlers and miners from entering the Lakotas' unceded territory—the Black Hills and the Powder River country.[21]

The Oglalas returned to the office of the commissioner on the tenth. Secretary Cox, Governor J. A. Campbell of the Wyoming Territory, and former peace commissioners Vincent Colyer and Felix Brunot were also present. Negotiations had proceeded smoothly up to this point, but Red Cloud created a furor when he angrily informed Cox, who had been carefully discussing the provisions of the 1868 treaty, that this was the first time he had heard of such terms. Moreover, he had no intention of honoring them. Instead, he contended that the paper he and others signed merely provided for the removal of the Powder River forts and the establishment of a formal peace between his people and Americans. The other delegates supported Red Cloud's assertions, openly accusing their interpreters of deceiving them during the Fort Laramie councils. One of the warrior representatives was so convinced that his relatives had been duped that he later threatened to commit suicide rather than risk public humiliation when the whites' interpretation of the treaty was made known to them.[22]

It is impossible to determine whether the treaty had been accurately translated, but if the delegates' sudden outbursts were ploys to wring concessions from federal officials, they were effective. The next day Secretary Cox announced that the president had agreed to modify the treaty. The Oglalas could live temporarily on the headwaters of the Big Cheyenne River northeast of Fort Fetterman, outside the boundaries of the Great Sioux Reservation but within the limits reserved for hunting. President Grant still expected the Oglalas to trade at the Missouri River posts but would arrange for their annuity goods to be delivered at a more convenient location. The commissioner also directed the delegates to submit a list of names of those they wanted as their agent and traders. Red Cloud responded that he disliked military officers because they frightened his kinsfolk, and poor men might be tempted to steal their treaty supplies. The Bad Face spokesman thought that Benjamin Mills would make a fine agent, and he could trust W. G. Bullock as a trader. The first request was soon rejected. Felix Brunot wrote Commissioner Parker that he did not consider Benjamin Mills a suitable candidate for the post. "Mr. Mills," he remarked, "is too nearly on a social level with the Indians, and has too long been identified with them." Furthermore, Mills did not have, in Brunot's opinion, "the inclination to do any serious work for the salvation of the Indians." The Indian Office was sufficiently swayed by Brunot's testimony, eventually appointing in lieu of Mills, John Wham, a member of the Protestant Episcopal Church, whose agents had been assigned to acculturate the Oglalas.[23]

The Oglala delegation reached New York City on 14 June, when Red Cloud and Red Dog were scheduled to deliver speeches at the Cooper Institute two days later. Addressing hundreds of Americans, a quiet but earnest Red Cloud epitomized the whites' conception of the noble chieftain. But in more private surroundings he displayed anxiety about his perceived role and status as the Oglalas' primary spokesman and "head chief." During a conversation with Colonel Smith and former peace commissioners Brunot and Campbell, Red Cloud stressed his determination to state the wishes of the multiband Oglala council, and certainly not to make promises he could not keep. "My people understand what I came here for," he tried to explain, "and I should lose my [authority to represent them] if I did not stick to one course." No councilor possessed the authority to make unilateral decisions for all the Oglalas. Indeed, very few *wakiconza* and *akicita* would dare to violate tribal customs by so doing, for such transgressions might result in their ostracism from the camp circle. Smith also proceeded cautiously, but suggested to Red Cloud that if the Oglalas sincerely desired peace, the president might at some future date permit them to settle permanently away from the Missouri River agency.[24]

The delegation returned to Fort Laramie by the end of the month. Soon after his arrival, Red Cloud set out again for the Powder River Lakotas, whom he hoped would accept binding peace terms with the United States. Col. Franklin Flint, the newly appointed commanding officer at Fort Laramie, telegraphed superiors that both Yellow Bear, a member of the recent Washington delegation, and Yellow Eagle had verified scouting reports that Red Cloud was doing his utmost to persuade the northern people to forgo war. Yellow Bear thought the Bad Face headman had enjoyed some early success, as no war parties had been organized lately. Red Cloud hoped that all the *tiyospaye* would reach the fort by mid-September, but first he must confer with prominent northern leaders before anything could be settled.[25]

During the Washington conference Felix Brunot had mentioned to Red Cloud that he planned to visit the plains sometime in the late summer or early fall. He and Robert Campbell, a member of the Board of Indian Commissioners, intended to bolster Red Cloud's efforts in coaxing all the Oglala bands to accept a temporary agency at Rawhide Buttes, forty miles north of Fort Laramie. On 21 September the two commissioners reached the fort, anxious to hear how the Lakotas had received Red Cloud's words. The Bad Face headman was in camp on the Cheyenne River, over one hundred miles from the post, but he sent his nephew and interpreter, John Richard Jr., to notify Brunot and Campbell that he would join them in early October to discuss the agency question.[26]

Interestingly, it was Man Afraid of His Horse, not Red Cloud, who was the first to come into Fort Laramie, having left the Bad Face headman at the forks of Laramie Creek. With the Hunkpatila *itancan* were Gray Bear and Grass. Man Afraid told the commissioners that he had journeyed over three hundred miles to see them and wished to know the purpose of their visit. Brunot explained that the president was eager to hear the results of Red Cloud's campaigning among his people, especially the Powder River bands. Brunot remarked that he regretted not meeting the Hunkpatila chief in Washington, and inquired as to whether the buffalo were scarce. Man Afraid of His Horse retorted that the commissioner ought to know, as he had come through his country scaring them away. This cutting remark, Brunot later recalled, had a "visible effect" on Man Afraid's entourage, but the commissioner declined to elaborate further. After receiving gifts of food, Man Afraid of His Horse set out for the Bad Face camp, promising to return shortly with Red Cloud.[27] Man Afraid no doubt realized that the federal emissaries would insist on doing business primarily with Red Cloud. Thus acting in the best interests of all the Oglalas, his symbolic children, Man Afraid believed it was his duty to reassure Brunot and Campbell that Red Cloud, the Great Father's "head chief," would indeed appear shortly.

Red Cloud finally came in to Fort Laramie on the fourth of October. The next day he, along with Man Afraid of His Horse, Red Dog, Sitting Bear, Grass, American Horse, Red Leaf, Little Wound, and a large number of warriors assembled in council.[28] Red Cloud spoke first. He avoided detailed reports of the Powder River talks, instead repeating the Oglalas' request for a trading post ten miles north of Fort Laramie, in an area that federal officials desired for American settlement. When Brunot reminded him that the 1868 treaty authorized trade on the Missouri River, Red Cloud exclaimed that the post should be located on the North Platte River and nowhere else. The Oyuhpe leader Red Dog motioned to speak next, immediately disrupting the council by demanding the interpreting services of Leon Palladay. At this point the tensions between the Bear and Smoke peoples resurfaced, when Sitting Bear and the southern Oglala *itancan* Little Wound strongly objected. Palladay had lied in previous councils, they claimed, expressing concern that erroneous translations might stir up trouble between the Oglalas and the Americans. Little Wound then criticized Red Cloud's defiant demeanor. He reminded the Bad Face that the Oglalas had suffered enough during the last war with the United States, chiding him that "if you go to war with the whites you have no country to go to. Now it is our duty and interest to be peaceable and mind what our friends here have to tell us." Red Cloud immediately deferred to the Kiyuksa *itancan*, proposing instead to adjourn the meeting until the following day. It became clear that the councilors could not reach a consensus and would require more time to settle their differences.

Brunot and Campbell arranged private talks that evening with Man Afraid of His Horse, Red Cloud, Red Dog, Grass, and John Richard Jr. The Oglalas now desired a trading post south of the Upper Platte River, Richard translated, but perhaps in a couple of years they might accept an agency north of the river. Campbell stated flatly that the president would never condone any trading south of the Upper Platte, where American settlements were sprouting rapidly. Indeed, he continued, the Oglalas should be satisfied with the Rawhide Buttes location as, after all, they found it more desirable than the Whetstone Agency. Little else was said until the following morning when another general council would convene.

Clearly the Oglalas had spent the previous evening privately debating the issues at hand, because their spokesmen presented the consensus of the councilors during the morning conference. Once the pipe had been smoked and passed to all in attendance, the Oglalas startled the commissioners by announcing that the *tiyospaye* would trade only at Fort Laramie. Moreover, they had emphatically rejected relocation to Rawhide Buttes. Man Afraid of His Horse, the senior *itancan* at the assembly, decided to intervene at this juncture, advising Brunot to set aside highly controversial subjects for the present time. The commissioner agreed, distributing gifts to the councilors to affirm his friendship. After the meeting broke up, Red Cloud remarked to Brunot that he personally longed for peace, but revealed that the final decision did not rest in his hands. It was the young men, Red Cloud explained, who had "picked out the place for a trading post," implying that the older councilors had decided to obey the warrior societies on this occasion.

Brunot waited two days before attempting once more to persuade the treaty Oglalas to select a mutually agreeable site for the new agency. He dispatched young John Richard to summon Red Cloud, who arrived accompanied by Man Afraid of His Horse, Red Dog, and American Horse, one of the head shirtwearers, whose presence had done little to prevent the open quarrels of the previous meetings. Commissioner Brunot warned Red Cloud that Fort Laramie's commanding officer had been issued strict orders not to distribute rations to the Oglalas while their leaders refused to resolve their current problems. Resuming his duties as primary spokesman, Red Cloud tried again to have the Oglalas' treaty supplies delivered to the south bank of the Platte. Brunot countered that if the bands wanted their goods, they must travel to the Missouri River for them, unless they agreed to live at Rawhide Buttes. With this ultimatum delivered, the commissioners departed.[29]

After the 1870 Fort Laramie councils broke up, many northern Oglala *tiyospaye* headed for the Powder River country but returned to the post in mid-December in need of provisions and ammunition. By February of the following year, nearly three thousand Lakotas, Northern Cheyennes, and Arapahos had gathered in the vicinity to receive supplies from Col. John Smith, who had since resumed his duties as Fort Laramie's commandant. A month later their numbers had grown by over five hundred and were increasing daily. Man Afraid of His Horse came in with sixty-five lodges; Red Cloud arrived with seventy-eight tipis, and Lone Wolf with fifty; Cut Forward, Big Foot, American Horse, and Rocky Bear claimed twenty, fifty-three, sixty-six, and seventeen lodges, respectively.[30]

In a series of communiqués to Maj. George Ruggles, assistant adjutant general for the Department of the Platte, Colonel Smith wrote that Red Cloud was "cooperating most heartily to induce all the Northern Indians" to accept peace terms with the United States. Moreover, the colonel regarded the Bad Face's views "worthy of consideration in the management of the Indians," and thought the Office of Indian Affairs should appoint an agent and licensed traders "in accordance with Red Cloud's recommendation." Interior Department officials dismissed Colonel Smith's advice, however, noting that Red Cloud had earlier nominated as an agent his close friend Benjamin Mills, a man they deemed unworthy of the post.[31]

Although repeatedly badgered to select the site of the Oglala agency (which federal officials had already decided to name Red Cloud Agency in honor of the Bad Face headman), Red Cloud refused to oblige. Many American leaders still dubbed him "head chief" of the Sioux—and he understood the expectations implicit in the title—but the Bad Face's subtribal status at this time cannot be easily surmised. Red Cloud's role was clearly that of an spokesman, but did the Oglalas themselves look upon him as a band chief, *wakiconza*, headman, or as an aging *blotahunka* with an exemplary military career?

Historian George Hyde contends that Red Cloud's own band, refusing to recognize him as an *itancan*, nevertheless acknowledged his talents for war. In her biography of the Oglala warrior and head shirtwearer Crazy Horse, Mari Sandoz describes how Crazy Horse disgraced himself by openly feuding with No Water, Black Twin's brother. Head shirtwearers were forbidden by custom to engage in public displays of anger; thus Crazy Horse's behavior obliged him to relinquish the fringed shirt symbolizing his role as protector of the people. Soon after Crazy Horse's "demotion," an Oglala councilor recommended bestowing the honor on Red Cloud in recognition of his contributions in Washington. If the Great Father considered Red Cloud a "big chief," it was said, then perhaps he would make a worthy head shirtwearer. Man Afraid of His Horse rejected the proposal, however, for reasons that are not clear.[32]

In line with peace policy objectives, the Protestant Episcopal Church was invited to nominate Captain Poole's successor as agent for the Oglalas. Poole served eighteen months at Whetstone Agency before being required by law to leave the Indian Service. Church member John Wham of Illinois won the appointment, reaching Fort Laramie at the end of March. Sparks flew almost immediately between Wham and Colonel Smith. The new agent wired his superiors that Smith's directive to feed the Indians from the quartermaster's supplies "robs me of the greatest power to their confidence, and will certainly lead to trouble between the military and myself." It was the agent's responsibility to provide for the bands camped around the fort, Wham protested, not the army's. The secretary of war obliged, authorizing Wham to dispense what remained of the ten thousand dollars' worth of goods made available to the quartermaster for supplying the needy Lakotas and their allies.[33]

While engaging in power struggles with Fort Laramie's commandant, agent Wham also pressed Red Cloud to name the site for the new agency. Red Cloud feared that if the president forced his hand, the Oglalas would "accuse him of selling out," and he would lose whatever influence he had mustered among his people. But if the Great Father would only establish a temporary agency south of the Upper Platte River, Red Cloud believed that eventually the Oglalas "can be induced to go on to the reservation without difficulty." Both Wham and Colonel Smith initially entertained this idea.[34]

Wham left for the American capital in the first week of April anxious to finalize plans for the Red Cloud Agency. For some reason he soon changed his mind about its location, remarking to H. R. Clum, acting commissioner of Indian affairs, that, in accordance with Felix Brunot's previous recommendation, the agency should be located "at some point thirty or forty miles north of the [Upper] Platte," presumably referring to Rawhide Buttes. But, surprisingly, Commissioner Parker ignored Wham's advice, opting instead for a temporary site just north of Fort Laramie.[35]

Wham contacted Red Cloud immediately upon his return from Washington in mid-April. During the agent's stay in the capital, someone had informed Red Cloud that the Oglalas would at last receive guns and ammunition. His people regarded these gifts as testimony not only of the Americans' good intentions but also as signs that the Great Father held their spokesmen in high esteem. When the articles were not forthcoming, the Oglalas questioned the success of their delegates' mission to the president and their overall ability to represent their people in negotiations with the whites. In contrast to his earlier optimistic stance, Wham wrote to the commissioner that if these often requested items were not delivered soon, Red Cloud, the prominent Oglala intermediary, "would lose his influence for good among his people," a result that could prove "ruinous" for future peace.[36]

By May the agency dilemma seemed hopeless. No one could say for certain where the Oglala people would live. Wham reported that the bands themselves were divided over the issue, some favoring an agency at Rawhide Buttes, and others opposed. Disregarding Commissioner Parker's recent suggestion for an agency just north of Fort Laramie, and his own earlier support of a site south of the Upper Platte, Wham now endeavored to convince the Oglala councilors to approve the Rawhide Buttes location. Those in opposition argued, however, that this region might draw the attention of whites who coveted the Black Hills. Colonel

Smith then tried his hand, browbeating the councilors that if they continued to delay their decision, the Office of Indian Affairs would withhold their rations. Following the colonel's lead, Wham declared he would indeed do so if he discovered any of the Oglalas camped south of the Upper Platte, a bold statement that incited Red Cloud to retort that he would personally kill anyone who dared to draw treaty supplies from the Rawhide Buttes site. Stalemated, Smith recommended that Special Commissioner Felix Brunot return to Fort Laramie to goad the Oglalas into settling the matter. Brunot later agreed to come, although having failed once before, he seriously doubted that he alone could influence the council this time.[37]

On 12 June, Brunot convened yet another series of meetings with northern and southern treaty Oglalas camped around Fort Laramie. Assembled in the grand council lodge (*tipi iyokiheya*) were the *itancan* Man Afraid of His Horse, Red Dog, Yellow Bear, High Wolf, and Brave Bear of the northern Oglala treaty bands, and Little Wound and Bad Wound of the southern Oglalas, along with the head shirtwearers Young Man Afraid of His Horse and Sword. Wazaza Brulé participants included the band chiefs Red Leaf and Quick Bear. Red Cloud (a relative of Red Leaf) served as primary spokesman.[38]

Brunot and Smith again admonished the councilors that if they failed to reach a consensus at this meeting, no more food supplies would be issued at Fort Laramie. Red Cloud responded defiantly: "If the rations are stopped we will all go to the north," that is, to consult the nontreaty Oglalas under Black Twin, Charging Shield, Crazy Horse, and Little Big Man, who had thus far rejected all overtures for peace. Brunot reminded Red Cloud that he had publicly vowed to settle north of the Upper Platte River before the end of winter. If the Oglalas remained in the vicinity of Forts Laramie and Fetterman, the commissioner added, disruptive whiskey traders would descend regularly on their camp circles. Red Cloud countered that he had never promised to relocate the bands, but at the same time he seemed anxious to know if the president truly intended to withhold rations. Brunot called upon other councilors to speak, but all remained silent; Red Cloud had expressed the consensus of the council, so nothing remained to be said.

Red Cloud's strong words during this assembly belied his concern of seeming utterly incapable of fulfilling the role of the Americans' "head chief," a man with far-reaching political power. In the privacy of Colonel Smith's quarters, Red Cloud informed Brunot that he personally was quite "willing to go over the river [north of the Upper Platte], but I want all the rest to agree to it." He feared that if he alone proclaimed the site for the agency, thereby breaching council protocol, "some of my friends will jump over me."[39] Even if Red Cloud were now a *wakiconza* (camp administrator) in his own Bad Face *tiyospaye*, the concept of making unilateral decisions of this importance for all his Oglala kinsfolk, including the nontreaty bands, was simply incomprehensible.

Brunot was puzzled as to why Red Cloud had not mentioned these misgivings during the last council. The Bad Face replied that he had been "afraid to do so," but hoped that eventually all the Oglalas could be persuaded to move to a mutually acceptable location. He now felt compelled to consult his northern relative Black Twin before rejoining the Fort Laramie council. Black Twin was a brother of No Water (Red Cloud's son-in-law) and a nontreaty Bad Face *blotahunka* greatly esteemed by the warriors. Red Cloud cautioned Brunot and Smith that in order to obtain unanimity on matters of such importance, as required by Lakota political customs, the northern leaders could conceivably debate an agenda for three to four days, especially if the issues were highly divisive. In the meantime, the Bad Face spokesman trusted that the colonel and the commissioner would remain patient.[40]

Convinced that Red Cloud was deliberately stalling, Brunot remembered that last fall several Oglala leaders had agreed to relocate north of the Upper Platte but Red Cloud had stymied their proposal. The Bad Face explained that he had merely advised his relatives to wait "until we had the goods and the guns," and doubted that the councilors would have promised anything unless these items had been distributed. Besides, the Oglalas were trying to be cooperative, having considered a site on the White River about eighty miles northwest of the Whetstone Agency. But Red Cloud had since learned that the Brulé bands under Spotted Tail and Swift Bear had already claimed the area.

Suspicious of Red Cloud's motives, Commissioner Brunot decided to adopt another approach, intimating that perhaps Red Cloud was not such a powerful man after all. If the Great Father discovered that the Bad Face was hindering official plans to move the Oglalas to the agency, he would conclude that Red Cloud "is not the great chief, but that there is some other great chief." Red Cloud uttered that he did not wish to be "the great chief," for, after all, Conquering Bear of the Wazaza Brulés in 1851 was named the "head chief" of the Sioux, "and the white man killed him." Taking the offensive, the Bad Face reiterated that if the Oglalas had only received the promised weapons, they would have already moved north of the Upper Platte, but now "they have been cheated so often they will not believe."

Moreover, Red Cloud questioned whether all the nontreaty Oglalas, who had not yet "eaten the white man's bread," would ever accept agency life. These *tiyospaye* were divided, the spokesman explained, "half want to go, and half do not," but he anticipated that the northern folk would at least review his proposals. If Red Cloud persisted in delaying a decision by journeying north to his nontreaty kin, Brunot announced, then he would personally ask the Laramie councilors to reconsider the matter in his absence. "Call them up at any time," Red Cloud responded, "they will talk, [but] their hearts are not all the same." In other words, consensus would be difficult to achieve whether Red Cloud was present or not. The Bad Face leader made plans to depart for the northern bands soon after without stating when he would return, but he thought Brunot and the Laramie councilors should grant him fifteen days before taking action.[41]

After Red Cloud left, on the fourteenth Brunot called upon the senior Oyuhpe chief, Red Dog, who confirmed that the Laramie Oglalas would postpone their council for fifteen days. Should Red Cloud return within this period, all would be well, Red Dog stated cryptically, but if he did not, the councilors would meet and subsequently notify the president of their decision. In the interim, Red Dog resumed where Red Cloud had left off, badgering Brunot for the long-overdue guns and ammunition. The commissioner declined to commit himself, and soon left the fort full of hope that Red Cloud would return imminently, after which "a proper place will be selected with [the] consent of all, or nearly all, [of] the Indians."[42]

Fifteen days passed without word of Red Cloud's whereabouts. Despite constant pressure exerted by the secretary of the interior and the commissioner of Indian affairs, the Oglalas camped in the vicinity of Fort Laramie refused to accept an agency at Rawhide Buttes. The councilors argued that the area was unsuitable for their *tiyospaye*, as the streams dried up in the summer months. They had resolved instead to remain near the banks of the Upper Platte River, choosing for the Oglala agency a site eighteen miles south of Fort Laramie, one that Wham had approved earlier.[43]

Both John Wham and Colonel Smith had now virtually given up cajoling the Oglala multiband council. Moreover, Wham was still fretting over having received renewed instructions to withhold food supplies until further notice. Despite promises of military assistance from Lieutenant General Sheridan, the agent dreaded executing the order, predicting grave consequences if the seven thousand Lakotas congregated around the fort were not adequately fed. Wham believed that federal authorities should simply bow to the Oglalas' wishes and permit them to remain off the Great Sioux Reservation for the present time. After reviewing a series of almost frantic communiqués from Wham, Commissioner Parker yielded, authorizing resumption of the sustenance program at Fort Laramie and consenting to the site for the Red Cloud Agency proposed by the councilors.[44]

Almost three years after the conclusion of the 1868 treaty, high-ranking members of the Interior Department had finally acquiesced to Oglala demands. Wyoming Territory governor Campbell strongly disapproved. In a letter to Commissioner Parker, Campbell wrote that by agreeing to such a poor location "it would be impossible to inflict a greater damage to the Indians themselves." The area was hardly conducive to subsistence agriculture, thus ensuring that the Oglalas would remain dependent on the federal government for food. It was Wham, however, who was blamed for the failed implementation of the peace policy that required the Lakotas to settle on reservation lands away from the Upper Platte valley. Interior Department officials strongly criticized Wham for prematurely promising the Indians an agency south of Fort Laramie. In late October, James Daniels, another nominee of the Protestant Episcopal Church, replaced Wham as agent for the Oglala people. In the interim, Colonel Smith was authorized to handle the administration of the Oglala agency until Daniels arrived.[45]

Over a generation later, Judge Eli Ricker, an amateur historian, interviewed George Colhoff, who had once lived and worked as an interpreter among the Oglalas. If Colhoff's recollections of this period are accurate, the Red Cloud Agency—or the sod agency, as it was dubbed—was "a mighty tough place," serving as a rendezvous for American "outlaws," sporting colorful names such as Black Doc and Fly Speck Billy, who "infested the Sidney Road, and the Black Hills route through Hat Creek and farther west."[46] Still, the "sod agency" was to be the treaty Oglalas' new home—one they had succeeded in establishing away from the Missouri River. Red Cloud, the Americans' "head chief," now appeared in their eyes to be unable or unwilling to dominate his kinsfolk. Moreover, neither civilian agent nor army officer, after three years of trying, had weakened, let alone destroyed, the political customs or influence of the Oglala multiband council.

# CHAPTER FIVE

# The Political Influence
# of the Warriors, 1871–1874

By the provisions of the 1868 Treaty of Fort Laramie, the United States government expected the Lakotas to settle peacefully on the Great Sioux Reservation—which spanned the present state of South Dakota west of the Missouri River—and to adopt the customs of the Great Father's people. The treaty was already three years old, however, before the first Red Cloud (Oglala) Agency was established on the Upper Platte River. Even then, Col. John Smith, commandant of Fort Laramie, expressed concern that the Office of Indian Affairs had failed to impress upon the Oglalas the necessity of relocating the Upper Platte or "sod" agency within the boundaries of the reservation itself.[1] A flurry of post–Civil War railroad construction helped bring many more American ranchers to the North Platte valley, and no longer would the Oglalas be welcome to trade their buffalo robes at the post. Thus by the early 1870s, federal agents for the Oglalas set their priorities on transferring the Upper Platte agency to the Great Sioux Reservation and persuading or compelling as many of the Oglalas as possible, nontreaty bands included, to settle there. Only then could agents, missionaries, and teachers begin the process of "Americanizing" the Lakotas.

The Oglalas (and their Wazaza Brulé relatives who lived with them and were often dubbed Oglala) seemed to view the 1868 treaty in a different light. Many camp leaders looked upon the agency as their personal commissary on the plains, from which to draw the food rations and other supplies guaranteed by the treaty. For some of them, peace with the Great Father's people was desirable, but convincing all their young men to abandon warfare as the traditional, principal means of gaining honor and prestige might indeed prove difficult. Moreover, it was unlikely at this time that the Oglala *tiyospaye* intended to forsake readily their traditional culture in favor of a more American lifestyle.

Hence in the late summer of 1871, Oglala *tiyospaye* came into the sod agency only to draw food rations and other supplies before heading out to prepare their meat caches for the coming winter. By the fall, most of the bands had dispersed again, and Colonel Smith knew only generally of their whereabouts. He believed that the *itancan* Man Afraid of His Horse with twenty tipis and Little Wound of the southern Oglalas with a large band of 120 lodges were hunting north of the Republican River, while Yellow Bear, a member of the 1870 Washington delegation, with thirty tipis, was presently encamped north of Fort Fetterman. These three band *itancan* had received rations from the agency during the summer but had not been seen since late September. By the end of the year only the head shirtwearer Young Man Afraid of His Horse, the Oglala headman Fire Thunder, and Red Leaf, a Wazaza *itancan* with a combined constituency of twenty-one lodges, still lingered at the Upper Platte agency, along with several small bands of Northern Cheyennes and Arapahos. Colonel Smith observed that all of them seemed "restless and uneasy" but nevertheless "well disposed."[2]

After preserving and storing buffalo meat for the cold months ahead, Oglala *wakiconza* directed their respective *tiyospaye* to start back for the sod agency. There several of the bands remained throughout the winter, enduring a shortage of wood or buffalo chips for fuel, and bartering their robes for jugs of fur trade whiskey. The potentially disruptive influence of whiskey in the camps concerned some of the Oglala councilors to such an extent that by February 1872 they began to admit publicly that the agency should be moved "to a more favorable place."[3] But such an important decision could not be made by merely a few.

American leaders still hoped that Red Cloud could influence the non-treaty Oglalas to forge a lasting peace with the United States and to settle on the reservation. He had left Fort Laramie the previous spring in search of his nontreaty kinsfolk and had not yet returned to the post. Lakota messengers reported that Red Cloud, with an estimated one hundred lodges of Bad Faces who had approved the 1868 treaty, had rejoined their relative Holy Bald Eagle (Black Twin) and a head shirtwearer and war leader, among the nontreaty Bad Faces, whose villages were located somewhere in the Black Hills or perhaps along the banks of the Tongue River. Clearly Red Cloud had elected to spend much of the winter in the sheltered camps of his northern kin, but Smith anticipated he would bring news from the nonagency Oglalas before spring arrived.[4]

In March, Colonel Smith at last received word from Red Cloud, who was coming in accompanied by three to four hundred lodges of Oglalas, Miniconjous, Hunkpapas, and Sans Arcs, all in need of supplies. The Bad Face spokesman relayed no messages from the war leader Black Twin nor from other nontreaty Oglalas, but he did ask the colonel to make preparations for a meeting in order to reopen talks concerning the agency's future location. Upon greeting Red Cloud at a spot just north of Fort Laramie, Smith mentioned that the former war leader "seemed much more reserved than I have seen him before," but nevertheless eager to meet the new "father," or agent, James Daniels. Many of the Bad Faces had decided to remain in the Powder River country, but members of the True Oglala band, whose *itancan* Bad Wound had died in 1865, had since selected Red Cloud as their *wakiconza,* persuading him to organize a hunt along the Republican River during the previous fall. These True Oglalas remained with Red Cloud until late 1871, after which they recognized Sitting Bear and American Horse as their *itancan.*[5]

The commandant and a number of councilors representing several Oglala and Wazaza bands assembled at the post on the fourteenth. Red Cloud, the primary spokesman, opened the proceedings by announcing that the Oglalas preferred their agency to remain near Fort Laramie, where they could trade and collect their rations. Smith replied that the Oglalas must soon leave the Platte valley, as some of their young men had killed an American rancher, one L. Powell, and captured army horses and pack mules. Further, the colonel expected Red Cloud to identify the men responsible for these deeds, adding that unless he could control the warriors' behavior, President Ulysses S. Grant would no longer recognize him as "head chief." Moreover, if the Oglalas did not move their agency away from the North Platte, the Great Father would withhold their rations. Red Cloud, whom Smith now described as "very insolent," retorted that he was not to blame for the recent violence, as he was not authorized to command the young fighting men.[6]

After the meeting broke up, Red Cloud retired to Colonel Smith's private quarters, where once again he softened his role as bold spokesman for the council and "talked over matters more pleasantly." The Bad Face informed the commandant, as he had done so many times before, that his duties as representative for the Oglala council did not empower him to make commitments he knew he could not keep, but added that if any of his kinsfolk waged war against the Great Father's people, "he would leave them." Red Cloud also reassured Smith that he would try to arrange the recovery of stolen army livestock, and vowed to continue working for peace. But now he would return to the Bad Face village on Rawhide Creek, northeast of Fort Laramie, to await his kinsman, Black Twin, whose arrival, Red Cloud claimed, was imminent. Moreover, once he had greeted Black Twin, Red Cloud promised to visit the sod agency for the first time. Colonel Smith did not know Black Twin personally but understood that he was a "very influential" man, who had thus far declined all invitations to negotiate with the United States.[7] Perhaps Red Cloud could persuade him to reconsider, he thought.

Red Cloud rode into the sod agency on 21 March. The following day he asked Daniels to not distribute any more of the provisions apportioned to the Bad Faces, as he desired to share some of them with Black Twin *tiyospaye* camped on Rawhide Creek. If he could demonstrate the "goodness of his Great Father," Red Cloud told Daniels, Black Twin's people might agree to settle at the agency. Daniels consented, arranging to have the provisions moved on the twenty-third. Red Cloud's strategy was politically astute. By bringing agency supplies to Black Twin's followers, thereby honoring them with a giveaway, Red Cloud could demonstrate the altruism expected of a band *itancan,* and, at the same time, stood to garner support and praise from Black Twin's warriors. Red Cloud almost certainly knew or suspected that Black Twin despised the very concept of agency life and would forever reject it. But by offering to share rations with Black Twin's Bad Faces, Red Cloud portrayed himself to Daniels as a cooperative chief committed to peace. Red Cloud had another incentive for taking treaty provisions to the Rawhide village, moreover. Several bands of Miniconjous, who had arrived at the sod agency just before Red Cloud, were demanding a share of the Oglalas' goods. These nontreaty Lakotas, Daniels asserted, were "restless" and "impudent."[8]

Daniels spent a rather busy week trying to devise ways of dealing with the Lakota visitors from the north, while remaining hopeful that the nontreaty Bad Faces on Rawhide Creek would venture to the agency. Within a few days, Red Dog, principal *itancan* of the Oyuhpes, reported to the doctor that several of his peers had recently approved the band chief's proposal to transfer the Oglala agency to the White River, near the tributaries of the south fork of the Cheyenne River. According to Red Dog, many of the agency *itancan* and headmen had grown impatient with Red Cloud's ambivalent stance.[9] After all, the Bad Face had enjoyed a relatively comfortable winter in the northern hunting grounds. Moreover, council elders could not be certain how much of Red Cloud was still symbolically bound to the northern *blotahunka*—Black Twin, Crazy Horse, Little Big

Man, and Charging Shield, who had rejected the 1868 treaty and ridiculed reservation life. Red Cloud had already displayed extraordinary talents for war before Crazy Horse and Little Big Man reached manhood, and by the mid-1860s Red Cloud epitomized to them and other young warriors the defiance and military might of the Lakota people. Were thoughts of past military glories now drawing Red Cloud to the village of Black Twin and his warriors, or was he truly expending his energies coaxing Black Twin's people to come in?

We can only speculate on how men like Crazy Horse, Black Twin, and Charging Shield regarded Red Cloud. When these war leaders looked at him, what did they see—a dedicated spokesman endeavoring to protect the interests of all Oglalas in the face of impending cultural change, or an aging *blotahunka,* softened by the flattery of the Great Father's people? Certainly the agency council would find consensus difficult to achieve not knowing precisely where Red Cloud stood; thus, Daniels wrote, Red Dog and the others had granted Red Cloud seven days to decide "whether he will join them or not."[10]

With his agency peers' ultimatum hanging over his head, and his reputation among the northern kinsfolk uncertain, Red Cloud elected to attend the grand council, convened at the agency on 10 April, to discuss moving the Oglala agency within the boundaries of the Great Sioux Reservation.[11] Representing the American government were agent Daniels, Colonel Smith of Fort Laramie, and Brig. Gen. E. O. C. Ord, who had replaced Christopher Augur as commandant of the Department of the Platte.

At this multiband assembly the councilors honored the *itancan* Man Afraid of His Horse, Red Dog, Blue Horse, Little Wound, Red Leaf, and Stabber, along with the head shirtwearers Young Man Afraid of His Horse, American Horse, and Sword. Also in attendance were the headmen and prominent warriors Spotted Horse, Three Bears, Fire Thunder, Sitting Bull (Little Wound's nephew), Black Bear, Red Dog's son Red Shirt, and former Washington delegates Rocky Bear and Sitting Bear. Red Cloud's role was clearly that of primary spokesman for the council; his status among the Oglalas and Wazazas as a whole remained conjectural. The small group of Bad Faces at the agency now regarded Red Cloud as their *itancan* and *wakiconza,* but it is difficult to ascertain whether the multiband council ceremonially recognized him as a prominent band *itancan*—one whose status ranked with that of Man Afraid of His Horse or Little Wound.

Red Dog of the Oyuhpes, who had initiated the idea to move the agency, opened the proceedings by invoking the guidance of the Great Mystery. Appealing for consensus, Red Dog began: "Today we are going to look to the welfare of the old people and our children. I want to see if you are all of the same mind. Last year I [meaning we] located this Agency here and today I look upon you to locate another one." Red Cloud also implored the council to reach a decision.[12]

As the conference continued, signs appeared that the older councilors were deferring to the warriors. During the early agency period, Oglala *tiyospaye* mingled for longer than customary periods of time, and as membership in the warrior societies cut across band, and even tribal, lines,[13] the *blotahunka* and warriors had a greater opportunity to present their respective societies' positions in multiband gatherings. Perceptible shifts in decision-making authority from the council as a whole toward the younger war leaders were not without precedent, having undoubtedly occurred numerous times throughout the years. When the moment came to break camp, for instance, the *wakiconza* commanded the people to strike their lodges and set out toward a new location, which the *wakiconza* chose. Once in transit, authority moved to the *akicita,* who ensured that the villagers remained together on the march and encamped at the appointed destination. However, if the column were suddenly threatened by enemies, such as the Crows, the *wakiconza* and *akicita* at once deferred to the war party leaders or *blotahunka* and their selected men.[14]

The persistent endeavors of Indian agents, post commandants, and federal commissioners to settle the Oglalas on the Great Sioux Reservation, and to impose upon them an alien lifestyle, represented much greater threats to the Oglalas' political autonomy after 1868 than did Crow or Pawnee war parties. Hence as the Oglala people depended on their *blotahunka* and warrior societies for protection during these unsettling times, decision-making authority naturally came to rest more often in the roles of *blotahunka* and warrior (*zuya wicasa*). In late March 1872, Man Afraid of His Horse informed agent Daniels that some of the young Oglala men had stopped heeding the advice of their agency elders, who advocated peace with Americans. Furthermore, J. J. Saville, Daniels's successor, also observed a temporary but perceptible increase in authority among the warrior societies, noting that when the young fighting men took action during periods of crisis, the council elders "hesitated to oppose them."[15]

Thus Oglala councilors were not surprised when Black Bear rose to announce, after Red Dog and Red Cloud had concluded their remarks, that he wanted "some of the young men to speak, as whatever they say we have decided to agree upon." Little Wound and Red Cloud immediately voiced their approval, and Black Bear called on Spotted Horse, No Flesh's younger brother, to address the assembly. But it was Young Man Afraid of His Horse, a protector of the people and a member of the Crooked Lance warrior society, who instead spoke up. As an Oglala head shirtwearer ceremonially recognized by the multiband council, Young Man Afraid exercised his right to intervene on behalf of all. The head shirtwearer entirely avoided the subject of the agency, proceeding instead to complain about the presence of white soldiers in Lakota lands. He consented to "go by the Great Father's words," but in turn expected the president to make good on his commitments to the Lakotas, including acknowledging their right under the 1868 treaty to live and hunt in the Big Horn country.[16]

Colonel Smith spoke next. Steering the conversation back to the transfer of the Upper Platte agency, he warned Young Man Afraid and the others that the Great Father would eventually cut off rations if they rejected resettlement, thereby jeopardizing their families' welfare if the hunt failed. Furthermore, if the assembly refused to name the young men responsible for Powell's murder and the stealing of horses, troops would be sent to hunt them down. Little Wound, the Kiyuksa head *itancan*, spoke up at this juncture. He also reminded Smith that the 1868 treaty entitled the Lakotas to hunt and live on unceded territory, and also did not waste the opportunity to voice his displeasure with the Great Father's failure to supply guns and ammunition.[17]

But despite differences of opinion voiced in the council session, the Oglalas finally agreed to move the Red Cloud Agency from its current location on the Upper Platte to the White River. After the decision had been announced, another head shirtwearer, American Horse, along with Fire Thunder and Big Foot, hinted that the warrior societies might be more inclined to cooperate with the agent if Smith agreed to drop the charges against their young men. The colonel emphatically refused to do so.[18]

The growing political influence of the young men did not entirely escape Daniels's attention. Throughout this protracted dispute over relocating the agency, the doctor appeared genuinely puzzled and worried by the inability of the Oglala and Wazaza band *itancan* and headmen to control the actions of the fighting men. The warriors, especially those younger than thirty-five years of age, the agent wrote, "have no respect for

1. *Little Wound.* National Anthropological Archives,
Smithsonian Institution, Washington DC. Photo no. 3214a.

2. *Young Man Afraid of His Horse*. National Anthropological Archives, Smithsonian Institution, Washington DC. Photo no. 3245a.

3. *Red Cloud.* National Anthropological Archives,
Smithsonian Institution, Washington DC. Photo no. 3237d.

4. *Sword.* National Anthropological Archives, Smithsonian
Institution, Washington DC. Photo no. 3202.

5. *American Horse.* National Anthropological Archives,
Smithsonian Institution, Washington DC. Photo no. 3214d.

6. *Red Shirt*. National Anthropological Archives,
Smithsonian Institution, Washington DC. Photo no. 3224a.

7. *Little Big Man*. National Anthropological Archives,
Smithsonian Institution, Washington DC. Photo no. 3215a.

8. *Delegation of Sioux to Washington DC, 1875.* National Anthropological Archives, Smithsonian Institution, Washington DC. Photo no. 3307C.

their chiefs," and "are greatly governed in their actions by the success of the hostile Sioux out north." Hence Daniels recommended to Commissioner of Indian Affairs Francis Walker that rather than negotiating with the Oglalas in open council, department employees should "have the chiefs and headmen designated, and do business with them only." That way, officials could block the warriors from challenging both the agent and their elders—a scheme the Oglalas quickly rejected.[19]

Shortly after the April meeting adjourned, Daniels, accompanied by Red Dog (whom the physician believed was "willing to do anything that I asked of him") and fifteen unnamed Oglalas, implemented the decision to find a new site for the agency, eventually selecting a spot near the confluence of the White and Little White Clay Rivers. Although a party of disaffected Oglalas camped near the sod agency had caused "no trouble of late," they continued to oppose vehemently any location that might prove suitable for agriculture, an occupation they considered unworthy of a warrior.[20]

Hoping to defuse some of the tensions at the Upper Platte agency, Red Cloud sought Daniels's permission to revisit President Grant in Washington. He especially hoped to take along "some [more] of my people and show them the white man's ways." The agent greeted Red Cloud's request enthusiastically, convinced that the first party of Oglalas to tour the American capital in 1870 had later worked diligently for peace. If Red Cloud could persuade other Lakotas, particularly those of the nontreaty bands, to put together other delegations, Daniels believed that "a certainty of future peace may be secured." Thus, he waited patiently for the Oglalas to name their spokesmen for the visit to Washington.[21]

On 17 May, after a month of preparations, Daniels escorted a group of twenty-seven Oglalas, including Little Wound, Red Cloud, Blue Horse, Red Leaf, Big Foot, High Wolf, and Red Dog, to the American capital, where they planned to air their grievances with the president. Also joining the party were the Oglalas' interpreters Joseph Bissonette, Jules Ecoffey, and Nick Janis. Ten days later the delegates met Secretary of the Interior Columbus Delano and Commissioner Walker at Interior Department headquarters. Red Cloud, Little Wound, and Red Dog immediately expressed their disappointment over not receiving the goods, guns, and ammunition they claimed were promised in earlier councils. Secretary Delano explained that the Great Father had withheld ammunition because of violent crimes committed against white settlers. But he was now satisfied that Oglala warriors had not participated in the attacks, so the bands would shortly receive some powder and lead with which to hunt.[22]

The next day the representatives had a private audience with the president. Grant broached the subject of resettling the Oglalas in the Indian Territory (later Oklahoma), but when the delegates ignored his suggestion the president let the matter drop. Instead, Red Cloud formally announced the Oglalas' agreement to relocate the agency on the White River. After the meeting, Delano cautioned the Oglalas to expect yet another move northward sometime in the future, as Americans settlers would soon desire the land around the White River site. But he assured the Lakotas that he would do everything in his power to keep them near the river for as long as possible. Although these Washington talks accomplished little by way of formally resolving longstanding disagreements, delegates and federal officials parted in good humor.[23]

Before embarking on his first trip to the American capital, Little Wound had dispatched *akicita*,[24] or messengers, to contact Lakota villages on the Yellowstone. One of them had returned during the first week of July to report that northern *tiyospaye* leaders, who were still divided over the "best course to pursue toward the whites," had convened a large multiband council at the mouth of the Little Powder River. Little Wound's *akicita* ventured that most of the nontreaty people supported peace, although some of the young men continued to advocate war in council meetings.[25]

Upon hearing this news Daniels resolved to contact several of the northern Lakota camps, requesting assistance from interpreter Joseph Bissonette. Red Dog, High Wolf, Two Elks, and Wolf's Ears, a young man "of considerable influence and promise," also agreed to accompany the agent on the journey to Fort Peck, Montana Territory, a small trading post five hundred miles south of Fort Benton, and presumably the point of contact. Daniels expressed his gratitude to Red Dog, praising him as "the best acquainted in the north of any man" at the agency. He especially trusted the Oyuhpe band chief's ability to communicate with Sitting Bull of the Hunkpapas, widely acknowledged by the Lakotas as the principal spiritual leader of the nontreaty bands.[26]

Red Cloud, Daniels soon discovered, was "too busy" to join the party. Some of his Bad Face relatives were still deliberating the wisdom of relocating the agency away from the Upper Platte, and Red Cloud contended he was occupied trying to persuade them to accept the multiband council's most recent decision. As Red Cloud had opted to remain with the agency Oglalas rather than move his household to Black Twin's *tiyospaye,* he sent a personal message with the agent pleading with Black Twin, Sitting Bull, No Neck, Crazy Horse, Red Horse, Fire Horn, and Black Moon to counsel their estimated three thousand followers for peace. "Friends," Red Cloud's message began, "I carried on the war against the whites with you until I went to see my Great Father two years ago." The president "spoke good to me," so "I went to see my Great Father a second time [and] he gave me good advice." Red Cloud had requested many items for his people, and the president "gave me those things [and] all the whites spoke well to me." If the northern *tiyospaye* still chose war over peace, Red Cloud continued, he would not support them this time. But if they would only come into the agency, the president would provide for them also. Finally, he beseeched the northern Lakotas to hear Daniels, whose "words are good." Red Cloud's advice fell on deaf ears, however, for the agent later admitted that many of the nontreaty people showed no interest in sending representatives to Washington, and instead seemed inclined to fight.[27]

It was during the second week of September that the Oglala council at Red Cloud Agency startled American officials by abruptly modifying its cooperative stance, having agreed all summer to leave the Upper Platte River. In one of several conferences arranged throughout the month, Red Cloud announced that his people had changed their minds about moving to the White River, as the 1868 treaty permitted them to reside in the North Platte valley for thirty-five years. When Red Cloud issued his statement, Little Wound added a few words in support of what had been said, and by the time the meeting broke up, only Red Dog, Blue Horse, and Red Leaf were still prepared to go. Daniels considered Red Dog staunchly loyal to him; Red Leaf's Wazazas felt no strong compulsion to heed the wishes of the Oglalas; and Blue Horse's Loafers had a long history of friendship with Americans. But the young Oglala men, especially those who slipped in and out of the northern Lakota villages, had persuaded—perhaps even commanded—Red Cloud, Little Wound, and most of the council elders to resist relocation. Indeed, during the session, a young Bad Face *akicita* had menacingly exclaimed that he would kill the first Oglala who started for the White River site.[28]

Thoroughly exasperated, Daniels singled out Red Cloud's relatives as the principal culprits in precipitating this turnabout. Recalling their previous aversion to moving the agency, Daniels wired Colonel Smith that the only way "to settle the Red Cloud party" was "to use force and compel them to do right."²⁹ Red Cloud's earlier efforts to sway the Bad Faces in favor of the White River site had obviously fallen short, leaving him to express, willingly or not, the revised consensus of the small Bad Face council at the agency, some of whose young fighting men admired, and at times joined, the *blotahunka* Black Twin.

Colonel Smith also attributed the current stalemate to Red Cloud's band, which he predicted would soon strike out northward to join the nontreaty Lakotas. The commandant quickly contacted the commissioner of Indian affairs, advising him to carry through with his oft-repeated threats to cut off rations until Oglala leaders acquiesced to American demands. When the families' provisions ran low, he thought, maybe then the councilors would come to their senses. Fearing violence would erupt at the agency if he withheld supplies, Commissioner Walker declined Smith's advice, much to the colonel's dismay. Against his better judgment, the commandant canceled plans to dispatch troops to the sod agency, later remarking to the assistant adjutant general for the Department of the Platte that "a golden opportunity to chastize these Indians as they richly deserve has been lost."³⁰

Daniels and Smith were too quick to condemn the agency Bad Faces for the latest impasse. Although Little Wound's southern Oglalas had earlier rejected alliances with northern Lakota bands in wars against the United States, some members of his Kiyuksa *tiyospaye* were now just as staunchly opposed to immediate resettlement as were Red Cloud's kin. Little Wound had warned Daniels on several occasions that his people intended to set out for the Republican River hunting grounds "whether they got permission or not," and on 21 October seventy-five lodges of Little Wound's followers left the agency without their *itancan*. When Daniels reported their departure, the Division of the Missouri's commanding officer immediately acted upon orders to intercept the Kiyuksas, and, if necessary, coerce them to return.³¹

Spotted Tail had invited the Upper Platte Oglalas and Wazazas to join the Brulés at their agency on the White River. But even though they declined his offer, some Oglalas, whose band or bands Daniels did not name, had decided by late October to move near the place marked out for the new Red Cloud Agency. Furthermore, Blue Horse notified the doctor that a number of "very timid" Miniconjous, Oglalas, and Brulés from the north had agreed to settle at the White River site if they could "get their rations at that place."³²

As the lodges came down at the sod agency, members of the warrior societies began to demonstrate forcefully against American policies, some even threatening to execute Daniels and his employees. Little Wound, Red Cloud, and other elders succeeded, however, in restoring some semblance of order. When November arrived the Oglalas and Wazazas had left the Upper Platte agency for wooded areas, and by the following month just over four thousand of them had established their winter villages in favorite sheltered spots along the banks of the White River. The Kiyuksa and Bad Face *tiyospaye* were not with them, however. Little Wound's people returned south in November, the band's *wakiconza* pitching the camps in the vicinity of Fort Mitchell, Nebraska; the Bad Faces selected Hat Creek, a tributary of the south branch of the Cheyenne River, 110 miles south of Bear Butte and about fifty miles west of the White River.[33]

On 9 November, Red Cloud and a party of young warriors rode into the sod agency to collect rations. The wording of Daniel's official correspondence to Commissioner Walker is ambiguous, but there is a hint that the Bad Face leader had thrown in his lot with the soldier societies. Red Cloud told Daniels that "they" had been "engaged in fighting the whites" around Fort Laramie but were now settled in the winter village on Hat Creek. Red Cloud informed Daniels that he and the warriors would return to the Upper Platte agency once a month to receive their provisions, but the agent soon thwarted their plans by transferring the supplies to the White River.[34]

Eager to unite all the Oglala people at the new location, Daniels resumed his efforts in December to win the confidence of the nontreaty bands. His hopes were raised after receiving a report that Black Twin had been spotted in the winter encampments of Lone Horn and Roman Nose, two prominent Miniconjous, whose people desired a share of the Oglalas' goods. Daniels thought that if he could convince Black Twin's followers to remain near the treaty camps, "it may be the means of overcoming the prejudices" of those Oglalas who had never drawn rations. Daniels had heard that the hunt was poor in the Powder River country this season; hence if Black Twin's people obtained provisions regularly, they might come to "appreciate the advantages of being at peace."[35]

No strong evidence exists indicating that Black Twin ever visited his agency kinsfolk. What seems clearer, however, is that Red Cloud's Bad Faces still opposed moving their *tiyospaye* to the White River. Red Cloud first demanded an agency for all the Oglalas on Rawhide Creek, north of

Fort Laramie, but in the following February, several weeks after Black Twin's putative sighting, he asked Daniels to notify the Great Father that "I want my agency on Hat Creek and I want to have it moved this moon."[36]

In response to Red Cloud's request, Daniels forwarded to Commissioner Walker in late March a description of the Hat Creek region, situated in the southwest corner of the Great Sioux Reservation. Those Americans familiar with the general area considered Hat Creek inferior for agricultural purposes to the terrain at the White River site. The water of the Cheyenne River nearby was stagnant, especially in the summer, but while the water in Hat Creek was potable where it emerged from the bluffs, it soaked quickly into the prairie sod. Red Cloud was aware of these conditions, having objected to a permanent agency at Hat Creek the previous summer, and his fellow Oglalas, Daniels wrote, "are not loth to call his attention to this fact now." The doctor surmised that Red Cloud had "very few friends in this move," and indeed had "made some very bitter enemies" among the treaty Oglalas, most of whom, Daniels contended, favored immediate resettlement at the White River spot but feared confronting the Bad Faces.[37]

When Edward Smith, an ordained Congregational minister from New York City and former agent to the Minnesota Chippewas, succeeded Walker as commissioner of Indian affairs on 30 March, he inherited this drawn-out dispute over the agency's location. As his predecessors had done, Smith first sought the opinions of former special commissioner Felix Brunot. Claiming he had never ventured more than a mile north of the Upper Platte's left bank, Brunot felt unqualified to evaluate the White River region. But as he considered it imperative that the Indian Department commit no further errors regarding "the supplies of good water, grass, and the capability of cultivation" at the new Red Cloud Agency, Brunot consented to chair another commission to examine the area, and coordinate the Oglalas' removal. E. C. Kemble, Henry Alvord, and Wyoming Territory Governor J. A. Campbell would serve as his colleagues.[38]

Kemble and Alvord were the first commissioners to reach the sod agency, arriving in late May to find approximately thirteen thousand Indians drawing rations there—over 1,000 lodges of Oglalas and Wazazas (representing about five bands), 262 tipis of Miniconjous and Sans Arcs, 168 lodges of Cheyennes, and 237 of Arapahos. On the last day of the

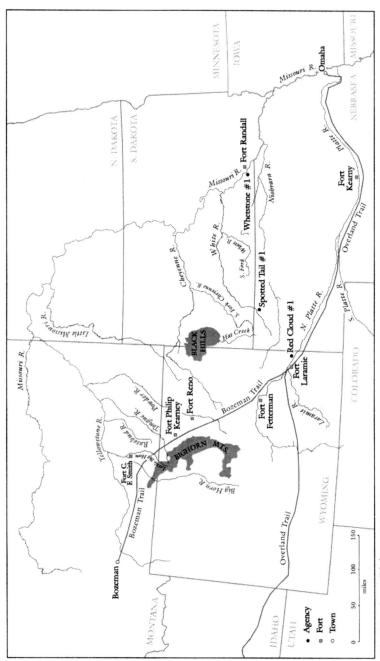

The Northern Plains, 1865–1873

month, the visitors met in council with Oglala and Wazaza delegates Young Man Afraid of His Horse, Blue Horse, High Wolf, Fast Bear, Slow Bull, the *blotahunka* White Crane Walking, and the *itancan* Red Leaf, the latter asking the young warrior Crooked Eyes to speak for him. For unknown reasons, neither Little Wound nor Red Cloud attended this preliminary conference, and Red Dog was confined to his lodge due to sickness.[39]

The commissioners began the proceedings by referring to the belligerent activities of Lakota war parties, sweeping in and out of the agency at will with stolen horses and other items. No band would claim responsibility, the Bad Face Oglalas and the Miniconjous at Red Cloud Agency both accusing the other group of condoning the young men's deeds. In light of these developments, Kemble mentioned that the president hoped the Lakotas would form their own guard of warriors, representing all bands, to protect the agency. If this could not be arranged, he continued, the Great Father would have no other recourse but to station troops near the Indian villages. The spokesmen replied that Red Cloud "had not done as he had promised" upon his return from Washington; instead of advocating peace, they claimed, he had stalled the relocation plans by inciting the young men. Furthermore, the delegates enumerated for the commissioners certain unfulfilled pledges made to their people: Lakota treaty rights to hunt along the Republican River had been restricted; guns, powder, and lead had not been issued; and rice, corn, and tea had been promised but had not yet arrived. Nevertheless, the councilors intended to defend their "father," approving the suggestion of recognizing agency sentinels—camp *akicita*, in their eyes. But the delegates refused to proceed without the consensus of the grand intertribal council, scheduled to convene in two days.[40]

On 2 June at least 150 Oglala, Wazaza, and northern Lakota chiefs, headmen, and warriors reopened talks with the Great Father's emissaries. Also invited were several Cheyenne delegates, including Morning Star and Turkey Legs. Only Little Wound and Red Cloud spoke in this assembly, representing primarily the southern (Bear) and northern (Smoke) divisions of the Oglalas respectively. Daniels and Commissioner Kemble had anticipated that Little Wound would favor an Indian guard, and also expected most of the other leaders to give their consent. Red Cloud's reaction was another matter, however. When the conference began, Red Cloud was asked to account for his questionable behavior. Defending himself against public criticism from his peers, Red Cloud exclaimed that

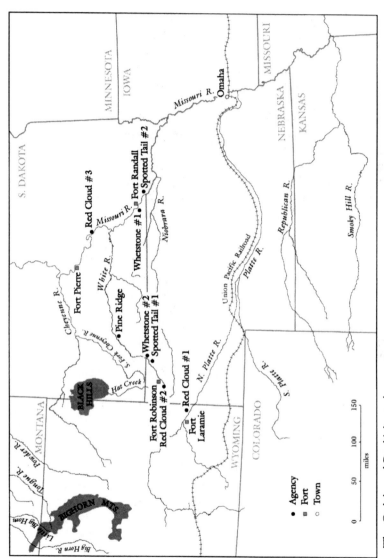

The Oglala and Brulé Agencies

he was not to blame for the problems encountered in moving the agency. His longstanding role as a principal spokesman for the Oglalas had not been an easy one. How could he properly influence all the Lakotas at the agency, his Bad Face relatives included, or fulfill his commitments to the Great Father while the president himself refused to issue weapons, ammunition, and food supplies, and all last winter the nontreaty bands were "playing over me"? If he could just obtain the ammunition and other articles promised the Oglalas, he could "better please [his] people."[41]

Furthermore, Red Cloud declined to discuss any additional proposals about moving the agency until the Wazazas under Stabber and the southern Oglala *blotahunka* Pawnee Killer, camped with over one hundred lodges near Sidney Barracks, Nebraska, had come in.[42] In an April communiqué to the assistant adjutant general, Col. J. J. Reynolds, commanding the Third U.S. Cavalry, had noted that the followers of Pawnee Killer, No Flesh, and Stabber had often refused to affiliate with Red Cloud even though one of Red Cloud's daughters was married to the prominent warrior Slow Bull, Stabber's nephew. Matters of such significance as establishing a new agency and creating an Indian guard required that the leaders of these southern Oglala and Wazaza *tiyospaye* also participate in a general assembly. As it was, the June council failed to achieve a consensus, specifically regarding the organization of an Indian guard, which some *tiyospaye* leaders, including Red Cloud, argued would "irritate" the warriors. Therefore, the commissioners adjourned the meeting.[43]

Afterward, Kemble penned a letter to Commissioner Smith in which he included some personal observations on Red Cloud. Presuming that the Bad Face leader held the authority to compel all the Oglalas to obey him, Kemble concluded that Red Cloud was simply being difficult, and that despite his repeated pledges to the president he had done very little to secure peace. Even more puzzling to the commissioner were the actions of the other Oglala councilors. While they grumbled constantly about Red Cloud's attitude, they declined "to act in any important measure apart from him."[44] As an American, Kemble, quite understandably, expected the voice of the majority to prevail in meetings. Lakota councilors, on the other hand, frequently deferred agendas indefinitely if a consensus was not forthcoming.

Moreover, Red Cloud had certainly earned his fame among the Lakotas as a prominent *blotahunka* in past wars against the United States, and he now sat at the *catku*—the "chief place"—in the Bad Face council at the agency. But while Red Cloud's peers might take exception, many federal officials in distant Washington still chose to regard him as the "head chief" of the Sioux—an influential man whose friendship and cooperation were crucial in any dealings with the Oglalas. The Americans honored Red Cloud by insisting that the agency bear his name, and only two months previously the president himself had entertained the Bad Face spokesman in his residence. Indeed, although Saville discovered that the treaty Oglalas recognized Man Afraid of His Horse as their "legitimate head chief," the agent also noted that when pressed, Lakotas "always add cautiously, 'the whites have made Red Cloud head chief, and of course we look upon him as our chief.'"[45] At a time when many *tiyospaye* leaders feared for the future welfare of their loved ones, it was not politically expedient to cast aside completely a man who might yet possess the means to prevail upon the Great Father's people.

Felix Brunot and Governor Campbell joined Kemble and Alvord in mid-June, meeting representatives of the Lakotas, Northern Cheyennes, and Arapahos on the twentieth.[46] For two days the councilors discussed whether to transfer the agency. Finally, they all consented to move, some more reluctantly than others, and soon formed an Indian guard as requested by Commissioner Alvord to assist in the agency's relocation. On 14 July, Daniels, who had since resigned his position as agent but who would not leave office until after the resettlement, wired Commissioner Smith that all preparations were complete and that he was merely awaiting official orders to proceed.[47]

Eleven days later the wagon teams were on the verge of starting for the White River site when Red Cloud and several young Bad Face warriors "menacingly" ordered Daniels to postpone the move until the agent's successor, J. J. Saville, arrived. Daniels had heard that several of Red Cloud's relations, including a son-in-law, had been spotted with the same Bad Face war party that had recently killed two American women in the Sweetwater River country. Worried that Red Cloud's kinsfolk might provoke another disturbance, and feeling unable to proceed without a military escort, Daniels directed the teamsters to turn back. Red Cloud was restating his demands for guns and ammunition, so Commissioner Smith authorized Daniels to placate the demonstrators with gifts from the local trader in order for the loaded wagons to leave uncontested.[48]

By August, despite the Bad Faces' eleventh-hour attempts to delay the convoy, the Oglalas and Wazazas had commenced their journey over seventy-five miles of sandhill trails from the old sod agency on the Upper Platte to the new Red Cloud Agency on the White River. The Oglalas' new home, Daniels wrote, was located in a pretty spot, "with good water and all the farming land" that the Lakotas would need for the next ten years.[49] When everyone had settled in, Saville and his employees intended to begin in earnest the process of Americanizing their Sioux wards.

Tribal leaders convened a council on 14 August at the White River to greet agent Saville for the first time. After the pipe had been smoked and passed around, Red Cloud rose to offer some prefatory words of welcome. He spoke up, not merely performing his customary role as council representative but also exercising his privilege as a band chief to be heard first. After his opening remarks, Red Cloud asked Daniels, who had not yet left the Oglalas, to remind the commissioner of Indian affairs once more that, as the *tiyospaye* had relocated the agency in accordance with the Great Father's wishes, they now expected guns, powder, and lead. The Oglalas deserved these items, Red Cloud pressed, having suffered extreme hardship and sacrificed much by leaving the North Platte. Moreover, distributing such treasured gifts might "pacify the Northern Indians and they would all come in."[50]

Other councilor members, especially the warrior representatives, were far from conciliatory. Delegates told Saville and Daniels that the Lakotas "should regulate all things at the agency" and that "everything would have to be done as they wished." American ranchers in their country were free to cut wood and graze their cattle between Crow Butte and the Little White Clay River, but the Lakotas expected reimbursement. After the meeting adjourned, the warriors organized "a large demonstration" in order "to intimidate and show their power," prompting one of the interpreters to caution Daniels not to distribute weapons at this time. Moreover, the former agent observed that the Oglalas appeared more independent at the White River agency, "as though they felt their security from molestation by white soldiers."[51]

Saville's first weeks as federal agent for the Oglalas were far from pleasant. The agency buildings were not yet complete, and, with no prior experience or guidelines, he was forced to administer official policies from his tarpaulin tent headquarters. But Saville's physical discomfort paled in comparison with the psychological torment that some of the young Lakota men had in store for him. Southern Oglala warriors belonging mostly to the *tiyospaye* of Little Wound, along with Brulés from the Spotted Tail Agency, attacked a Pawnee hunting party on the Republican River in the summer of 1873, killing upwards of one hundred people before returning to Red Cloud Agency with Pawnee horses and other property. (Little Wound, Two Lance, and Pawnee Killer claimed they later surrendered the Pawnee prisoners—eleven women and children—at Fort Sidney, Nebraska.) Having ordered the Kiyuksas to return the Pawnees' horses, hides, and buffalo meat, Saville arranged a conference to hear their arguments and to confer with other agency leaders. The agent judged the current situation to be serious but not grave, and, hoping that the council would prove productive, he decided against requesting troops from nearby Camp Robinson.[52]

When Saville joined the multiband assembly on 27 September, he found the Oglalas already in an angry mood over a recent Indian Office directive banning the distribution of weapons and ammunition and forbidding hunting trips to the Republican River country. Little Wound, head *itancan* of the Kiyuksas, addressed his audience. According to his interpretation of the 1868 treaty, it was not the Great Father's prerogative to demand the forfeiture of Pawnee property, as the Oglalas had never concluded a peace treaty with either this tribe or with the Poncas and Utes. Little Wound asserted that his Kiyuksas had merely contracted to live peacefully with the Americans and had thus far honored the treaty with them. Besides, the *itancan* added, most of the property taken from the Pawnees actually belonged to the Oglalas, as they had been the victims of Pawnee raiding parties throughout the previous spring. If the president now insisted that they return these articles to their enemies, the Oglalas would in turn expect everything the Pawnees and Utes had already seized from them.[53]

Two Lance, a well-respected warrior whose older brother, the *itancan* Whistler, had just been murdered by American settlers, interrupted at this point, asserting that the commandant at Fort Sidney, Nebraska, had actually authorized the southern Oglalas to raid the Pawnees should the latter cross Plum Creek westward into Lakota country. After Two Lance's brief statement, Little Wound resumed his oratory and abruptly changed the subject, requesting permission instead to camp on the banks of the Republican River for the fall hunting season. Saville was at a loss for words. As he was not yet fully conversant with either departmental procedures or the 1868 treaty, his initial reaction was to propose that the Oglalas simply avoid future intertribal disputes by negotiating peace treaties with the Pawnees and Poncas.[54]

Life at the agency remained fraught with tension for the remainder of the year. Tempers flared over minor incidents, and the Oglalas tested the agent's courage and stamina on more than one occasion. Like Daniels before him, Saville played host to a number of nontreaty Lakotas—Miniconjous, Sans Arcs, Oglalas, and Hunkpapas—who periodically appeared at the agency to collect food and sundry supplies. Saville considered the visitors "exceedingly vicious and insolent" in their demands for rations, virtually impossible for him to intimidate, and possessed of "a very exalted idea of their ability to resist the Government."[55]

Furthermore, the treaty Oglalas and Wazazas complained constantly about the inferior quality and quantity of the goods issued to them. More than once, groups of young warriors had broken into the warehouse where Saville stored the provisions allocated for the few bands of Northern Cheyennes and Arapahos residing at the agency. In addition, the Lakotas resented their "father's" insistence on counting them. Saville was particularly determined to estimate the number of nontreaty Lakotas at the Red Cloud Agency, as their sporadic movements in and out of the agency distorted the number of persons officially registered on the beef ration rolls.[56]

Hence the agent ventured eight miles from his headquarters to the north bank of the White River to count tipis but soon encountered a small Lakota war party intent on destroying his horse. Retreating hastily to the agency compound, Saville found waiting there a large group of young men led by the northern Oglala warriors Little Big Man and Pretty Bear, whom he described as "two rather notedly vicious characters." One of them commanded the agent to approach, but he refused, retorting that they should meet him in his office if they had anything to say. Upon hearing this, about two hundred warriors slowly advanced only to find that Little Wound with several armed Kiyuksa *akicita* had suddenly appeared on horseback to their left, with Red Cloud and a number of Bad Face and Oyuhpe *akicita,* also armed and mounted, to their right. Predicting dire consequences for all the agency bands should the northern warriors harm Saville, Little Wound, Red Cloud, and Red Dog had called upon the *akicita* of their camp circles to defend their "father" against the young men's taunts and threats. Momentarily subdued by this show of force and unity, they jumped on their ponies and sped back to their villages, but not before hurling insults at the agency chiefs.[57]

After this incident Saville thought it prudent to visit Washington in late fall to obtain firsthand advice from his superiors on handling his Oglala charges and their northern relatives. Hearing of the agent's plans, Red Cloud, Red Dog, and Blue Horse asked him to deliver messages from them directly to the president, as they had long suspected that "when we send words to the Great Father they go through so many ears that they are all lost before they reach him." Blue Horse of the Loafers wanted Saville to know that the elder councilors had not found the opportunity to discuss fully the relocation of the agency, as "our young men have done all the talking." The bold and at times rebellious behavior of the warriors, especially those of the northern camps, alarmed them. But they wished to reassure the president that most of their people desired to live peacefully at the agency "and keep all the Indians here that we can."[58]

Red Cloud added that the agency camps were humming with rumors that Maj. Gen. Philip Sheridan was en route to Fort Laramie with orders to commence a road survey through Lakota country. If this were true, Red Cloud earnestly hoped Saville would tell the president "not to permit him to come yet," as the presence of army engineers would only infuriate the warriors. Furthermore, Red Dog and Blue Horse asked the agent to notify the Great Father that the clothes he sent were too small. Blue Horse remarked that when he visited the president a few years ago, he and other Lakota delegates toured a factory in Philadelphia, where they observed the manufacture of blankets and clothes. Upon returning home, Blue Horse continued, they decided to examine their own blankets, and concluded that the Indian Office had sent the Oglalas "all the worst goods." Finally, the three *itancan* reminded the doctor that the *tiyospaye* were growing impatient waiting for guns and ammunition.[59] Failure to secure these valued items only furnished the *blotahunka* and the warrior societies with another excuse to humiliate the agency *itancan* and headmen, whose political influence hinged considerably on their ability to provide for their respective camp circles.

Saville promised to deliver the chiefs' messages, and just before leaving for the American capital he also sought authorization to bring some of the northern Lakotas with him. The agent theorized that the nontreaty people challenged Indian Office policies merely because they were ignorant of American cultural and military superiority. Thus if more Lakota councilors could witness the splendor of Washington, he reasoned, they might be more inclined to confirm the 1868 treaty with the United States. But despite his momentary optimism, Saville failed at this time to induce any of the northern people to accompany him.[60]

Before arriving at Commissioner Smith's office, Saville learned that his superior was contemplating punitive action against Little Wound and one hundred lodges of his Kiyuksas, who, unknown to the agent, had departed for the Republican River, ignoring the commissioners' order prohibiting hunting parties in that region. Both the commissioner and Maj. Gen. William Sherman had deplored the Oglalas' August attack on the Pawnees, contending that the Lakotas' actions justified the forfeiture of their treaty guarantees to hunt in the Republican valley. Consequently, Smith recommended mobilizing troops to drive Little Wound's followers back to the agency, and even entertained the notion of holding them hostage to be bargained for in future American negotiations with the Oglalas.[61]

Commissioner Smith's response to the situation horrified agent Saville, who respectfully urged him to proceed cautiously in forcing the southern Oglalas to abandon the chase. The doctor hoped especially that no blood would be shed over this incident, as he and his employees were "at present defenseless at the agency" and any misguided decisions on the part of the Indian Office "would endanger our lives."[62] Little Wound's people were therefore left to return on their own accord.

Saville arrived back at the Red Cloud Agency in the second week of December to find the supplies of beef almost depleted. Determined to avert a riot over inadequate rations, he resolved once and for all to obtain an accurate census of Lakotas at the agency. Before embarking on his trip, Saville had considered appointing a mixed-blood Oglala to supervise the count, speculating that the bands would be more inclined to cooperate with one of their relatives. He was mistaken.[63] With the exception of the Oyuhpe chief Red Dog, the Lakotas at Red Cloud joined their nontreaty relatives in hindering the census, convinced that it might encourage the agent to reduce the amount of rations band leaders already deemed inadequate.

Transportation problems compounded the frequent shortage of essential goods at the agency. In late December, Saville fretted that "the amount of stores now in transit is not enough for more than half rations for the number of Indians here." The man largely responsible for this dilemma, the agent contended, was D. J. McCann, who had been contracted by the federal government to furnish timely and adequate transportation for the agency's supplies. Saville asserted on several occasions that McCann had violated his agreement, and the contractor was eventually indicted on charges of fraud.[64]

Some documents support the Oglalas' contention that they were receiving insufficient food.[65] Samuel Walker, a chief clerk employed by the Board of Indian Commissioners in the early 1870s, claimed that fraud was commonplace at Red Cloud and other Lakota agencies. Walker even accused Saville of colluding with government beef contractor L. H. Boster to obtain payment from the Indian Office for cattle that had never been delivered. At this time no complete records were kept of the quantity of supplies issued to the Oglalas, nor were there scales at Red Cloud Agency capable of weighing cattle. In fact, Samuel Walker stated that beef contractors determined the average net weight of beef allocated to the bands by slaughtering only a few selected beasts, and sometimes falsified even these records by weighing the four quarters of a carcass with the endgate of a wagon. Congress tried to correct abuses in the contracting service by empowering five inspectors to suspend anyone employed by or under contract to the Indian Office who engaged in fraud. In 1876 military officers stationed at posts near the agencies began overseeing the delivery and distribution of all goods; three years later, most of the agencies had installed platform scales calibrated to weigh live cattle.[66]

When agents compiled a census, the Oglalas, like other reservation Lakotas, resorted to padding the ration rolls to ensure they would not be shortchanged.[67] In order to do this, families would not report the names of their deceased, or would pass around their very young children from lodge to lodge so that even childless adults could claim rations for their "dependents." Moreover, when one considers that many Lakotas had several names, which they often added to the ration lists, the likelihood of obtaining an accurate census was remote.

The Oglalas reckoned a population of fifteen thousand by the end of 1873; Saville had been issuing for about thirteen thousand, requiring a monthly beef supply of approximately 800,000 pounds—a total twice that of the Indian Office's original estimate. The agent promised Commissioner Smith that he would try to compile a more correct census in order to reduce the quantity of beef distributed, but he feared that troops might be needed if his endeavors failed.[68]

Despite his official instructions to implement the Americanization program, Saville was not averse to honoring Lakota customs as a means of communicating more effectively with agency leaders. Presumably accepting the advice of mixed-blood Oglalas and American men married to Lakota women, he purchased a supply of gifts, not exceeding five hundred dollars in value, to be "kept on hand" and donated "in such cases as I may think for the best interest" of the Indian Office. In November the doctor bestowed gifts of clothing on band chiefs Little Wound, Red Cloud, Man Afraid of His Horse, Red Dog, High Wolf, Red Leaf, and Blue Horse in order to affirm his friendship and secure their cooperation. Saville clearly enjoyed some success with the giveaway, because on 25 December he decided to arrange a feast for Lakota leaders. He anticipated that a substantial meal of boiled and roasted puppy (a Lakota delicacy), rice, tea, and dried apples would bring together as many leaders as possible and "get them to decide upon counting their lodges."[69]

Little Wound, Red Dog, Red Cloud, Slow Bull, and Blue Horse had come out in favor of the census before the December council even convened. But when the time arrived for the meeting to commence, Red Cloud had to be summoned twice before he would leave his tipi. When the others gathered, Saville explained the necessity of counting the people—namely, that the Great Father could only provide sufficient food and supplies if he knew how many Lakotas lived at the agency.[70]

Red Cloud gestured to reply, his words reflecting the sentiment of all present. After praying for guidance, he made no mention of the census in his opening remarks, outlining instead his peers' concerns regarding Americans "running over" their country. The president had assured him in Washington, Red Cloud recalled, that the Oglalas could reside on the north bank of the Upper Platte River for thirty-five years. Then emissaries came, making promises that his kinsfolk would receive weapons and ammunition if they would only relocate the agency on the White River. Red Cloud doubted their sincerity at that time and now felt justified in so doing. Then, in a display of defiance that surely gladdened the younger warrior representatives, he announced that the Oglalas should not submit to the census until they had received guns. Both High Wolf and Red Dog publicly endorsed Red Cloud's speech, and none challenged him. Saville countered that he could do nothing for them until they agreed to obey his orders. But Red Cloud stood his ground, ending the council on a rather ominous note. The Oglalas would wait at the agency for the weapons and ammunition, but only until spring. After then, no one could say what might happen.[71]

After the meeting broke up, Saville admitted to the commissioner of Indian affairs that, as the warriors at Red Cloud Agency were becoming "more overbearing in their demands" each day, he had given up trying to limit the amount of rations distributed. Moreover, Red Cloud's closing comments at the last conference strongly implied that the young men intended to fight in the spring, and the agent feared that the elder councilors would not, or could not, guarantee his personal safety. In Saville's opinion, the band chiefs and headmen had grown "jealous of each other," each striving to "gain favor among" the "dissatisfied, insolent, and unreasonable" young men. Saville speculated that he could depend on a few Lakotas, most notably Man Afraid of His Horse's followers, to protect him. Consequently he appealed to the chief for assistance, but while Man Afraid's people were sympathetic, the agent lamented that even they were often "overruled and silenced" by the disaffected Oglala majority. Man Afraid did caution the agent, however, that Miniconjou *wakiconza* had ordered all their followers to leave the agency "as soon as the grass started." The doctor saw this as a sign of impending war and began to fret that the disgruntled Lakota faction at Red Cloud Agency was "gaining ground." Several Wazaza warriors, for instance, had taunted Saville, threatening to kill him if he did not issue guns and blankets as compensation for timber cut on Lakota lands. Saville refused to comply with their demands, diverting his energies instead to shoring up the agency's defenses. He was now convinced that troops would be needed before spring appeared.[72]

Saville and his nervous employees celebrated their New Year festivities quietly, but the strain of living among so many emboldened warriors was beginning to take its toll. In the second week of January, H. W. Moore, storekeeper for Oglala supplies, wrote Commissioner Smith that Saville was at his wit's end. The agent had earlier dashed off an urgent letter stating that unless he secured additional teams to transport provisions, the young Lakota men would surely resort to violence. D. J. McCann had failed yet again to lay on the necessary number of wagons to haul the provisions, and consequently the agency warehouse was almost bare. As it was the agent estimated that he required at once 500 sacks of flour, 200 sacks of corn, 3,000 pounds of coffee, over 6,000 pounds of sugar, and 13,000 pounds of bacon. Saville himself almost precipitated a riot when he renewed his efforts to count the Oglalas. Pleading with the band chiefs and headmen to help him, the agent was mortified to discover that they had become merely the "representatives" of the young fighting men, expressing "the opinion of the majority" of the warriors when goaded to speak in council. Saville lashed out at the Bad Faces, again designating them as the most stubborn Oglala group, composed of people whom he believed were strongly antagonistic to the Indian Department's policies. Only the Bad Faces' old rivals, the Kiyuksas, offered Saville limited support.[73]

The agent was cheered briefly when the gifts he had previously ordered for northern Lakota councilors at last arrived. Hoping to make a favorable impression on them before they left for the Powder River country, Saville dispatched messengers to the camp of Lone Horn, a prominent Miniconjou *itancan*, informing him that the agent desired to honor him with a present. Accompanied by twenty warriors of his *tiyospaye*, Lone Horn arrived at the agent's office, where they found assembled a number of Oglala and Wazaza chiefs, headmen, and warriors, whom the agent did not name. With the aid of an interpreter, Saville proceeded to explain the terms of the 1868 treaty. The Miniconjous and other Lakotas had broken it by organizing war parties against Americans and other tribes, he told Lone Horn; thus the Great Father would no longer cater to their needs. But as it was not Saville's intention to seem unfriendly, he quickly proffered Lone Horn a gift as a sign of the father's affection. But before the *itancan* could accept it, thereby forming an amicable relationship with the agent, one of the Miniconjou warriors, who had been eavesdropping outside Saville's office, "hollered at him," compelling Lone Horn to refuse the token. Saville then distributed the presents to the assembled Oglalas, who "pledged themselves to defend the agency and obey the orders from the Great Father at Washington." Disgusted by the perceived weakness of these Oglalas, the northern warriors stepped up their threats against Saville's life.[74]

Several war parties left the Red Cloud Agency on the seventh of February, heading toward the Black Hills and the Powder River. The next day Saville rode to the Spotted Tail Agency, which had been established for the Brulé Lakotas on the White River east of the Oglala Agency, to consult with Spotted Tail agent E. A. Howard, who was embroiled in his own struggle with northern Lakota warriors. During Saville's absence, High Foretop, a young Miniconjou man belonging to Lone Horn's band, scaled the agency stockade wall before dawn on the ninth, awakening Frank Appleton, the agency clerk. Mistaking Appleton for Saville, whom he intended to murder, the Miniconjou mortally wounded the clerk and fled on foot. Shortly after, High Foretop appeared in Roman Nose's camp near the Spotted Tail Agency where an Oglala, Afraid of the Eagle, identified him as the assassin. Brulé camp *akicita* later killed him.[75] At the same time, other warriors began to threaten the sawmill employees at the Red Cloud Agency, forcing Saville to move the mill inside the agency compound. The agent suspected that the young men responsible for the recent violence were not Oglalas or Wazazas but Sans Arcs, Hunkpapas, and Miniconjous—the latter harboring, Saville believed, a "particular desire" to kill him.[76]

Concerned that a well-armed cavalry detail might be dispatched to the Indian villages as punishment for Appleton's murder, a number of agency warriors, most notably Wazazas, momentarily halted their demonstrations, prompting Saville to rejoice that he had "gained a victory over" them. Even though Wazaza warriors had earlier terrorized the agent, some now agreed to perform guard duty outside the stockade day and night, and White Crane Walking, a Wazaza *blotahunka*, asked a member of his soldier society to watch over their "father." Saville did not explain in his correspondence to superiors why the Wazazas would defy other Lakota warriors by coming to his aid. Perhaps they were remembering the tragedy that befell their old chief Conquering Bear in 1854, when inexperienced American soldiers marched into their village. In addition, over at the Spotted Tail Agency, the Wazazas' Brulé relatives moved in council to impede northern war parties from revisiting the agencies.[77]

Although several northern Lakota war parties had left the Red Cloud Agency by the sixteenth, a number of their young men still lingered in the Oglala camps, "for no good purpose," in Saville's opinion. The agent bemoaned the fact that they "have had a great influence over the young men of the Oglalas [and] Brulés," forever haranguing them to abandon reservation life and commanding their "father" to remove all agencies from Lakota country. Indeed, as February drew to a close, Saville discovered that Lakota warriors had also been mingling in Little Wolf's Northern Cheyenne band, trying to recruit young men for the war faction. Crazy Horse planned to fight the Americans, it was said, and even now a number of Oglala warriors from the Red Cloud Agency were heading for the Powder River country with the "avowed purpose of joining" him and other nontreaty people. Furthermore, as the band *itancan* and headmen had persistently failed, or refused, to suppress the warriors' actions, Saville was faced with "a constant struggle" to avert a major conflict.[78]

Not all the Oglalas advocated violence, however. While northern Lakotas lobbied for the war effort, Kiyuksa *wakiconza* directed their people to strike the lodges and move south. Little Wound's people had rejected participation in "Red Cloud's War" almost a decade ago, and this time they vetoed an alliance with Crazy Horse and other Lakota *blotahunka*—a decision that incited some Oglalas at the agency to become "as hostile to them as to other [enemy] tribes."[79]

In the midst of this pending crisis Red Cloud called on Saville with news that Black Twin and Crazy Horse *tiyospaye* had divided. Black Twin's nontreaty Bad Faces were ostensibly en route to the agency, whereas

Crazy Horse's band had elected to stay with the northern war faction. But Saville's hopes that Black Twin would come in were dashed when additional reports indicated that the his village had been sighted in the Bighorn Mountains, a stronghold of the northern Lakotas. Moreover, of the Miniconjous, Sans Arcs, and Hunkpapas who had left the agency in recent weeks, sixty lodges under Lame Antelope were camped on the Cheyenne River near the Black Hills, and north of them was the Miniconjou Black Shield with his forty-lodge following. In addition, eighty lodges of Lakotas were on Hat Creek, south of the Black Hills, and 140 were in camp on Bear Creek, their *tiyospaye* names unknown. Sitting Bull's Hunkpapas and Sans Arcs had also been seen heading for the Black Hills after a fight with Crow warriors. Although no white settlers had encountered the northern Lakota war parties in weeks, Saville's employees refused to occupy their posts unless troops were present. The agent therefore felt obliged to request military reinforcements from Fort Laramie.[80]

While Saville endeavored to keep the agency on an even keel, Col. John Smith accused him of oversupplying the Oglalas and Wazazas and neglecting to inform neighboring military commands of the movements and locations of Lakota war parties, to which charge Saville responded that he had done his best to report such information. Besides, most of the fighting men, he continued, were Miniconjous and Sans Arcs, who were not his responsibility. Saville conceded that these warriors often drew rations at the Red Cloud Agency but added that their general whereabouts "are not known to me any more than to" Colonel Smith.[81]

The seriousness of the current situation induced Yellow Hair, whom Saville considered "one of the most intelligent and best men" of the Lakotas, to convene a private meeting for Oglala and Wazaza leaders in late February. After the councilors had met, Yellow Hair contacted the agent. Speaking through interpreter Todd Randall, Yellow Hair promised the agent that he would do his utmost to prevent further violence at the agency. In accordance with Yellow Hair's advice, other *tiyospaye* leaders had agreed to obey their father's directives, even permitting him to compile a census. Yellow Hair understood why Saville had summoned troops; nevertheless, he dreaded the possible outcome of stationing them so close to Lakota families. Several council delegates would call on Saville within a couple of days, Yellow Hair continued, to discuss fully what had transpired in the meeting, but for some reason they later changed their mind. After conferring again on the 1 March, Oglala and Wazaza spokesmen invited Saville to attend a general meeting to be held in the agency's warehouse on the third. The agent explained to the councilors why soldiers had been summoned, and that as long as their people remained calm and followed his orders, no one would be harmed.[82]

On 5 March, Colonel Smith arrived at the Red Cloud Agency with eight troops of cavalry and eight companies of infantry (a total of 949 men). A similar force was also dispatched to the Spotted Tail Agency, but as many of the Oglalas and Brulés had already dispersed before the soldiers reached their destinations, Smith ordered six troops of the cavalry to return to their base. Later that day a wagon rolled into the Red Cloud Agency packed with the weapons that Saville had ordered for defensive purposes. He immediately corralled it inside the stockade, unloading the guns during the night "without exciting the suspicion of the Indians."[83]

Tranquility descended over the Oglala agency in the shadow of Smith's garrisons. Despite sporadic interference from small groups of northern Lakotas who had not left with the main war parties, Saville had almost completed the census by the third week of March. The final July tally of nearly eight thousand Oglalas and Wazazas surprised him, especially as a number of families had fled when troops arrived. The agent had thought a more accurate aggregate would be around six thousand people, excluding the Northern Cheyennes, who had already departed for Hat Creek and the Powder River.[84]

In the interim Saville took advantage of the Miniconjous' absence to arrange internal protection for the agency. He hoped that guard duties would give employment to many of the young men, thereby discouraging them from "going off in war parties," fostering peace, and settling "the claims and disaffections growing out of the removal of the agency." Assuming to some extent the role of a *wakiconza,* Saville selected a small Oglala and Wazaza guard, his *akicita,* arming them with Springfield needle guns and paying them between five to twenty-five dollars a month to defend the agency. Those initially chosen—all of them either Kiyuksa, Loafer, Wazaza, or Oyuhpe. Little Wound's nephew Sitting Bull, the agent's "warm friend," was appointed the first leader of the guard.[85]

But this peaceful period was merely the calm before the storm. Saville's spirits sank in late July when he received word that a large number of Miniconjous and Hunkpapas who had spent previous winters at the agency intended to return sometime during the fall. The number of Oglalas and Wazazas at Red Cloud was already higher than his estimates, and now that many more Lakotas were heading to the agency, Saville knew from experience that warehouse supplies would soon be exhausted. By mid-August, with over ten thousand people to sustain, the storekeeper was entirely out of provisions except for beef. Bracing himself, Saville predicted that his only chance of defusing potentially explosive incidents at the Red Cloud Agency rested on arming twenty Oglala and Wazaza guardsmen, whom he hoped would bring him firsthand reports of the warrior societies' actions.[86]

American officials had succeeded in transferring the Red Cloud Agency to the Great Sioux Reservation but they had not silenced the Oglala band chiefs and headmen, and most certainly not the *blotahunka* and their young fighting men, whose political influence in agency affairs during this period was most perceptible.

# CHAPTER SIX

# Oglala Warriors
# and Agency Affairs, 1874–1876

The 1868 Treaty of Fort Laramie recognized the Lakotas' unconditional rights to occupy the Black Hills (Paha Sapa), but by the summer of 1874, American authorities had been largely unable to hold back a surging tide of gold prospectors in the Black Hills. Officials hoped to discourage miners from illegally invading Lakota country by proving conclusively that no substantial deposits of the precious metal could be found in the hills. During the summer of 1874, Lt. Col. George Custer led an expedition into the Black Hills in order to demonstrate that rumors of panhandlers knee-deep in gold dust were false. Custer soon reported, however, that his surveying teams had discovered rich veins of gold. Alarmed by the likely impact of Custer's dispatches, the U.S. Congress employed Professor Walter Jenney of the New York School of Mines to evaluate Custer's account.[1]

In the interim, private companies began to form with the purpose of mining the Black Hills. In late August a Yankton, Dakota Territory, company launched an expedition into the hills from the west via the Wyoming Territory in order to circumvent a recent military order from Brig. Gen. Alfred Terry warning Americans not to invade the Lakotas' unceded territory. Concerned that such orders would be generally disregarded, Lt. Gen. Philip Sheridan threatened to use military force if the citizen companies of Sioux City and Yankton trespassed on Sioux lands—at least until federal authorities had concluded some type of an agreement with the Lakotas. Sheridan's directive inflamed the staff of the *Sioux City Daily Journal*. One editorial stated that "the gold-seekers might as well break the [1868] treaty as for Congress to do it—and, any way, the army ought to be kept busy" fighting Indians.[2]

After Custer's return, Professor Jenney set out with a military escort led by Lt. Col. Richard Dodge, remaining in the Black Hills until the fall.[3] The following year the professor submitted his findings to Congress. Although Jenney confirmed that the Black Hills did contain gold deposits, he reported that they did not exist in the quantities that Custer had enthusiastically claimed. But gold seekers continued to trek into the Dakota Territory as if Jenney's report had never been written. In fact, Professor Jenney mentioned in his official account that Lieutenant Colonel Dodge had exerted little effort to evict prospectors already panning in the hills, even authorizing some of them to remain. Furthermore, Capt. John Bourke predicted that within a year the Black Hills would be "swarming with a hardy industrious population; not merely self-sustaining but productive."[4]

Angered by the invasion of Paha Sapa, Oglala, Wazaza, and Miniconjou warriors frequently dominated the multiband councils at Red Cloud Agency. Indeed, the years spanning the period from the summer of 1873 to the final surrender of Crazy Horse's people in 1877 highlighted a time when Oglala warriors often challenged the opinions and advice of their elders—the band *itancan* and headmen—and, like their nontreaty relatives, enjoyed flouting their agent's rules and regulations. But in the true spirit of Oglala political customs, not all of them did so. Although many of the young fighting men acted as if they held the fate of their agent, J. J. Saville, in their hands, others felt equally free to support whomever they wished, even shifting their loyalties from their own kinsfolk to the agent.

The first bands of northern nontreaty Lakotas began arriving at Red Cloud Agency as early as 7 August 1874, and by the end of the month over ten thousand Lakotas, along with some Northern Cheyennes and Arapahos, had raised their lodges in the vicinity. Saville anticipated violence as government contractors had not yet delivered the agency's food supplies and other essentials. The doctor notified the commissioner of Indian affairs that the agency warehouse contained only beef, compelling him to issue extra rations from this already depleted supply in lieu of pork, sugar, flour, and coffee. At the same time, he sought permission to arm twenty warriors, whom he selected to assist him in maintaining order and to "spy on" their agency kinsfolk and the nontreaty Lakotas.[5]

Aware that Commissioner Edward Smith disapproved of the proposal to arm Oglala warriors, Saville wrote again to elaborate on his plan. The agent had come to realize that he could not depend on the band chiefs and headmen to control the behavior of the warriors, as he concluded that the elders were now dominated by the younger men and "conform to their wishes in everything." Indeed, if Saville wished to implement any of his plans or regulations at the agency, he felt obliged to contact the war party leaders, or *blotahunka,* first, rather than the band *itancan* and headmen.⁶ As Col. David Mitchell and Brig. Gen. William Harney had tried over twenty years ago, Saville also endeavored to modify the political customs of the Oglalas. The Lakota people, the agent assumed, did not have what he termed a "regular government." Hence he thought it prudent to establish his Oglala guard by enlisting several of these influential *blotahunka,* who would serve as "a nucleus around which I hope to form a government among them." This small group, salaried at fifty to seventy-five cents a day, would presumably compel the agency Lakotas to obey them and their agent. Saville did not name the warriors he favored at this time, although he later issued weapons, with departmental permission, to the prominent warrior White Crane Walking of the Wazazas; the headman White Tail, a future follower of the northern Oglala *blotahunka* Big Road; the Oglala headmen Three Bears and Yellow Hair; Little Wound's nephew, the young Sitting Bull; and Sword, presumably the same man who was a head shirtwearer among the Bad Faces and a son of the *itancan* Brave Bear.⁷

Saville exaggerated the initial effectiveness of his small corps of guardsmen, however, for they failed to prevent their kinsfolk from leaving the agency. By the end of September, despite the secretary of the interior's desire to settle as many Lakotas as possible at the Red Cloud Agency, only 599 remained, compared to the previous month's total of almost ten thousand, most of whom had undoubtedly departed to procure their own meat supplies for the fall and winter seasons.⁸

The tensions that had slowly simmered all summer finally came to a boil in October, over the construction of a flagstaff within the agency compound.⁹ Saville complained that the band chiefs and headmen had fallen into the "habit of bothering" him every day, including Sunday. Therefore he proposed to fly the U.S. flag on Sundays in order to remind the Oglalas that it was the Sabbath day for his employees. Many Lakota warriors, already enraged by the presence of miners in the Black Hills, opposed the idea, countering that the flag symbolized the power of the U.S. Army and transformed the agency into a military fort. Red Leaf's Wazazas, it was claimed, were particularly "troublesome. . . , finding fault with every little thing" the agent suggested.¹⁰

Saville did not take their objections too seriously at first, but on the twenty-fourth a party of armed and painted warriors, many of them Wazazas, entered the agency stockade while he was in his office conducting business with the Oyuhpe *itancan* Red Dog and Red Cloud of the Bad

Faces. Alarmed by the young men's sudden appearance, the agent immediately asked Red Cloud to intervene, but the Bad Face leader "carelessly remarked" that many of the warriors had earlier convened a meeting and resolved "to destroy the pole." When several Wazaza men began to chop down the flagstaff, Saville dispatched a Lakota messenger, aptly named Speeder, or Racer, to summon troops stationed at Camp Robinson, which had been established by Col. John Smith about a mile and a half west of the agency.[11]

The Oglalas enjoyed wagering on the horse races that took place around the agency compound almost daily, and when Lt. Emmet Crawford, commanding twenty-five soldiers of Company G, Third U.S. Cavalry, arrived, he found a crowd of four hundred Lakota men, including a substantial Miniconjou contingent, already assembled for the races. When the soldiers were sighted, Saville instructed his employees to open the large double gates of the compound through which Crawford and his detail rushed in. Quickly ordering his men to dismount, the lieutenant commanded them to face the still ajar stockade gates with guns pointed toward the Lakotas outside, many of whom were enraged or confused by the troops' sudden appearance. Chaos erupted among the crowd, and several of the young cavalrymen became so disoriented that they pointed their rifle butts toward the yelling Lakota warriors who were threatening to storm the stockade.

At this juncture the Oglala head shirtwearers, Young Man Afraid of His Horse and Sword, the traditional peacemakers, along with Sitting Bull, Spider (Red Cloud's younger brother), and other camp *akicita* and guardsmen intervened, repulsing the angry throng with threats and a show of weapons. Sitting Bull brandished a gun-stock club into which were set at right angles four knife blades, and, in the words of agency employee Benjamin Tibbitts, many Oglalas "were afraid of him."[12] At the same time, Three Bears, with some of his armed camp *akicita*, formed a human cordon in front of the open gate, thus preventing Lakota warriors from attacking the soldiers within and enabling agency personnel to shut the heavy stockade gates. Once the compound had been secured, Sitting Bull told Saville that if the frightened cavalrymen would quietly return to their barracks, he, Young Man Afraid, and Sword would subdue the crowd and defend the agency.

Soon after, mixed-blood interpreters William Garnett and Louis Richard slipped through a side door adjacent to the main gates. When they stepped outside they saw that the Lakotas had started to fight among themselves. Within moments several camp *akicita* from unnamed bands clubbed from his horse young Conquering Bear of the Wazazas (the nephew of Red Leaf, and the son of the *itancan* Conquering Bear, who was killed in the wake of the 1854 Grattan incident). Placing a bow across Conquering Bear's throat, the *akicita* stood on both ends as punishment for severely beating and cutting Speeder as he returned from delivering Saville's message to Camp Robinson. Bear Brains, Red Cloud's "brother-in-law," also attempted to curtail the violence. As the crowd fought among itself, Bear Brains shouted that Conquering Bear had precipitated the ruckus by resolving to retaliate against American troops for killing his father. Bear Brains continued to harangue the throng, yelling that Conquering Bear was a "troublesome fellow," that he did not belong among the Oglalas but with Spotted Tail's Brulés, and that the Oglalas should not permit him to foment such a disturbance at their agency.

Sitting Bull also remained at the scene, wielding his terrifying knife and knocking over men and horses "right and left" with "the power of a giant" while he commanded the crowd to scatter. One mounted warrior attempted to shoot Sitting Bull, but as he leveled his gun to fire, Grey Eyes seized and held the barrel. Turning and boasting to the would-be assassin that he had already survived several bullet wounds in battle, Sitting Bull continued to drive away the mob. Moreover, other Lakotas volunteered to protect the agency by surrounding the stockade, thus guarding against arson.[13]

In all, the primary motivation of these warriors for mounting a defense against their own kinsfolk, some of whom could conceivably have belonged to the same warrior societies as the volunteers, was not simply to serve agent Saville but to prevent American troops from being permanently stationed at the Red Cloud Agency. When Young Man Afraid of His Horse, Sitting Bull, Sword, Three Bears, and Bear Brains had restored peace, the *itancan* Man Afraid of His Horse, Red Dog, and Red Leaf, along with Ribs, Pretty Bear, and White Tail, scolded the demonstrators before telling them to return home peacefully.[14]

Although Conquering Bear had played a part in exciting many of the warriors, other Oglalas accused Red Cloud of causing the disturbance. Even some of the Bad Face leader's own relatives later contended that he had wished only to protest the weekly flag-raising but had in the process "overplayed his hand and lost control" of the situation. Capt. William Jordan, commandant at Camp Robinson, also claimed that during the ruckus Red Cloud had "remained passive inside the stockade" appearing "afraid to do anything." Furthermore, Ben Tibbitts mentioned that Red Cloud did not once leave the stockade, as the Bad Face *itancan* had "sat on a pile of lumber" next to him, remaining "right through the scene." Still, Saville expressed his gratitude for the assistance he received from some of the Oglalas who risked their lives defending the agency and Crawford's men by bestowing upon them blankets and other small gifts.[15]

Army reports present a different version of the flagpole incident. Even though prominent Lakota warriors, including two head shirtwearers, had quelled the disturbance, in his official brief Col. L. P. Bradley of the 9th Infantry praised the "judicious action of Lieutenant Crawford" for preventing "loss of life and property." In addition, Professor Othniel Marsh, a Yale University palaeontologist who would soon become embroiled in a formal investigation at the Red Cloud Agency, wrote that the lieutenant, with a handful of men, had "saved the agent and all the white people at the agency from destruction."[16]

Although military officers praised the actions of Camp Robinson's commanders during the recent affair, they severely criticized Saville's decisions, remarking that a shrewder agent would have anticipated the consequences of flying Old Glory in the presence of Lakota warriors, bold young men who often discounted the advice of their band elders. Captain Jordan contended that the doctor had jeopardized the safety of the 140 troops at Camp Robinson, and considered him "too nervous and excitable a man for so important a position" as agent for the Oglalas. Ben Tibbitts refused to take sides, but added that it was fortunate that "no one fired a shot" as one volley "would have set the trouble to going and the agency would have been burned."[17]

Army personnel also ridiculed Saville's administrative abilities, particularly his recent move to arm and pay an Oglala guard. When Lt. Gen. Philip Sheridan got wind of the agent's plan, he retorted that "what we want at the Red Cloud Agency is more troops instead of more guns for the Indians." In his opinion the Oglalas had "no real use for arms but war." Brig. Gen. William Sherman concurred, adding that war between the Lakotas and the United States seemed not only inevitable but imminent. That Saville would provide weapons to the Oglalas at this time was surely "an act of liberality that no man conversant with the subject can dispute." Besides, Sherman concluded, the Oglalas already possessed "all the arms needed for game and too many for a people who profess a desire to learn the arts of husbandry and agriculture."[18]

A semblance of order had barely returned to the Red Cloud Agency when violence broke out again over the perennial problem of the census. Predictably, Saville threatened to withhold rations at the end of October unless the Oglalas agreed to be recounted.[19] For over a week the agency councilors deliberated both day and night, struggling to reach a consensus. On the evening of 4 November, Red Cloud summoned Saville to their conference, where he found waiting *itancan*, headmen, and warriors from all the agency bands. Resuming his role as principal spokesman, Red Cloud announced the Oglalas' decision: the council would not permit another census to be conducted. Saville reacted by telegraphing Captain Jordan to place his troops on alert.[20]

The thought of losing their provisions and the presence of military forces from Camp Robinson forced the Oglalas to reconsider, however, for the following morning Saville received word that the councilors had reversed their initial decision. Honoring their responsibilities to protect their people at all costs, the head shirtwearers Young Man Afraid of His Horse and Sword had exercised their authority in the multiband assembly and had taken "a very firm stand against Red Cloud" (Sword's uncle), and even Young Man Afraid's father, the Hunkpatila *itancan* Man Afraid of His Horse, compelling them both to yield. Shortly thereafter, many of the families began to move their lodges closer to the agency compound in order for Saville to count them. But despite the agent's assumption that Red Dog was loyal to him, most of the Oyuhpe chief's people, along with several camps of Hunkpapas, Sans Arcs, and Miniconjous, left the agency before the census could be completed. Assisted by his own "*akicita*," the small Oglala guard, Saville recorded an Oglala and Wazaza population of 9,339, excluding eight to nine hundred Oyuhpes and Kiyuksas who were hunting on the Republican River.[21]

Silenced by the head shirtwearers during the last meeting, Red Cloud demanded to air his grievances with the Great Father. The chief's unwillingness or inability to intervene during the flagstaff affair, along with Young Man Afraid's success in thwarting Red Cloud's efforts to block the census, had shaken the Bad Face's influence in the eyes of his peers and of the agent. Saville blamed Red Cloud for hampering his attempts to negotiate with leaders of the nonagency Oglalas. Little Big Man, whom Saville regarded as one of "the most irreconcilable" of the northern warriors, had recently visited the Red Cloud Agency. The agent had seized the opportunity to open channels of communication by proffering Little Big Man gifts for his followers and requesting that he distribute the rest to Black Twin and Crazy Horse. Little Big Man assured Saville that his kinsfolk would come into the Oglala agency after the late February hunt, but Red Cloud was so envious of the northern war leaders' influence, the agent claimed, that "he does much to prevent" their arrival.[22] Did Red Cloud therefore hope that a private audience with the president might enable him to shore up his failing reputation as an influential man among the agency *tiyospaye* by discrediting Saville?

There is some evidence that Red Cloud used the animosity between the U.S. military and the Interior Department to intimidate the agent. By February, Red Cloud's request to visit the president had placed Saville in the center of yet another bitter squabble with Captain Jordan, whom the agent charged with actively inciting the Oglalas to question his authority. The previous December, Saville informed Special Commissioner C. C. Cox that some of Camp Robinson's officers had promised Red Cloud that they would escort him to Washington if the agent denied the chief's request. When Captain Jordan learned of the communiqué he responded by pointedly suggesting that Saville should have first corroborated the facts with the commandant before firing off a written complaint to Cox based solely on the testimony of Red Cloud, "who was probably lied to by the interpreter."[23]

While Saville and Jordan quarreled (Jordan, for instance, had once claimed that the agent was "robbing" the Oglalas), Fort Laramie's trader, J. S. Collins, invited Oglala leaders to the post for an unauthorized council during which he erroneously announced that President Grant wished him to pose certain questions "relative to matters of great importance." Collins warned the councilors that the president was powerless to prevent gold prospectors from invading the Black Hills. He therefore advised them to sell that portion of Lakota land between the Cheyenne River and its southern fork rather than risk the Americans' stealing it from them later. Furthermore, in order to discuss the matter, the Oglalas should weigh the options of either receiving at the agency itself a special government commission or dispatching delegates to the Great Father.[24]

Red Cloud replied, unaware that the Office of Indian Affairs had not sanctioned the Fort Laramie conference. The Oglalas had grown to distrust special commissions, he began, as they rarely delivered the gifts promised during formal sessions; therefore a delegation, which would almost certainly include himself, should visit Washington. Red Dog of the Oyuhpes concurred with Red Cloud, proposing that their white relatives ("men of the country"), along with mixed-blood Oglalas, should accompany the travelers to ensure accurate translations of the president's words.

As it was, the people were still debating the exact meaning of the 1868 Fort Laramie treaty. Crazy Horse's followers, it was said, had denounced Red Cloud as a "cheap man" who had seriously compromised Lakota sovereignty by signing the treaty. After further deliberation, Blue Horse of the Loafers adjourned the meeting by announcing that as all present had resolved to send representatives to the Great Father, nothing more would be said at this point.[25]

The following week Collins penned a letter to President Grant insisting that most of the Oglalas were "anxious to sell" the Black Hills while they could still obtain a good price. Some councilors had demanded money, he continued; others also wanted mares and cows. The trader predicted, however, that the war leaders would oppose any negotiations regarding the Black Hills, but if federal emissaries failed to consult them, "trouble of a serious nature may come from it." It was Collins's understanding that the Oglalas desired to send spokesmen to the American capital, but Man Afraid of His Horse notified him that the councilors were already arguing bitterly over who should represent them in Washington. The Hunkpatila *itancan* complained that Red Cloud's white kinsfolk had heavily influenced the tone and content of the Bad Face's council speech, and that Red Cloud's public comments did not reflect the general wishes of the Oglalas. In fact, Man Afraid remarked that most of the elders wanted their *blotahunka* and warriors to select their delegates. Furthermore, the warrior societies wanted the Red Cloud Agency moved to the Tongue River, away from army camps and other American settlements that served as a magnet for gold prospectors; they were adamant that the *tiyospaye itancan* and headmen would not determine the Oglalas' future once they arrived in Washington. Hearing this, Collins cautioned President Grant that any Oglala delegation would have to include at least three to five leading warriors from each band in addition to the *tiyospaye* elders.[26]

Saville was displeased that Collins would dare to usurp his authority by convening an unauthorized meeting with the Oglalas; nevertheless, he focused his energies on exploring the possibility of persuading several of the northern Lakota leaders to join the Washington party while trying to reconcile the agency bands that had since become completely "broken into factions." On 8 April, Saville's Oglala envoys set out from the agency, battling the deep snow of an early spring storm and bearing gifts to honor the northern people. Despite the conditions, the agent anticipated the messengers' return within fifteen days. In the meantime he continued his plans to assemble the Oglala delegation at Cheyenne, Wyoming Territory, by the first of May.[27] The agent soon learned, however, that both Crazy Horse and Black Twin had spurned his request to send spokesmen from their camps. With this knowledge Saville decided to limit the delegation's size to no more than fifteen men—a decision that threatened to stall the party's departure, as Red Cloud continued to insist that at least twenty men would be required to represent the agency *tiyospaye*. Although the bands had often assembled to discuss important issues, they nevertheless remained autonomous, and certainly there was no one man among them authorized to conclude binding agreements with federal authorities. Thoroughly exasperated, Saville, who vented his anger on interpreters Todd Randall and Louis Richard, sought official permission to bring along the recognized leaders of all the agency warrior societies, "without whom the chiefs cannot or will not act."[28]

After much discussion the Oglala multiband council finally settled on just thirteen spokesmen. Only Scalp Face (or Face), Sitting Bull, and possibly American Horse (if this man was the Kiyuksa warrior of that name) had served as members of Saville's agency guard. Accompanied by their interpreters Nick Janis, William Garnett, and Leon Palladay, they left for Washington, where delegates from other Lakota agencies were also gathering.[29]

When Saville and the Oglala spokesmen reached the capital in mid-May, the agent was greeted with the startling news that he was under investigation for fraud. During the previous November when Professor Othniel Marsh organized with the secretary of the interior's approval an archaeological expedition to a location in the Bad Lands just ten miles north of the Red Cloud Agency, Saville advised the professor that northern Lakota bands would most likely oppose his presence in their country. Undeterred, Marsh arrived at the agency on the eleventh with a military escort from Camp Robinson. Although many of the agency Oglalas questioned Marsh's intentions, a few promised to accompany the professor to the Bad Lands if he agreed to dismiss the unwelcome American soldiers but withdrew their offer when Marsh refused to proceed without troops.[30]

Before commencing his search for fossils, Professor Marsh met Red Cloud and Red Dog at the Camp Robinson quarters of Lt. Cols. L. P. Bradley and T. H. Stanton. The Bad Face and Oyuhpe *itancan* brought the professor substandard specimens of coffee, tobacco, beef, flour, and sugar, which they claimed were "fair samples of the provisions issued" to the agency bands and illustrative of Saville's determination to defraud their people. When Marsh delivered these samples to the Board of Indian Commissioners in late April, a public outcry ensued, prompting federal officials to press charges against the agent for mismanaging the Oglalas' food rations. And it was these charges that Red Cloud and Red Dog wished to discuss during the Washington summit.[31]

The Oglala delegates met the commissioner of Indian affairs on 19 May but did not speak with Secretary of the Interior Columbus Delano until the twenty-seventh.[32] In the interim the Lakotas argued among themselves, casting aspersions on each other's personal character and reputation. Lone Horn, a well-respected Miniconjou *itancan* who had ties to both the nontreaty and Cheyenne River Agency bands, suggested that the combined Lakota delegations should settle once and for all the Black Hills controversy while they still had the opportunity to meet with the Great Father himself. If the *New York Times'* coverage of this dispute is accurate, Lone Horn's proposition is particularly intriguing in that here was a man accustomed to consensus politics but who presumably considered the president the embodiment of American decision-making authority. Moreover, Red Cloud immediately criticized Lone Horn's cooperative gesture, retorting that the Miniconjou was not a great *itancan* and that he was personally "disgusted with his boasting."[33]

While Red Cloud and Lone Horn questioned each other's status, the Oglala representatives began to contest the decisions they had earlier reached—so much so that a member of the party asked an American official to telegraph the Red Cloud Agency, instructing the head shirtwearer, Young Man Afraid of His Horse, to come east as soon as possible. A *New York Times* reporter covering the Lakota delegations' visit to the capital referred to Young Man Afraid as the Oglalas' "hereditary chief," whose status the "usurper" Red Cloud had long since appropriated. Young Man Afraid, the journalist continued, "heads the opposition to Red Cloud," and was most likely to give the Bad Face "a hard fight for the chieftainship of the Oglalas."[34] The reporter's comments more accurately encapsulate the conventional American wisdom that "chieftainship" among the Oglalas granted a man the power to dictate the actions of others. As long as he embraced the American concept of a Sioux "head chief," the *Times* reporter understandably failed to consider other reasons why Young Man Afraid, Red Cloud's putative adversary, was summoned. Young Man Afraid was indeed the son of the Oglalas' head *itancan*, Man Afraid of His

Horse, but he also enjoyed the prestige and bore the responsibility of a head shirtwearer, a peacemaker. In the aftermath of heated quarrels over the fate of the Black Hills that threatened to open an unbridgeable chasm between the delegates, someone had elected to send for their most prominent head shirtwearer, whose pipe would help soothe tensions, restore order, and perhaps encourage consensus.

When Secretary Delano finally greeted the Lakota spokesmen, he set aside the Black Hills question, discussing instead the recent entry of American settlers into favorite Lakota buffalo ranges in Kansas and Nebraska. If the Great Father could not prevent the migrations of his people, Delano stated, would it not benefit the Lakotas to relinquish their treaty rights to hunt along the Republican and Smoky Hill rivers? Moreover, Congress had already appropriated twenty-five thousand dollars for the Oglalas and Brulés if they would abandon the chase in this area.[35]

Red Cloud expressed bewilderment, believing that the primary purpose of this visit was to discuss with the president current affairs at the Oglala agency, particularly the substandard quality of government rations that he and Red Dog had previously shown to Professor Marsh. Hence the Oglala party returned to the Indian Office on the twenty-eighth to elaborate on their specific complaints. Desiring to question Red Cloud in person, Professor Marsh arrived at the meeting, accompanied by B. R. Cowen, the assistant commissioner of Indian affairs. The professor informed the Bad Face *itancan* that he had passed on the poor food samples to the president, and urged Red Cloud to speak candidly about any hardships that the agency Oglalas were experiencing. Red Cloud's testimony was vague and fraught with inconsistencies, however, and it soon became clear that the Bad Face chief could not adequately support the charges of mismanagement leveled at Saville. While Red Cloud continued to insist that the Oglalas had endured a food shortage during the previous winter, he nevertheless admitted that neither he nor Red Dog had wished to create the impression that the specimens were typical of those the *tiyospaye* had customarily received throughout the years.[36]

At this juncture the commissioner and secretary momentarily curtailed Marsh's impromptu investigation, resuming instead the debate concerning off-reservation hunting in the Republican River valley. Most of the Oglala delegates now seemed poised to relinquish their treaty rights to hunt there, but they disagreed over the best means of compensation. Little Wound refused to cooperate, however, as the Republican River region had long been his followers' most cherished buffalo range. Thus as the day quickly approached for the Oglalas' departure and the document remained unsigned, the Indian commissioner advised them to take home a draft of the proposed agreement for all the agency councilors to consider.[37]

Before leaving, young Sitting Bull reminded Delano of the importance of the warriors in the current political affairs of the Oglala people. "The young men," he began, "have their opinions about matters as well as" the *itancan,* who "only tell the business of the people." The Oglala councilors had instructed their Washington delegates to present all the viewpoints expressed at the last agency conference to the president, and they most certainly did not possess the authority to make solemn agreements without first consulting the warrior societies. When Sitting Bull concluded his remarks, Scalp Face spoke. With little respect for Red Cloud's status as a band *itancan,* Scalp Face pointedly told him, "We came here with divided councils; we have accomplished nothing, and we have no one to blame but ourselves. The Red Cloud agent is a good man; he is a brave, true man. We tried to break him down, but we could not. . . . We have tried him enough."[38] Bravery was one of the cardinal virtues of the Lakota people, and Saville's tenacity had won him the respect of some of the young men such as Scalp Face and Sitting Bull, both founding members of the doctor's Oglala guard who had come to acknowledge, at least temporarily, Saville's authority as a white *wakiconza.*

Red Cloud fell silent, but not Little Wound of the Kiyuksas. He felt that the Great Father had not paid the Lakotas the respect they deserved as spokesmen for the agency bands. "We came here at the invitation of the president," he began, "and we expected to go home with horses, equipment, and guns so that our people would receive us gladly." If they returned empty-handed their kinsfolk would "all laugh at us"—mere shadows of men whom the Great Father held in such contempt that he had refused to honor them with even a modest gift. Therefore, when the Lakotas bade farewell on the fifth, neither they nor federal officials were in particularly cheerful spirits.[39]

After the delegation arrived home, the councilors, including Little Wound, eventually approved the federal agreement abrogating Oglala rights to hunt in the Republican River valley.[40] But although the *tiyospaye* had abandoned the chase in Kansas and Nebraska, the Black Hills question continued to loom large, and Red Cloud and Red Dog had still not succeeded in proving wrongdoing on Saville's part. Sensitive to public criticism generated by Marsh's exposé, however, the commissioner of Indian affairs appointed on 1 July a special commission, chaired by Thomas Fletcher, to conduct a thorough investigation of affairs at the Red Cloud Agency. While the commission assembled, Secretary Delano directed Professor Marsh to submit a personal account of his earlier visit to the agency.[41]

The hearings commenced in the first week of August, the commissioners conducting extensive interviews with Oglala and Wazaza band chiefs, headmen, and warriors, army personnel from Camp Robinson and Fort Laramie, mixed-bloods, traders, and Americans employed at the Red Cloud Agency. Interpreter Jules Ecoffey was one of the first men summoned for questioning at Fort Laramie. He testified on the fourth that he had spoken with Young Man Afraid of His Horse, Sword, Sitting Bull, and other Oglalas and Wazazas. All had complained, Ecoffey asserted, that their food rations and goods were insufficient and of an inferior quality. The translator added, however, that the visitors should not take such grievances to heart, as the Lakotas, he insisted, had "a habit of complaining."[42]

Man Afraid of His Horse and young Sitting Bull spoke informally with the commissioners on the ninth, the day before the general council was scheduled to convene. Sitting Bull took issue with Ecoffey's statements, claiming that the *tiyospaye* had received plenty of rations last winter and that the quality of food was generally satisfactory. His only grievance centered on the shortage of blankets, which became threadbare within months of receipt. Man Afraid refused to say anything, however, neither supporting nor challenging Sitting Bull's remarks.[43] As a band *itancan,* it was his perogative to remain silent; besides, he had decided to wait for the grand council to open before offering an opinion.

The following day, just before the assembly convened, the commissioners interviewed trader F. D. Yates at Camp Robinson. Yates claimed that he had overheard Red Dog admit to interpreter Leon Palladay that he and Red Cloud had rummaged through a large quantity of coffee beans, pulling out all the inferior "black grains." When questioned, Red Dog countered that he and Red Cloud had done this simply because Professor Marsh had requested such a sample. But commanding officer William Jordan contended that the Oglalas often received inadequate provisions, remarking that he would never issue to his own troops the quality of flour the Lakotas were forced to accept. On the other hand, he considered both

Red Cloud and Red Dog unreliable witnesses, claiming they could be "bought with a bottle of whiskey."[44]

After concluding these preliminary interviews, Fletcher, Harris, and Faulkner addressed the multiband council at the agency warehouse. Red Cloud rose first to speak. Saville, he began, had distributed only thirty-seven bales of blankets to all the agency *tiyospaye*. Furthermore, because these bands had shared blankets with their northern Lakota relatives camped near the agency, many of the Oglalas had gone without blankets during the frigid winter months. But rather than seizing the moment to publicly accuse Saville of fraud and mismanagement, Red Cloud seemed more conciliatory, swayed perhaps by the stinging remarks the warrior Scalp Face had thrown at the *itancan* before they left Washington. "My father," Red Cloud addressed the doctor, "we don't blame you about our provisions and goods, because you don't buy them, but you ought to see that they do well by us." The agent had angered the Oglalas for summoning troops during the flagpole affair, Red Cloud continued, but for the most part they all liked and respected him.[45]

Kiyuksa *blotahunka* Sitting Bull spoke next. Recalling that Man Afraid of His Horse had refused the previous day to comment on the current investigation, Sitting Bull boldly challenged the elderly *itancan* to offer an opinion. "If there is anything that Red Cloud has said that you don't like, get up and speak," as the commissioners "have not come here for nothing." But the Hunkpatila chief remained reticent. George Hyde claims that many of the northern Oglalas still regarded Man Afraid of His Horse as their nominal head chief. Man Afraid, Hyde writes, was upset that Saville had failed to issue him the extra rations a head chief required to feed and entertain those who came to his lodge. He therefore used silence to demonstrate his displeasure.[46]

Chairman Fletcher broke the silence by inviting other Oglalas to speak. He explained that the Americans admired Red Cloud as a great warrior, wise man, and leader, but would be happy to hear from others if they had anything to contribute. After another pause, Little Wound offered a few words on behalf of his old friend Man Afraid, who surely felt his words were worthless, as the Americans had always respected Red Cloud's opinions more than his. Little Wound stated that the Oglalas did indeed lack adequate supplies, especially warm blankets and canvas cloth for their lodges. The days of the great communal buffalo hunts were slipping away, and as his people had fewer skins from which to construct tipis, as many as two to three families were obliged to share a single lodge. Moreover, when the Oglalas relinquished their treaty rights to hunt along the Republican and Smoky Hill Rivers, they did not "expect to sell the ground; at least that was not told to us." His kinsfolk accepted the twenty-five-thousand-dollar compensation mainly because they could not prevent American hunters from recklessly slaughtering the buffalo merely for their tongues and hides. The Oglalas believed that if they accepted the money, the president would purchase horses, cows, and wagons for the benefit of their children. After Little Wound concluded his remarks, the commissioners decided to adjourn the council, convinced that it was not the best vehicle for continuing their investigation. But they did invite Red Cloud and several others to join them in closed session, where, presumably, fewer conflicting viewpoints would be presented.[47]

When the meeting broke up, Red Cloud, Sitting Bull, Scalp Face, Shoulder, Tall Lance, Scraper, Slow Bull, Fast Thunder, and Man Afraid of His Horse remained behind. Little Wound refused to attend this private gathering, which was dominated by prominent warriors, some of whom supported Saville and the recent abrogation of the Oglalas' hunting rights. Sitting Bull, head of the agency guard, represented the Lakotas while Red Cloud listened. In his opening remarks Sitting Bull spoke of Man Afraid of His Horse, who was present but still silent. The Hunkpatila *itancan* "is a man of sense," Sitting Bull began, in a more respectful tone. Man Afraid "used to be the brave man of the Sioux Nation; we used to follow him, and everybody under him used to follow him, and listened to what he said." But later many of the Oglalas called on Red Cloud to speak for them in negotiations with the Great Father's people. Red Cloud had repeatedly requested a new agent, but, Sitting Bull added, "this [does not] please us, we young men sitting in here now." He considered Saville a good man, but "just about the time he is trying to do something for us," the council elders such as Red Cloud and Little Wound tried "to throw him away." Red Cloud intended to press for Saville's replacement, Sitting Bull continued, although the warrior members of the guard "don't know where he will find a better one."[48] The *itancan* and headmen were powerless to prevent some of the young men from enlisting in Saville's guard, and the agent's evolving status as a *wakiconza,* with an agenda the council elders often deemed disruptive, threatened what influence they could still muster among the warrior societies as a whole.

After completing their exhaustive investigation, the commissioners concluded that the food samples given Professor Marsh during his stay at the agency and the subsequent interviews with Red Cloud, Red Dog, and

Scalp Face in Washington yielded insufficient evidence to convict Saville of fraud and mismanagement. But the commissioners did deliver a scathing attack on the agent's character and demeanor. In their opinion Saville was "incompetent, weak, and vacillating," "unfit for the responsible position he occupies." Furthermore, the agent had "a nervous and irritable temperament, inordinate loquacity, undignified bearing and manners, a want of coolness and collectedness of mind, and of firmness and decision of character." Finally, the investigators recommended the dismissal of several government contractors, most notably J. W. L. Slavens, the pork merchant; J. H. Martin, the flour vendor; and D. J. McCann, the principal freighter for the Red Cloud Agency.[49]

The threat of war between the Lakota people and the United States had been building steadily, and while the investigation was under way at the Red Cloud Agency, Congress moved to acquire all or part of the Black Hills. On 18 June 1875 the secretary of the interior, with the president's permission, had appointed William Allison chairman of a commission authorized to secure American rights to the region of the Black Hills between the north and south forks of the Cheyenne River, and to an area of the Bighorn Mountains lying west of a line running roughly from the Niobrara to the Tongue River.[50]

While the Allison commission prepared itself, Saville endeavored once more to open the lines of communication with the nonagency bands. Messengers returned in mid-August, having contacted on the Tongue River a very large intertribal encampment of nearly two thousand lodges of northern Oglalas, Miniconjous, Hunkpapas, Sans Arcs, Northern Cheyennes, and Arapahos. These people were all too aware of the events transpiring in the Black Hills, and the runners reported that they were "much divided in their councils" concerning the fate of the sacred Paha Sapa. Many Bears of the Sans Arcs and the Miniconjou Many Ground Squirrels—followers of the Hunkpapa spiritual leader Sitting Bull— flatly rejected all invitations to bargain with the Americans. The Cheyennes, however, along with the followers of Little Big Man (an Oglala *blotahunka* and a close friend of Crazy Horse), did plan to attend the grand council. Neither Crazy Horse nor Black Twin sent word, but for some reason Saville was led to believe that the two would "agree to any treaty" signed by the agency Lakotas.[51]

When Allison and his colleagues reached the vicinity of the Red Cloud Agency they discovered that the Oglalas and the Upper Brulés of the

Spotted Tail Agency were arguing over where the formal sessions should be held. The Oglalas wanted all meetings convened at their agency, whereas the Brulés insisted that all participants should assemble at Chadron Creek, about twenty-five miles equidistant from the Red Cloud and Spotted Tail Agencies. So bitterly did the Lakotas dispute the location of the scheduled meetings that the commissioners began to wonder if negotiations would ever commence. Eventually, on 17 September, a spot was selected on an open plain directly north of Crow Butte on the White River, approximately eight miles from the Red Cloud Agency.[52]

Before embarking on their mission to the Lakotas, the Allison commission had been instructed to honor the 1868 Fort Laramie treaty, especially article 12, which required, for the purpose of concluding agreements with the United States, the consent of three-quarters of the adult Lakota male population. On 20 September, after greeting the Lakotas in the first of the several formal sessions, Chairman Allison outlined the purpose of the visit: "We have now to ask you if you are willing to give our people the right to mine in the Black Hills, as long as gold or other valuable metals are found, for a fair and just sum. If you are so willing, we will make a bargain with you for this right. When the gold and other valuable minerals are taken away, the country will again be yours to dispose of in any manner you wish." The Great Father, Allison continued, only desired peace with the Lakotas and their relatives and friends, the Dakotas, Cheyennes, and Arapahoes, and hoped they would approve this agreement with his people.

No sooner had Allison concluded his prefatory comments than had Red Cloud found a way to disrupt the meeting. The Bad Face *itancan* had earlier refused to attend this council, apparently displeased with the chosen site, but Red Dog brought a brief message from him stating that, as so many different *tiyospaye* had gathered, it would take at least seven days for all the autonomous band councils to discuss the issues in private before rescheduling the general assembly. The majority of the delegates agreed with Red Cloud, and, accompanied by their families, soon left the council arena, except for twelve members of the Tokala warrior society who served as *akicita*, or "policemen," of the council camp.[53]

Two opposing groups among the Sioux and their allies emerged during the closed sessions. The larger one consented to lease the mineral rights for Paha Sapa for what the commissioners considered an exorbitant sum of money, whereas the smaller group, composed mostly of young warriors, rejected all American offers.

In the hope of expediting matters, the commissioners pressed the councilors to announce their decisions, only to learn that by the twenty-sixth, convinced that no mutually satisfactory agreement could or should be made with the United States, at least half of the *itancan,* headmen, and warriors from all the bands had left the council grounds. However, the Lakota band chiefs Red Dog of the Oyuhpes, Red Cloud of the Bad Faces, Lone Horn of the Miniconjous, and Spotted Tail of the Brulés, along with other Lakotas, promised to attend another conference to be held at the Red Cloud Agency.

For the next three days the representatives delivered their carefully rehearsed speeches, which the commissioners judged "a mixture of complaints and demands, the latter of so extraordinary a character as to make it manifest that it was useless to continue the negotiations." Red Dog summarized the Lakota position, stating that his kinsfolk expected rations and supplies "for seven generations to come" if they approved the Great Father's agreement. One by one, other spokesmen issued their demands. High on their lists were guns, ammunition, horses, cattle, oxen, wagons, clothes, tobacco, knives, and food—in short, as Little Bear added, "a great deal more than we get now." Spotted Tail announced that the delegates expected $7 million for permitting mining in the Black Hills, a figure large enough to earn sufficient interest on which all the bands could live comfortably throughout the coming years. In addition, the Brulé *itancan* reminded the commissioners to state in writing the exact sum of money they were prepared to offer for the Black Hills, along with the government's payment plan.

Allison and his colleagues were astounded. They had come prepared to engage in lively, even heated debates with the councilors, but they had not anticipated haggling with the Lakotas. Indeed, the native spokesmen appeared anything but cowed by the Great Father's representatives. "Now, beware, and be lively," Stabber told the commissioners, "and don't be discouraged." Stabber expected them "to try and give us as many millions as we have asked for the hills," for "we know that those hills will support us for generations to come." Crow Feather was also unimpressed by the power of the American government and the president of the United States. "I never call anybody our Great Father but" the Great Mystery, he stated. The *tiyospaye* chiefs had honored their responsibilities to provide for their followers' welfare by requesting support for all bands for seven future generations, and Crow Feather hoped that the president would "not be so stingy with his money as not to grant" their wishes. Crazy

Horse's close friend, Little Big Man, who had recently arrived from the north, also spoke, but in more threatening tones. "My heart is bad," he cautioned the commissioners, "and [I] have come from Sitting Bull to kill a white man."[54]

With the delegates' demands and stinging words ringing in their ears, the Allison commission submitted its final proposal. If the Lakotas and their allies permitted American prospectors to mine gold in the Black Hills, the president would pay the bands a combined total of $100,000 per year, with the added stipulation that he could terminate the agreement at any time after giving two years' notice. However, if the Lakotas and their allies wished to sell the disputed land outright for $6 million, the president would deposit the money in a special fund to finance their annual subsistence and educational expenditures.

When the commissioners departed Lakota country without a satisfactory agreement, they left behind uncertainty, confusion, and resentment. Many Lakota councilors, especially the warriors, had stormed out of the proceedings angry with the Americans' attempts to acquire the sacred Black Hills and disgusted with some of their relatives for putting a price on the land. By this time at least one thousand miners had staked out claims in the hills, establishing mining associations for mutual aid and protection. As reports listing illegal mining activities continued to pour in, Secretary of War W. W. Belknap was forced to conclude that the young fighting men would soon take up arms to protect their unceded land.[55]

In mid-October Saville observed that many Oglala warriors were leaving the agency, heading northward, but he did not believe they intended to join the northern war faction. Buffalo had been sighted crossing the Yellowstone River and moving slowly toward the Tongue River, and as the young men's families were still in camp near the agency, Saville presumed the warriors had left simply to hunt. The agent was otherwise busy compiling the annual census, and although the *itancan* and headmen had started to rehash old complaints, he considered them more cooperative and amiable than on previous occasions.[56]

Lieutenant General Sheridan and Brigadier General Sherman disagreed, almost pro forma, with Saville's assessment of agency affairs. The generals, along with U.S. Inspector E. C. Watkins, who visited the Lakota agencies in early November, speculated that many of the warriors did indeed plan to fortify the northern bands, and that the fate of the reservation policy rested on the War Department's ability to destroy the Lakotas' military strength. In December, Commissioner Smith requested that all fed-

eral agents for the Lakotas, Northern Cheyennes, and Arapahos immediately notify the numerous bands that they must report to their respective agencies by 1 January 1876. Those who failed to obey the order would
be considered hostile by the U.S. Army.[57]

As the deadline approached, James Hastings made preparations to replace Saville, who had resigned his post shortly after he had been accused
of corruption. When Commissioner Smith directed Hastings to prohibit
the sale of arms and ammunition to the Oglalas, the new agent balked, insisting that, contrary to the sensational articles printed by local newspaper
editors, the Lakotas were "perfectly quiet and have evinced no disposition
to be otherwise." Banning the sale of weapons at this time, Hastings protested, would only make it difficult for the young men to kill the live cattle
delivered to the Red Cloud Agency as part of the Oglalas' food ration. Instead, licensed traders should be permitted to sell arms and ammunition
in limited quantities, a proposal that the Indian Department quickly
rejected.[58]

In late January, Hastings was delighted to telegraph Commissioner
Smith that Black Twin and Crazy Horse, prominent leaders of the Oglala
war faction, along with three to four thousand supporters, had been spotted moving toward the Red Cloud Agency. Their progress was difficult
due to deep snow and freezing temperatures, but scouts sent word that
they were presently encamped somewhere in the vicinity of Bear Butte,
one hundred miles from the agency. The last report relayed that the followers of Sitting Bull the Hunkpapa were heading for the Yellowstone
River country, but few details were forthcoming. But like his predecessors, Hastings would never see Black Twin and Crazy Horse, who rejected
peace with the United States. By the end of the following month, however, over one thousand Lakotas from other *tiyospaye* had arrived at the
Red Cloud Agency in compliance with federal orders. Although relieved
to see them, Hastings informed the commissioner that food supplies were
now so low that the warehouse contained only one issue of bacon, flour,
and sugar.[59]

By the summer of 1876 estimates of the war faction's strength ranged
from over two thousand to nine thousand Lakota, Cheyenne, and Arapaho fighting men. Valentine McGillycuddy, an army surgeon who served
with a cavalry reconnaisance unit in the Black Hills during the mid-1870s,
stated vaguely that half of the young male population from all Lakota
agencies moved to the war camps during 1876, but how many of these

were warriors from the Red Cloud Agency is unknown.[60] Nor can one accurately assess the opinions of all the agency *itancan* and headmen concerning the impending war with the United States; but certainly, as on previous occasions, the council elders could not prevent the young men from fighting if they so wished.

# CHAPTER SEVEN

# Going Home to Pine Ridge: The Resiliency of the Oglala Multiband Council, 1876–1879

The battle of the Little Bighorn, the climactic conflict of the 1876 war between the Lakotas and the United States, has spawned an entire historiography. Countless publications have appeared over the years, a number devoted to the now legendary statures of George Armstrong Custer and his nemesis Crazy Horse.[1] Moreover, the Battle of the Little Bighorn, a symbol of defeat for a United States celebrating its centennial, had a profound impact on the continuing political and diplomatic relations between the Oglala people and the United States. Within weeks after the last shot was fired at the Little Bighorn battleground, Congress issued a directive ordering federal agents to withhold rations until the Lakotas relinquished the Black Hills country. The Office of Indian Affairs also stepped up its efforts to settle the Oglalas and other Lakotas at agencies on the Missouri River. Furthermore, the death of Crazy Horse and the surrender of the pro-war camps marked another major turning point in the history of the Oglala people. Even though they did not always share their feelings with federal Indian agents, many Oglala councilors surely questioned their war leaders' abilities to protect the *tiyospaye* from external threats.

From the end of 1876 to the establishment of the Pine Ridge Reservation just over two years later, the Oglalas endured one of the most critical periods in their history, marked by the Americans' theft of the Black Hills, the unsettling appearance of the last of the pro-war Lakotas among their camps, and the uncertain future of the Oglala agency itself. But if waging a protracted war with the United States was becoming less than a viable strategy, what paths should the multiband councilors now take to prevent losing all control of their followers' welfare during these difficult years?

On 14 August 1876 the president of the United States appointed George Manypenny chairman of a commmission authorized to recommence negotiations for the acquisition of the Black Hills.[2] After preliminary talks with the commissioners on 7 September, the Oglalas withdrew to Chadron Creek, where the various camps discussed yielding this sacred land. The following week Little Wound notified Manypenny that the Oglala multiband council would conduct business with him and his colleagues shortly. "Our councils may not seem of much importance to you," the Kiyuksa *itancan* told Commissioner Manypenny, "but to us it seems a very serious matter to give up our country. You must have patience and bear with us."[3]

By the nineteenth the Oglalas were ready to proceed. Speaking for the council were the *itancan* Red Cloud, Red Dog, Little Wound, Man Afraid of His Horse, Young Man Afraid, and American Horse, all of whom had pledged by virtue of their status and role as *itancan* and head shirtwearers to consider carefully the future welfare of their followers. It was immediately apparent that the rather hurried camp councils on Chadron Creek had failed to produce a consensus. Red Cloud mentioned that the Oglalas might be prepared to cede the Black Hills (Paha Sapa) to the United States, and that a few Bad Face camp *akicita* would visit the Indian Territory to assess its potential as a possible home for the Oglalas. Young Man Afraid of His Horse announced, however, that he would not consider parting with the Black Hills until he had spoken with the president himself. Furthermore, most of the warriors refused to be hurried or intimidated into signing any document with the United States.

Believing that some of the *itancan,* headmen, and head shirtwearers were proceeding too hastily, the Oglala *blotahunka* Sitting Bull rushed into the council ground brandishing a club with three knives attached, a revolver, and a Winchester rifle. He yelled that the Oglalas would never move to the Indian Territory, and that nothing as important as ceding the Black Hills could be decided without consulting their northern relatives, most of whom were not in attendance. The *itancan* White Bird opposed Sitting Bull's actions, but the warrior continued to harangue the councilors, ordering them to leave the stockade. Most complied, anxious not to provoke Sitting Bull, who had hurried White Bird out of the enclosure by striking him with the flat side of his club.[4] Under most circumstances, beating an elderly *itancan* before his followers was a disrespectful act. But Oglala political customs provided for a crisis such as the impending loss of the Black Hills by granting significant "police" powers to the roles of *blotahunka* and *akicita.*

Hoping to weaken the influence of the younger men, which was still considerable in the multiband councils, the commissioners informed the elders the following day that they expected a "chief" and two headmen from each band to sign the Black Hills agreement that afternoon.[5] Lt. O. Elting, interim agent at the Red Cloud Agency, had already wired the commissioner of Indian affairs that there were "no supplies on hand except corn," and the *itancan* and headmen feared that the families would lose the rest of their rations if they did not acquiesce to the commissioners' orders. Therefore, with great trepidation, many of the most prominent *itancan* and headmen eventually came forward to "scratch the paper," but not before offering brief remarks on the proceedings. Little Wound hoped that the president would provide for his relatives' welfare, and intended to visit the White House in order to "finish the business with him." Young Man Afraid of His Horse spoke defiantly before placing his mark on the paper. He rejected the notion of becoming a farmer, calling on the president and his successors to sustain the Oglalas for at least one hundred years. Shamed and humiliated, Fire Thunder actually covered his eyes before signing the document; Crow Feather refused outright.[6]

From the outset there is some indication that the Oglalas did not fully understand the terms of the agreement; Red Cloud, for example, later contended that he was unaware that he was negotiating a land cession. Most importantly, the band *itancan* and headmen who signed the agreement did not comprise three quarters of the adult male population, whose consent was required, under article 12 of the 1868 treaty, in any future negotiations with the Lakota people. Despite this fact, the United States formally seized possession of the Black Hills in February 1877, claiming that the Lakota people had ceded it under the 1876 Black Hills Agreement. When the commissioners had departed, a small Oglala contingent, led by Red Dog and Young Man Afraid of His Horse, prepared to visit the president to air their grievances concerning the Black Hills councils. Red Cloud declined to go on this occasion, however, explaining that his *tiyospaye* needed his guidance and protection.[7]

After Custer's defeat, the Red Cloud and Red Leaf villages had withdrawn from the Red Cloud Agency to Chadron Creek. Believing that these bands were still allied with the northern war faction and therefore potentially dangerous, military commanders had recently ordered destroyed a number of lodges in these two camp circles.[8] In mid-October, Col. Ranald Mackenzie sent the interpreter William Garnett to inform Red Cloud and Red Leaf that all food supplies would be withheld if their people did not return to the agency. Red Cloud refused, and on 22 October, Mackenzie left Camp Robinson with eight companies of cavalry, reconnoitering with Maj. Frank North, his brother Luther, and forty-two Pawnee scouts. Four miles from Chadron Creek, Mackenzie divided his command, ordering Maj. George Gordon to lead one battalion and half of the Pawnee contingent to Red Leaf's village, and Capt. Clarence Mauck, with the remaining twenty-one scouts, to Red Cloud's camp. Shortly before sunrise the two bands were surrounded, and troops quickly confiscated without resistance 722 horses, a few guns, and small quantities of ammunition. Brig. Gen. George Crook praised Mackenzie for his judicious handling of the incident, which represented for him the "first gleam of daylight we have had" during the 1876 war with the Lakotas.[9]

When the bands had returned to the agency, Crook requested all Oglala men to assemble within the agency stockade. The general announced that Red Cloud had betrayed the American government; consequently, officials would no longer recognize him as the "head chief" of the Sioux. As Crook considered Spotted Tail of the Brulés the "only important leader who has the nerve to be our friend," the general named him head chief instead. The Oglalas, and especially the Bad Faces, paid little attention to Crook's pronouncement, however.[10] In fact, the general's actions could well have bolstered Red Cloud's standing among the warriors, who saw the Bad Face leader's defiance as his own symbolic assault on American forces.

From the standpoint of the Department of War, the 1876 war against the Lakotas could not be officially closed until all bands had surrendered at the various agencies. By the end of the year the *tiyospaye* under Sitting Bull the Hunkpapa had crossed the U.S. border into Canada, but Crazy Horse's village still remained somewhere in the lower Yellowstone and Upper Tongue River country. Information gleaned from bands arriving at the agencies indicated that the remnants of Crazy Horse's pro-war group were themselves dividing. Those who now advocated peace were largely agency Lakotas who had temporarily joined Crazy Horse's followers after army officers confiscated their weapons and ponies. The Lakotas who desired to continue the war were mostly the *blotahunka* such as Crazy Horse, Little Big Man, and Big Road.[11]

Hunts the Enemy (later George Sword) and Few Tails set out to find Crazy Horse's village. The scouts took with them separate bundles of blue and red cloth containing gifts of tobacco to honor Crazy Horse and the other *blotahunka* Iron Hawk, Big Road, Little Hawk, He Dog, and Iron Crow. Opened packages would symbolize the smoking of the pipe and hence peace; but if the tobacco pouches were discarded or returned unopened, war would continue. Few Tails and Hunts the Enemy returned within a month, bringing with them several Oglalas from Crazy Horse's village who had opposed the camp council's decision to fight on.[12] Col. Nelson Miles eventually located Crazy Horse's band on 1 January, and a week later violence erupted as each side tried to overcome the other. After the engagement, which ended in an impasse, the Crazy Horse *tiyospaye*, which also included several Northern Cheyenne families, returned to the Little Bighorn valley, hungry, weary, and ill clad.[13]

Shortly after, Crook received news from scouts that the peace advocates within the village were continuing to recommend negotiations with the Americans. Crook asked Crazy Horse's maternal uncle, Spotted Tail, to visit his nephew to persuade the young man to forgo war. Spotted Tail agreed to Crook's request, but warned him that his nephew's followers would most likely reject the general's terms of unconditional surrender and relocation to the Missouri River. Crook would not modify his terms, however, but promised that the militant Lakotas could have an agency in the northern country, somewhere between the Black Hills and the Powder River. After careful consideration, Spotted Tail with several Oglalas departed around 12 February. When the travelers reached the northern camps, they were welcomed by the Oglala *blotahunka* No Water, who had opposed Crazy Horse's decision not to surrender. A council was immediately convened. Crazy Horse refused to attend but sent word through his father, Worm, that he would accept the consensus of the council. It was soon decided that each band *itancan* would lead his followers to the agencies, and on 5 April, after a fifty-day sojourn, Spotted Tail returned to Camp Sheridan with the news.[14]

During Spotted Tail's absence, Red Cloud and General Crook settled their personal grievances, and the Bad Face *itancan* agreed to assist Crook in escorting the northern Lakotas to the agencies. When the time came for Oglala scouts to approach Crazy Horse's *tiyospaye*, they spotted about seventy warriors assembled on a knoll awaiting their arrival. Suddenly, a youth from the village charged down the knoll, quickly followed by Black Fox, an *itancan* the Americans did not know who was "magnificently decked in war costume" and had a knife clenched between his teeth. Galloping toward the halted line of scouts and soldiers, he cried out: "I have been looking all my life to die; I see only the clouds and the ground; I am all scarred up." But as Black Fox advanced, head shirtwearer American Horse, who was in charge of the scouts, walked toward him holding a pipe in his outstretched hands. American Horse replied, "Think of the women and children behind you; come straight for the pipe; the pipe is yours." Black Fox yielded when he saw the peacemaker's pipe, and the two smoked in friendship, reforging their bonds to one another and affirming their connectedness to the Great Mystery. When Black Fox spoke again, he told the scouts that Crazy Horse had fled with his wife, who was gravely ill with tuberculosis. He had urged Crazy Horse to embrace peace, but when the young *blotahunka* left, Black Fox assumed the role of band *itancan* and protector of the camp. "I [had] come to die [for the village]," Black Fox added, "but you saved me." While Black Fox spoke, the warriors stationed behind him on the knoll continued to drill their horses in magnificent fashion until Black Fox called to them: "All over. Go back." American Horse then directed Black Fox to relocate the camp at the agency, while Lt. W. P. Clark, whom the Oglalas called White Hat, directed thirty scouts under No Flesh to pursue Crazy Horse.[15]

By May, Crazy Horse had decided to surrender with about nine hundred of his followers, two-thirds of them women and children. Appearing from the north, they headed toward the Laramie River and the Black Hills Road, three miles south of the Hat Creek stagecoach station. Red Cloud, who had earlier agreed to assist Crook, rode out with fifty scouts under American Horse and Lieutenant Rosecrans to greet Crazy Horse. When the young war leader, along with two hundred warriors, arrived, they presented a pony to Rosecrans and to each Oglala scout. After this brief ceremony, Crazy Horse shook hands with the lieutenant, which marked, according to William Garnett, the first time the *blotahunka* had touched the hand of an army officer. Lieutenant Clark also welcomed Crazy Horse, who gave him a pipe, a beaded tobacco pouch, a warbonnet, and a fringed shirt. Clark in turn honored Crazy Horse by immediately putting on the shirt and the headdress. The warriors then surrendered their weapons, and the rest of their ponies were given to the scouts. Finally, on 25 May, Crazy Horse's followers, including a number of Northern Cheyenne families, pledged peace, requesting an agency near Bear Butte in the Black Hills.[16]

After Crazy Horse's surrender, General Crook displayed good faith by supporting the Oglalas' desire to hunt and to put on a grand feast. Around 4 June, Young Man Afraid of His Horse suggested holding the festivities in the camp of the *blotahunka* Crazy Horse and Little Big Man, and James Irwin (the agent at Pine Ridge) promised to issue them three cattle along with some coffee and sugar. No one objected to these plans at this time, but Red Cloud and several other Bad Faces left the gathering at Irwin's office without uttering a word.[17]

That evening at ten o'clock a small group of Oglalas appeared at Irwin's quarters demanding to speak with him. The agent agreed, quickly summoning his interpreter. The visitors explained that they represented Red Cloud and several other agency band *itancan* who disapproved of the recent decision to organize the feast at Crazy Horse's village. These *itancan* were offended because Crazy Horse had refused to visit their camp circles, and they had no intentions of going to his lodge as "such action indicated a disposition to conciliate him." Moreover, the band *itancan* feared that Crazy Horse's popularity with the warriors would weaken the elders' efforts to maintain peace at the agency. Crazy Horse, many of the older leaders now believed, was an "unreconstructed" individual "only waiting for a favorable opportunity to leave the agency and never return." If the young war leader were permitted to hunt, the vistiors told Irwin, Crazy Horse and his warriors would take the ammunition furnished for the hunt and use it to renew hostilities. "He was tricky," they added, "unfaithful," and "very selfish as to the personal interests" of the Oglalas.[18]

Irwin concurred, later adding that Crazy Horse "has not been acting in good faith with the Army. He has all the time been silent—sullen—lordly and dictatorial and even with his own people and other bands of Sioux at this and Spotted Tail Agency." The *blotahunka* repeatedly demanded an agency in the Black Hills and refused to endorse receipts for the agency provisions allocated to his camp. Indeed, Crazy Horse's behavior, especially his unwillingness to accept food rations, signified his refusal to assume the role and status of an agency *itancan*. By July most of his hungry followers had drifted away to other agency *tiyospaye*.[19]

Despite Crazy Horse's request for an agency in the Black Hills, the Office of Indian Affairs decided to relocate all the Oglalas along the Missouri River. Not even the pleas of Irwin could move the commissioner. At the end of July the agent mailed a candid letter to the commissioner, stating his opinion that the Indian Department was mistreating the Oglalas. Irwin had been "determined to steel my heart against all sympathy" for the Oglala people, but "when I was called into their council and heard their simple tale of wrongs and their earnest appeal for the Government not to move them to the Missouri River where they would not live and as long as they were peaceable to let them stay where they are I could not help feeling that justice should not overreach itself in dealing with these troublesome people." Irwin suggested establishing agencies for the Oglalas and

Brulés near the mouth of the south fork of the White Earth River, describing the terrain there as magnificent, with broad and fertile valleys containing a good water supply, ample stands of oak and pine trees, and abundant grass. This was an area that the agent believed was especially suitable for cultivation.[20]

On 1 September over eight hundred Oglala men attended a grand assembly to discuss the Indian Office's policy and the ongoing repercussions of Crazy Horse's presence at the agency. All the most prominent agency *itancan* and headmen were present except Yellow Bear, who sent word to Irwin that "his mind was the same as of those" in attendance. American Horse took over from Red Cloud as the principal speaker for the multiband council. The agency *itancan*, headmen, and head warriors had been meeting almost daily to discuss what they considered to be Crazy Horse's antagonistic attitude. The elders, the head shirtwearer American Horse announced, had done their best to "quiet" Crazy Horse, hoping to "bring him into a better state of feeling" toward agency life. They regretted, however, that they could do "nothing with him," as "he had not attended our councils." Finally, American Horse announced that Oglala leaders had agreed to accept another agency anywhere on the White Earth River rather than to settle at the Missouri.[21]

After the council adjourned, General Crook decided to restrict the freedom of Crazy Horse and his followers. Assisted by band *itancan*, headmen, and young men of all the Oglala bands, the general placed a tight cordon around Crazy Horse's camp but failed to prevent him from escaping. Crazy Horse was later captured at the Spotted Tail Agency and brought back to Camp Robinson on the fifth.[22]

Shortly after his arrest, Crazy Horse was confined to the guardhouse, where he was fatally stabbed. Carrying him in a blood-soaked blanket, the head warriors Two Dogs and Red Shirt bore the critically injured leader to the Adjutant's office, where army surgeon Dr. Valentine McGillycuddy treated his wounds. Crazy Horse died shortly before midnight, his last words reported to have been, "Let me go; you've got me hurt now." When dawn broke, Crazy Horse's father, Worm, sat near his son's lifeless body; so, too, did the warrior's close friend, Touch the Clouds of the Miniconjous, who, placing his hand on the still chest of Crazy Horse, uttered, "It is good, he has looked for death, and it has come."[23]

The circumstances surrounding Crazy Horse's death remain controversial. Maj. H. R. Lemly contended that the Oglala war leader had been murdered by a bayonet-wielding officer of the guard. American Horse asserted, however, that the guardsman had unintentionally stabbed Crazy Horse when the warrior fell against the bayonet. Still others have suggested that Crazy Horse was accidentally stabbed with his own knife when Little Big Man, who himself sustained a deep cut, attempted to restrain him. According to Capt. John Bourke, Little Big Man claimed that Crazy Horse's death had been a tragic accident, but that Little Big Man had allowed the Oglalas to believe that the white soldier had killed Crazy Horse for fear that the *blotahunka*'s grieving family would retaliate against him.[24]

Crazy Horse has been considered the personification of Lakota military defiance—a man capable of inspiring warriors but also of alienating and even frightening his own people. By the time of Crazy Horse's death, American soldiers had retaliated for the defeats they suffered during the previous year. Furthermore, federal officials were threatening to starve the Oglalas and to resettle them along the Missouri River where they believed misfortune would befall them. What strategies remained for the Oglala councilors as they guided their people into a future fraught with uncertainty and fear?

Red Cloud, Young Man Afraid of His Horse, Three Bears, Little Wound, American Horse, Little Big Man, He Dog, Big Road, and Yellow Bear, along with the Brulé delegates, visited President Rutherford B. Hayes in late September 1877 to protest the relocation of the agencies to the Missouri River.[25] Fearing that whiskey peddlers and thieves who lived along the river would prey upon their kinsfolk, the spokesmen expressed their desire to remain either in their present location or at an agency near the Bighorn Mountains. In addition, Red Cloud asked for the Oglalas' provisions to be shipped back to their agency, because he feared that if they remained much longer at the Missouri River warehouse, "long tailed rats" (thieves) would "go into the boxes, and we would probably lose half of them." President Hayes thought the Lakotas had consented to resettle when they signed the Black Hills agreement, but as these spokesmen before him were unanimously opposed to the Missouri River site, he promised that their councils could select new locations for the agencies sometime in the spring. But until then the Lakotas would have to spend the winter on the Missouri, as he had already instructed the Office of Indian Affairs to divert supplies and rations from their old agencies to the river. In turn, the Oglala delegates assured the president that the elders would try to persuade the young warriors to accept the "decisions and promises" of the Great Father.[26]

At the end of October, Irwin informed Ezra Hayt, the newly appointed commissioner of Indian affairs, that General Crook expected the Oglalas to depart immediately for the Missouri River. The weather was already turning cold and winter storms would soon be upon them. The Oglalas lacked adequate transportation and the teams Crook ordered had still not arrived. Furthermore, the food rations were again seriously depleted and would not be replenished at the present Red Cloud Agency. Despite these difficulties, Irwin felt confident that the Oglalas could leave by the twenty-eighth, and he vowed to do his best to care for the women and children who already had little protection from the cold.[27]

The doctor's optimism faded by the first week of November, however. The Oglalas had traveled only sixty miles before frigid temperatures and deep snow drifts forced them to remain in camp. Irwin was so concerned about the shortage of food that he requested permission to purchase cattle from the ranching outfit Barker and Boster, which owned a small herd near the Missouri that could be driven westward to the winter village. The cattlemen agreed to provide beef but, much to the agent's dismay, demanded (and later received from the Indian Department) a monthly payment of fifty dollars for their services.[28]

By the end of November the Oglalas were within sixty miles of the Missouri River agency. All the agency bands had endured blizzards, short rations, and a constant barrage of threats and taunts from some of the northern Lakotas, who tried to prevent them from continuing their journey.[29]

The agency Oglalas were not submissive, however. When December came the councilors refused to resettle their followers at the Missouri River site. Irwin was told on the third to withhold rations and supplies until the Oglalas agreed to obey him, but the elders stood firm, forcing acting Indian Commissioner A. Bell to authorize the establishment of a winter village on the south fork of the White River, about sixty miles from the Missouri. But Bell still expected the family heads to haul their rations weekly from the Missouri agency warehouse, so the *wakiconza* of the winter camp appointed Little Big Man head *akicita* of those traveling to pick up the supplies. Valentine McGillycuddy, acting assistant surgeon for the U.S. Army, considered Bell's directive ludicrous, however, as it would keep the men "traveling all the time" in deep and drifting snow.[30]

Despite the hardship of hauling the rations from the Missouri River warehouse, Irwin agreed that the Oglalas should remain in the winter camp on the White River. Good timber and potable water were in short supply at the Missouri River location; besides, the agent believed that the Oglalas had already suffered enough. Brig. Gen. William Sherman disapproved of the decision, however, cautioning Secretary of War George McCrary that the Oglalas would simply interpret Bell's concession as a sign of weakness. Sherman expressed concern that the warriors were only subdued, not conquered, and that in his opinion the threat of war still lingered. Irwin threatened to resign should the general's views prevail, but Interior Department officials abided by their initial ruling to establish the White River encampment.[31]

The village remained peaceful until the second week of January 1878, at which time several northern Lakotas, including the Miniconjou *blotahunka* Touch the Clouds, organized a demonstration. When the agent visited the camp he found most of the agency Oglalas "considerably excited about the Northern Indians behaving so badly, fearing that they would be blamed," too. Moreover, news had been traveling around the lodges that some of the northern Lakotas had just left to join Sitting Bull the Hunkpapa, who had sought refuge in Canada. The *wakiconza* immediately offered to send some of the camp *akicita* in pursuit, a proposal that prompted Touch the Clouds to chastise the *wakiconza* for their "submissive" behavior. Irwin later reported, however, that the agency elders were "very proud of having done their part" in maintaining the peace.[32]

Irwin later discovered that the actions of a Miniconjou scout, Bull Eagle of the Cheyenne River Agency, had helped precipitate the ruckus. Several days earlier, Bull Eagle had received a pass from Maj. Charles Bartlett, the acting agent at Cheyenne River, to visit relatives at the Oglala winter village. Bull Eagle claimed that Bartlett granted him the pass because the major wished to learn from the scout how well Irwin was doing among the Oglalas. Bull Eagle mentioned that Shavings, a Northern Cheyenne warrior, had recently brought a message from Sitting Bull, urging his supporters among the agency Oglalas to help him plan another war against the United States. Although Bull Eagle later stated that he did not believe Shavings's story, the scout claimed that many of the Oglalas desired war and the destruction of the agencies.

Bull Eagle believed that Little Wound wanted a permanent home somewhere on the White River, but Red Cloud, whom the scout claimed was influenced by the *blotahunka* Big Road, preferred an agency on the Tongue River, as the warriors "could then get our supplies [for war] from that place." Bull Eagle told this story to Bartlett, adding that Irwin was instrumental in generating unrest in the winter village. Irwin responded by asserting repeatedly that the Oglalas were well disposed toward the United States, and that Bull Eagle had a reputation among the Oglalas for stirring up trouble. Nevertheless, Bartlett condemned the physician's alleged misconduct in a statement to the *Chicago Times*.[33]

The actions of Touch the Clouds and Bull Eagle prompted the band *itancan* and headmen to resume discussions on relocating the Oglala agency. Red Cloud had indeed suggested the Tongue River as a suitable site during the last Washington conference, but added that his followers would live along White Clay Creek if necessary. By the new year, signs of the old Bull Bear–Smoke division had become evident again. Many Bad Faces lobbied once more for an agency on the Tongue River, while the Kiyuksas openly opposed them, favoring instead White Clay Creek, a tributary of the White Earth River near the Nebraska border. When the councilors met in mid-February, Irwin reminded the Bad Face council that the president had already rejected a site on the Tongue River, claiming that the Lakotas had already ceded this part of their country to the United States. Much to Irwin's relief, the Bad Faces yielded and decided for the sake of consensus to accept the White River site, at least for the time being.[34]

Irwin was not familiar with the proposed location, but he had been told that it was "the most desirable place on the reservation," with fresh water and arable land. Some of the Oglalas had even hinted that they might like to begin farming if they could reach their new home by spring. Irwin was pleased to hear this and urged Commissioner Hayt not to reject the Oglalas' decisions, for if he should do so there would be "a great distrust and indignation on their part, and perhaps an attempt to go North, setting everything back for years to come."[35]

Irwin soon discovered, however, that bureau officials had made other plans for the Oglalas. While conducting business in New York, Commissioner Hayt transmitted instructions to Irwin through W. M. Lee, an aide at bureau headquarters in Washington, that the doctor should refrain from making any promises to the Oglalas or expressing his personal opinions in their councils. Moreover, the agent must prevent the bands from starting for White Clay Creek, as President Hayes had since ordered an official to examine other possible locations for the new Oglala agency. Irwin immediately assembled the councilors to inform them of the president's decision and the imminent arrival of J. H. Hammond, a U.S. Indian inspector, whose visit ultimately proved unproductive in fostering unity among the bands.[36]

By April, Red Dog of the Oyuhpes had grown weary of the impasse, and with the assistance of former Oglala agent James Daniels, sent a curt letter to the president. "You know how we have moved at the wish of the white man from the Platte River to the head of the White River," Red Dog's message began, "having our Agency changed two or three times and each time under promises in which [the Great Mystery] was called upon to witness the truth . . . that each time would be the last." The Og-lalas had listened to the president, and now their only wish was for a home in the region between Wounded Knee and White Clay Creeks. But should the incumbent president refuse to aid them, Red Dog cautioned, the Og-lala council would expect his predecessor "to send us back the papers [the Black Hills agreement] that we signed." Irwin begged the Oglalas to re-main calm, but Red Cloud took it upon himself to petition General Crook for his support, as the Great Father had obviously grown deaf.[37]

As the days wore on, Oglala leaders stepped up their demands for an agency on the White River. Their kinsfolk had been living on short ra-tions for some time and were now anxiously awaiting word from the pres-ident's office. Inspector Hammond sensed their frustration, reminding Hayt that "the force stationed at Red Cloud is inadequate to meet any troubles should such arise." Week after week came and went, and the agency wire service had fallen silent. Moreover, the bureau's tardiness had begun to try Irwin's patience, not to mention that of the Oglala council. On 7 May the agent dashed off a rather brusque letter to the commis-sioner wondering if it was not "asking too much that I should be in-formed" of his plans. The suspense of not knowing was "intolerable" to the Oglalas, Irwin continued, and "places me in an awkward situation, as I can tell them nothing." Irwin finally received news that Congress had passed the Indian Appropriation Bill on 20 June, authorizing the secre-tary of the interior to establish yet another special commission—the Stan-ley commission—to investigate the issue, but the agent quickly re-sponded that the Oglalas were by now "not in a mood to talk with any person or commission." When Irwin threatened once again to resign if the government did not honor its promises to the Oglalas, Hayt countered that the department was experiencing "more trouble with the Agent than with the Indians." Furthermore, the commissioner considered Irwin's "insinuation of bad faith" on the part of the bureau "simply insulting."[38]

The Stanley commission arrived in July to commence its investigation

among the Oglalas, and to recommend a permanent site for both the Oglala and Brulé agencies. Irwin hoped that its appearance would at least
"open the way for relief." The Stanley commission soon proposed resettling the Oglalas near Wounded Knee Creek, but a final decision had not
yet been made. Before the commissioners left to visit the suggested site,
James O'Beirne, a special agent employed by Hayt to supervise the relocation of the bands, mentioned to them a request he had received from Little Big Man, whom O'Beirne considered "one of the most influential"
leaders of the Oglalas. Little Big Man desired to pursue and bring back his
friend Big Road, who, with forty lodges of his relatives, had left to find
Sitting Bull; O'Beirne believed Little Big Man's suggestion warranted the
commissioners' immediate attention.[39]

The special agent remarked that everyone in Red Cloud's camp regarded Little Big Man "with respect if not awe," and although the Indian
Department still looked upon Red Cloud as the Oglalas' "directing
mind," O'Beirne thought that it was actually Little Big Man, along with
Young Man Afraid of His Horse and Three Bears, who represented "the
leadership of the Sioux." O'Beirne's reasons for naming these men are unclear. Little Big Man was a noted war leader and ally of Crazy Horse, thus
his reputation may have garnered for him the attention and support of the
warriors and their families. Young Man Afraid of His Horse was an important head shirtwearer and the son of the nominal head chief of the Oglalas. However, such high status would not correspondingly bestow upon
him any more decision-making authority that was customarily permitted.
Three Bears was a headman, or possibly a *tiyospaye itancan,* who helped to
organize scouts during the search for Crazy Horse. While American officials no doubt appreciated his efforts, it is difficult to see how Three Bears
commanded any more authority among his own people than leaders such
as Red Cloud, Little Wound, and Red Dog. O'Beirne argued that if officials slighted Little Big Man at a time when he stood poised to embrace
agency life, future peace might be jeopardized. Lt. Gen. Philip Sheridan
questioned Little Big Man's sincerity, however, suggesting that his request was simply an excuse to relay information on agency affairs to the
Sitting Bull village.[40]

Little Big Man later tried again, with O'Beirne's support, to obtain
permission to pursue Big Road. The special agent argued that if the commissioner would only approve Little Big Man's request, the Oglala *blotahunka* would come to trust the government, and perhaps one day might
prove "of great assistance in keeping the factions of turbulent spirits in a

condition of peace, and good behavior." Moreover, O'Beirne believed that Little Big Man would eventually become "one of the best and most reliable of the" former war leaders.[41]

O'Beirne and Irwin had every reason to be concerned about the mood of the Oglalas. Commissioner Hayt seemed trapped in a web of indecision. He acknowledged O'Beirne's recommendations but still seemed unable unable to resolve the dilemma regarding the agency's new and presumably permanent location. By the end of August the councilors, especially the band *itancan* and headmen, were on the verge of taking matters into their own hands without regard for the consequences. Not only were the councilors displeased, having endured a harsh winter with food shortages, inadequate clothing, internal dissension, and general uncertainty, they were also "suspicious of the delay, and would not promise to remain quiet." Most Oglalas were now determined to move the two hundred miles west to White Clay Creek despite a lack of essential transportation and food supplies. Moreover, Irwin realized that he was losing control of the situation when the *wakiconza* began organizing the lodges into a caravan, commanding the camp *akicita* to control the people, "by force" if necessary.[42]

Irwin estimated that the westward trek to White Clay Creek would take at least forty days. Deciding that nothing would be accomplished by pleading with the commissioner, who had threatened to dismiss him rather than accept his resignation, Irwin contacted Secretary of the Interior Carl Schurz. The agent wrote candidly that "winter will shortly be upon us, and to repeat the frightful experiment of the last winter in moving six thousand destitute people at such a season, when the judgment of the world will be that they could and should have been moved before the cold weather, is an urgent reason for immediate action, independent of common humanity."[43] In Irwin's opinion the commissioner had simply been stalling for time by insisting that bureau employees erect a warehouse for the incoming supplies at the site of the new agency before dispatching transportation teams to the Oglalas' temporary encampment. The agent deemed this ruling preposterous, explaining to Secretary Schurz that he and his staff could easily live in huts and tents until houses were constructed. In the meantime, tarpaulins would protect the supplies. Furthermore, Irwin was incensed by one of Hayt's recent comments that it was the Oglalas' duty to "preserve order and keep their promises." These Lakota people, Irwin reminded the secretary, had been most patient and tolerant throughout.[44]

What actually shocked the agent the most, however, was Commissioner Hayt's suggestion that perhaps the Oglalas should remain near the Missouri River after all. Irwin had repeatedly promised the Oglalas that the president and the secretary of the interior would not "sell them out." But it was now obvious in Irwin's mind that Hayt was "running the agency," and was more concerned with protecting his own government's interests than those of "the helpless creatures" who regarded Irwin as "their agent and friend."[45]

The Oglala councilors were anything but helpless. By 19 September they all agreed to move the bands as best as they could, planning to leave for White Clay Creek within two days. Irwin notified Hayt that no one should attempt to stop them, for they were "not now to be trifled with"— a remark that Hayt deemed illustrative of the agent's "want of loyalty" to the government and "a want of heartiness in its service."[46]

Traveling ahead of the main Oglala caravan, Red Cloud, his brother Spider, Little Wound, Red Dog, and No Flesh reached White Clay Creek on the 8 October, where they waited for the rest of their kinsfolk, expected to arrive during the following week. In the meantime, the *itancan* and headmen contacted James O'Beirne (who had departed even earlier than the Oglalas), thanking him for whatever preliminary arrangements he had been able to make on their behalf.[47]

Irwin arrived with his family a few weeks later only to discover that there was no beef fit for issue, and that the Oglalas' supplies had not been shipped from the Missouri River warehouse to the new agency. Furthermore, the railroad companies refused to cooperate with the Indian Department, forcing agency employees to borrow old and rotten wagons from Camp Robinson. O'Beirne blamed Irwin for the "terrible mismanagement" of the agency and transportation teams even though the agent had repeatedly pleaded for instructions from his superiors.[48]

Snow began falling and temperatures plummeted, but although the Oglalas had endured months of interminable delays, hunger, and a shortage of clothing, they had succeeded in moving their camps away from the Missouri River and in remaining on good terms with Irwin and his colleagues. O'Beirne continued to supervise building construction at the new agency, renamed Pine Ridge, suggesting that Red Cloud, the Americans' "head chief," had at last fallen out of favor with the Office of Indian Affairs.[49]

In February, Red Dog, Little Wound, Red Cloud, Lone Bear, and other *itancan* and headmen received invitations to attend a ceremony celebrating the founding of the agency schoolhouse. O'Beirne was especially delighted to hear that Red Cloud had consented to participate in the laying of the cornerstone, believing that this symbolized the *itancan*'s acceptance of a new way of life and a "triumph quietly effected over his haughty disposition." But as Red Cloud placed a gold ring inside the box that would be buried beneath the cornerstone of the Pine Ridge schoolhouse, he invoked the guidance of the Great Mystery to "put it into the hearts of the white man not to disturb us in our present home, but to remain here in peace" at last.[50]

# Afterword

Throughout the years from the death of Bull Bear in 1841 to the establishment of the Pine Ridge Agency in the winter of 1878, the U.S. government endeavored to modify the political customs of the Oglala people and to weaken the influence of their leaders. The broadly applied accultura-tionist policies of the federal government failed, however, to destroy Oglala political customs, whose fluid and adaptable nature afforded the Oglalas the means and strength to cope with external threats to *tiyospaye* and subtribal autonomy.

Both the *tiyospaye* and especially the multiband councils, which became more commonplace as the bands assembled to discuss various strategies for dealing with the growing American presence in their country, continued to recognize all the roles associated with the various forms of Oglala leadership. Ideally, councilors desired to reach a consensus on all issues raised before them, a deliberate and formal process sometimes requiring days or even weeks to achieve, if at all. Depending on the circumstances, however, decision-making authority could flow to and from any one of several types of leadership positions, such as the *wakiconza* (camp administrators), the *akicita* (the enforcers of decisions), the *blotahunka* (war party leaders), the *zuya wicasa* (warriors), the headmen, holy men, head shirtwearers, and band *itancan,* or chiefs. During periods of perceived crisis, for example, Oglala political customs permitted decision-making authority to shift when necessary from noncombatant leaders to the *blotahunka* and their warriors. Moreover, the *wakiconza* and their hand-picked *akicita* moved the villages more often during wartime in order to keep them out of harm's way. Under these circumstances, decisions reached through council consensus frequently yielded to the immediate commands of the *blotahunka, wakiconza,* and *akicita.* It must be remembered, however, that the decision-making authority of these leaders was circumscribed by the occasion, and did not symbolize radical or permanent modifications in the political customs of the Oglalas.

This is not to suggest that the Oglalas' political customs were destined never to change. When the Oglala people began to settle down at Pine Ridge, the old band structure gave way to the more static district organization. Around 1891 these reservation districts selected their own delegates to participate in a loosely organized political body called the Oglala Council. The 1868 Treaty of Fort Laramie provided that all binding decisions made by the Oglalas required the consent of three-quarters of the adult males. When the Oglala Council was formed, this three-quarters majority rule became the model for all subsequent decisions. Over the years, however, the Pine Ridge superintendent played a major supervisory role over the council's organization and activities. Permitted to assemble only at the superintendent's discretion, the council was convened very infrequently and by 1920 was defunct.

The Oglalas tried to resurrect the concept of a tribal council in the mid-1920s, most notably the three-quarters majority rule council, or *okaspe yamni*.[1] Some traditional practices did continue. For example, all adult Oglalas were permitted to speak in council meetings. Furthermore, the council delegates, chosen by the people from the various reservation districts, continued to view themselves as "word carriers," individuals whose primary task was to present the opinions of their respective districts. However, the Oglalas still did not have an elective council that was officially recognized by the federal government. Thus in 1928 the Pine Ridge superintendent appointed three delegates from each of the seven districts to serve two-year terms on the Council of Twenty-one, often referred to as the Big Council. Oglala leaders drafted their own constitution, but the Bureau of Indian Affairs promptly restructured it, vastly undermining the council's decision-making authority. Federal recognition of the Council of Twenty-one did not prevent the old three-quarters majority rule council from assembling, however, nor from opposing the activities of the Council of Twenty-one.

In 1923 former social worker and Indian rights activist John Collier organized the American Indian Defense Association to promote reform in federal Indian policy. A decade later, Collier, acting in the capacity of commissioner of Indian affairs, drafted the Indian Reorganization Bill which advocated, among several things, the reversal of the allotment policy and the establishment of new tribal governments with the power to write constitutions and bylaws. With the exception of the Crow Creek and Sisseton Sioux, all the Lakotas approved the Indian Reorganization Act's provisions for establishing tribal governments, although the Oglalas accepted self-government by the narrowest of margins. Under the 1934 legislation, political officers, such as the president and the vice president, were now to be elected by the tribe. Thus in just over sixty years the old customs of making decisions by consensus had given way to political campaigns, elections, and committees. But during the timeframe selected for this present study—1841 to 1879—interactions with Americans did not drastically alter the remarkable fluidity of Oglala political customs.

Federal emissaries attempted, with little success, to create among the Oglalas "head chiefs"—a title that Americans hoped would grant those men selected the right to make unilateral decisions binding on not only the Oglalas but on the Lakota people as a whole. Moreover, federal officials anticipated that the appointment of head chiefs would eventually undermine the significant influence of the young warriors in council meetings and *tiyospaye* affairs. At the Horse Creek assembly of 1851, treaty commissioners selected Conquering Bear as the "head chief of the Sioux"; and in the wake of the 1868 Fort Laramie treaty proceedings, Americans bestowed the same title on the esteemed war leader Red Cloud, with whom they erroneously believed they must negotiate if peace were to be obtained and preserved between the Lakotas and the United States.

By the late 1860s Red Cloud of the Bad Face Oglalas was approaching his midforties, a time of life when most distinguished *blotahunka* had made the transition to council elder. Red Cloud, however, still maintained the support of many prominent warriors who admired his superb talents for war. Indeed, by 1867 Red Cloud claimed an estimated following of 250 lodges, mostly young warriors and their families, representing a constituency as large as that of the prominent Oglala *itancan* Man Afraid of His Horse. During this period Red Cloud's supporters recognized him as a war leader, committed to removing the American presence from the Powder River hunting grounds but not as a band *itancan*. Bad Face, son of Smoke and father of Woman's Dress, retained the status of *itancan* among the band that bore his name, even if his own following had dwindled by this time. Although Red Cloud's decision-making authority as a *blotahunka* might have been quite extensive during the war years of the late 1860s, it was nevertheless temporary and always bound by Oglala customs. Red Cloud cared deeply about the future of the Oglala people, and eventually the agency Bad Faces honored him as their *itancan*, but the decision-making authority he wielded in the preagency period scarcely resembled the degree of political power that Americans had come to associate with their concept of a "head chief." An Oglala *itancan* bore the responsibility of providing for his *tiyospaye*, ensuring, among many duties, that food and supplies were adequately and fairly distributed to all of his "children." The *itancan* whom the Oglalas recognized were highly esteemed as their people's protectors, but such status did not empower them to control their followers at will. Individuals who disagreed with the actions or opinions of their *itancan* were free to recognize another man as their chief or to leave their *tiyospaye* to follow another. When Crazy Horse came into the agency, for instance, his unwillingness to accept government rations to feed his followers—thereby fulfilling the customary role of an *itancan*—forced many of them to abandon him for other *tiyospaye* leaders.

When the Great Sioux Reservation was established by the provisions of the 1868 Treaty of Fort Laramie, ongoing negotiations with the United States brought into sharper focus for the agency Oglalas the necessity of selecting men capable and willing to represent the viewpoints of their multiband councils. By 1870, Red Cloud's status among his own people had changed from that of *blotahunka* to Bad Face headman, the senior male of his extended family. Moreover, as federal emissaries usually insisted on speaking with Red Cloud, their head chief, during formal assemblies, the Bad Face leader came to assume the role of primary council spokesman for the protreaty Oglalas, and also that of a Washington delegate.

This transition presented Red Cloud with a significant personal dilemma. After he agreed to peace with the United States he found himself struggling to acquire rations for the camps—and weapons and ammunition for the many warriors who had since changed their allegiance from him to the younger *blotahunka* Crazy Horse, Black Twin, Big Road, Touch the Clouds, and Little Big Man—while at the same time negotiating with those Americans still intent on viewing him as the Lakotas' supreme authority. Furthermore, Red Cloud had many influential peers in both the agency and war camps—a fact that employees of the Office of Indian Affairs often overlooked. On several occasions Red Cloud desired to impress the war leader Black Twin of the pro-war Bad Faces and deferred to the hereditary *itancan* Little Wound of the Kiyuksas and the Hunkpatila Oglala Man Afraid of His Horse. Moreover, it was the Oyuhpe *itancan* Red Dog, not Red Cloud, who initiated the relocation of the Red Cloud Agency to White River in the spring of 1872.

Intense factionalism existed at times in Oglala society, most notably in the wake of Bull Bear's murder in 1841, during the years of sustained warfare with the United States when the Oglalas divided into pro- and anti-war *tiyospaye,* and also after the founding of the Red Cloud Agency. Such factionalism, however, did not render the Oglala people entirely helpless, docile, or politically dependent. Although the councilors who pursued diplomatic accords with American officials at the Red Cloud Agency respected the right of their kinsfolk, especially the young men, to join the war villages whenever they felt compelled to do so, they did not consider themselves subordinate to the Indian agents. Indeed, even when the shortage of food and other necessary supplies finally forced Crazy Horse, Big Road, and other *blotahunka* to surrender after the 1876 campaign closed, at the same time leaving the agency Oglalas fearful that the Great Father would also try to starve them, Oglala councilors took matters into their own hands. Fulfilling their responsibilities to the camp circles, Oglala leaders moved their respective *tiyospaye* away from the Missouri River, which they had long considered an undesirable location, to a new home at the Pine Ridge Agency. Increasingly obliged after 1877 to plead with the American government to provide adequate rations, clothing, and transportation for their followers, Oglala leaders, regardless of their political role and status, never permitted personal feelings of frustration, anger, or humiliation to erode their dignity or jeopardize the welfare of their families.

# List of Abbreviations

AGO1     Records of the Adjutant General's Office. Record Group 94. Selected Letters Received by the Office of the Adjutant General (Main Series), 1822–1860. Microfilm M567. NARS.

AGO2     Records of the Adjutant General's Office. Record Group 94. Selected Letters Received by the Office of the Adjutant General (Main Series), 1861–1870. Microfilm M619. NARS.

AGO3     Records of the Adjutant General's Office. Record Group 94. Selected Letters Received by the Office of the Adjutant General (Main Series), 1871–1880. Microfilm M666. NARS.

ARCIA     Annual Report of the Commissioner of Indian Affairs.

ARSI     Annual Report of the Secretary of the Interior.

ARSW     Annual Report of the Secretary of War.

BIA     Records of the Bureau of Indian Affairs.

BIAM     BIA. Record Group 75. General Records. General Correspondence: Copies of Miscellaneous Correspondence Received, 1871–1879. NARS-KC.

DDL     Records of United States Army Continental Commands. Record Group 393. Department of Dakota, Headquarters Records, General Records, and Correspondence: Letters Received Relating to the Sioux Indians, 1863–1876. NARS.

DDT     Records of United States Army Continental Commands. Record Group 393. Department of Dakota, Headquarters Records, General Records, and Correspondence: Selected Telegrams Received, 1872–1877. NARS.

DM     Records of United States Army Continental Commands. Record Group 393. Military Division of the Missouri, General Records and Correspondence. Special Files of Letters Received, 1863–1885. Microfilm 1495. NARS.

DP     Records of United States Army Continental Commands. Record Group 393. Department of the Platte, Headquarters Records, General Records, and Correspondence, 1866–1880. NARS.

DS        BIA. Record Group 75. Records of the Superintendencies and Agencies of the Office of Indian Affairs. Selected Records of the Dakota Superintendency, 1861–1870 and 1877–1878, and the Wyoming Superintendency, 1870: Dakota Superintendency. Microfilm M1016. NARS.

LDR       BIA. Record Group 75. Records of the Land Division. Irregularly Shaped Papers: No. 68—The Great Peace Commission of 1868. NARS.

NARS      National Archives and Records Service. Washington DC.

NARS-KC   National Archives and Records Service. Kansas City MO.

PR        BIA. Record Group 75. Pine Ridge Indian Agency. Legal and Legislative Records. Legal Records: Council Proceedings, 1875–1879; Petitions, 1875–1879; Records of Controversies, 1867–1879. NARS-KC.

PRM       BIA. Record Group 75. Miscellaneous Letters Sent by the Agents or Superintendents at the Pine Ridge Indian Agency, 1876–1879. Microfilm M1229. NARS.

PRT       BIA. Record Group 75. General Correspondence, General Records: Telegrams Received and Copies of Telegrams Sent, January 1876–November 1879. NARS-KC.

RCA       BIA. Record Group 75. The Office of Indian Affairs, Letters Received, 1824–1881: Red Cloud Agency, 1871–1880. Microfilm M234. NARS.

STA       BIA. Record Group 75. The Office of Indian Affairs, Letters Received, 1824–1881: Spotted Tail Agency, 1875–1880. Microfilm M234. NARS.

UPA       BIA. Record Group 75. The Office of Indian Affairs, Letters Received, 1824–1881: Upper Platte Agency, 1846–1870. Microfilm M234. NARS.

# Notes

PREFACE

1. For detailed biographical information on Walker, see Walker's *Lakota Belief and Ritual*, pp. xiii–xvii, 3–61, and *Lakota Society*, pp. ix–xiv.
2. DeMallie, in Walker, *Lakota Society*, pp. xii–xiii.
3. DeMallie and Jahner, in Walker, *Lakota Belief and Ritual*, p. 18.
4. Sword and Walker, quoted in Walker, *Lakota Belief and Ritual*, pp. 23, 75.
5. Walker, *Lakota Belief and Ritual*, pp. 7, 18.
6. See for example Abel, *Tabeau's Narrative*; Burpee, *Journals and Letters of Pierre Gaultier*; DeMallie, "Nicollet's Notes"; Frémont, *Narrative*; Hennepin, *A New Discovery*; Lowe, *Five Years a Dragoon*; Nasatir, *Before Lewis and Clark*; Pike, *Journals*; McFarling, *Exploring the Northern Plains*; Radisson, *Voyages*; and Sage, *Rocky Mountain Life*.
7. Lowe, *Five Years a Dragoon*, p. 51.
8. Ortiz, "Indian-White Relations," p. 1.

1 THE SACRED HOOP

1. Quaife, *Journals*, p. 17.
2. For thoughtful discussions on the westward migration of the Lakotas, see White, "The Winning of the West"; and Anderson, "Early Migration and Intertribal War." For information on the vastness of the Oglala tribal domain, see DeMallie, in Walker, *Lakota Society*, p. 72; and Denig, *Five Indian Tribes*, p. 19.
3. The seven Lakota subtribes, or *ospaye*, are the Oglala, Sicangu (Brulé), Miniconjou, Hunkpapa, Oohenonpa (Two Kettle), Itazipco (Sans Arcs), and Sihasapa (Blackfeet). Each tribe was divided into two or more bands, or *tiyospaye*.
4. See Jahner, "The Spiritual Landscape."
5. Brown, "Becoming Part of It," p. 12.
6. See Mirsky, "The Dakota," pp. 384–85, 391–92; and Bad Heart Bull, *Pictographic History*, p. xx.
7. Walker, *Lakota Society*, pp. 44, 46–47; DeMallie, "Sioux Social Organization."

8. See Mirsky, "The Dakota," pp. 394–403; and Eggan, *Social Anthropology*, pp. 75–81.

9. Walker, *Lakota Society*, pp. 5–6; Deloria, *Speaking of Indians*, pp. 19, 21–22. A Lakota woman informed DeMallie in 1970 that "relationship," or *wotakuye*, has more to do with "feeling" and the way someone acts toward another than with blood or affinal ties; see DeMallie, "Change in American Indian Kinship Systems," p. 233.

10. Walker, *Lakota Belief*, pp. 195, 198, 211.

11. George Hyde portrayed Bull Bear in quite a different light. Bull Bear, he claimed, was "something of a tyrant, holding his turbulent followers in check by roaring at them and promptly putting a knife into any man who did not heed his orders" (Hyde, *Red Cloud's Folk*, p. 53).

12. DeMallie, "Pine Ridge Economy," p. 244.

13. DeMallie, "Nicollet's Notes," p. 261; Dorsey, "Siouan Sociology," pp. 220–21; Wissler, "Societies and Ceremonial Associations," p. 7.

14. See Wedel, "Le Sueur and the Dakota Sioux"; Keating, *Narrative*, pp. 393–94; and Abel, *Tabeau's Narrative*, pp. 105, 107.

15. DeMallie, "Nicollet's Notes," pp. 255–57, 261–62; Anderson, "The Letters of Peter Wilson," p. 261; Lottinville, *Paul Wilhelm*, p. 363.

16. See Wissler, "Societies and Ceremonial Associations."

17. Only "husbanded" tipis were counted when determining the size of a camp. Even if a man had several wives, each one with her own lodge, the camp counted only the tipi in which the husband "officially" resided. See Walker, *Lakota Society*, p. 58.

18. Wissler, "Societies and Ceremonial Associations," pp. 7–11, 39; Walker, *Lakota Belief*, pp. 101, 263, 303 n.4; Thwaites, *Jesuit Relations* 54:191.

19. Walker, *Lakota Society*, pp. 22, 27.

20. Walker, *Lakota Belief*, pp. 75, 83; Valentine T. McGillycuddy to Walter S. Campbell, 2 December 1929, box 107, Campbell Collection.

21. Quaife, *Journals*, pp. 120–22. For a concise discussion on Arapaho consensus politics, see Fowler, *Arapaho Politics*, pp. 1–17.

22. Walker, *Lakota Society*, pp. 5–6; Powers, *Oglala Religion*, p. 25; Black Elk, *Sixth Grandfather*, pp. 319–20.

23. Walker, *Lakota Society*, p. 30.

24. Statement of Robert P. High Eagle, box 104, Campbell Collection; Walker, *Lakota Society*, pp. 24–27.

25. Walker, *Lakota Belief*, p. 297 n.41; see also Walker, *Lakota Society*, pp. 24, 26.

26. Walker, *Lakota Society*, pp. 17, 24, 27, 30; Black Elk, *Sixth Grandfather*, p. 320.

27. Jackson and Spence, *Travels from 1838 to 1844*, pp. 228–30.

28. Walker, *Lakota Society*, p. 30; High Eagle, in Campbell Collection; Ricker, interview with George Colhoff, roll 1, Ricker Manuscripts.

29. Walker, *Lakota Belief*, p. 80; Walker, *Lakota Society*, p. 60.

30. For detailed information on Oglala warrior societies, see Wissler, "Societies and Ceremonial Associations," and Lowie, "Plains Indian Age-Societies," p. 904.

31. Mirsky, "The Dakota," pp. 409–10; Standing Bear, *Land of the Spotted Eagle* p. 91.

32. Black Elk, *Sixth Grandfather*, pp. 300, 321–22, 387, 389–90.

33. Culbertson, *Journal*, p. 132; Walker, *Lakota Society*, pp. 60–61.

34. High Eagle, in Campbell Collection; Walker, *Lakota Society*, pp. 39, 60; Wissler, "Societies and Ceremonial Associations," pp. 8, 11. Smaller camps might have only one *wakiconza*.

35. Black Elk, *Sixth Grandfather*, p. 323.

36. Black Elk, *Sixth Grandfather*, p. 321; Walker, *Lakota Society*, p. 25, 59–60, 78; Walker, "Sun Dance," p. 77.

37. Walker, *Lakota Society*, pp. 29, 59; Walker, "Sun Dance," p. 66.

38. Walker, *Lakota Society*, pp. 7–8, 29, 31, 60–61, 71, 79, 84, 86–87, 94.

39. Walker, *Lakota Society*, pp. 7–8, 29, 31, 60–61, 71, 79, 84, 86–87, 94.

40. Walker, *Lakota Society*, pp. 76, 78; Black Elk, *Sixth Grandfather*, p. 146.

41. Walker, *Lakota Society*, pp. 29, 59; Black Elk, *Sixth Grandfather*, p. 320.

42. Walker, *Lakota Society*, pp. 30, 31, 33, 34, 59; Black Elk, *Sixth Grandfather*, p. 321; High Eagle, in Campbell Collection.

43. Abel, *Tabeau's Narrative*, p. 117. See also Sage, *Rocky Mountain Life*, pp. 242, 244.

44. Walker, *Lakota Society*, pp. 59–60, 79; Ricker, interview with Colhoff.

45. Hinman, "Life of Crazy Horse," p. 19.

46. Hinman, "Life of Crazy Horse," p. 19.

47. See James Saville to E. P. Smith, 30 November 1874, file S1804-74, roll 718, RCA. For an alternative perspective on the authority of head shirt-wearers, see Hassrick, *The Sioux*, p. 7.

48. Walker, *Lakota Belief*, pp. 181–82; Amiotte, "Lakota Sun Dance," p. 78; Ricker, interview with Red Cloud and Clarence Three Stars, roll 5, Ricker Manuscripts.

49. For an excellent discussion on the stereotyping of Native American women in various media, see Stedman, *Shadows of the Indian*, pp. 17–41.

See also Green, "The Pocahontas Perplex," and Grumet, "Sunksquaws, Shamans, and Tradeswomen."

50. Hassrick, *The Sioux*, pp. 41, 47; Walker, *Lakota Society*, p. 63. See also Kehoe, "The Shackles of Tradition," and Weist, "Beasts of Burden and Menial Slaves."

51. Anderson, *Kinsmen of Another Kind*, p. 13.

52. Deloria, *Speaking of Indians*, p. 26; DeMallie, "Male and Female in Traditional Lakota Culture," p. 261.

53. See Wissler, "Societies and Ceremonial Associations," pp. 98–99.

54. Deloria, *Speaking of Indians*, p. 26; Sneider, "Women's Work," p. 117; Walker, *Lakota Society*, p. 30.

55. Strayer, "Fur Trappers' Attitudes," p. 39.

56. McDermott, "Joseph Bissonette," pp. 50, 52, 60; McDermott, "James Bordeaux," p. 69; Robinson, "Journals and Letter Books," p. 177; Unrau, *Tending the Talking Wire*, p. 107n.

57. Anderson, *Kinsmen of Another Kind*, p. 56.

58. Anderson, "Fur Traders as Fathers," pp. 246–47, 251.

59. Grange, "The Garnier Oglala Winter Count," p. 75; Dorsey, "Siouan Sociology," pp. 220–21.

60. White, "The Winning of the West," p. 334; Alfred Cumming to George W. Manypenny, U.S. House of Representatives, Executive Document no. 65, 34th Cong., 1st sess., p. 2; "The No Ears, Short Man, and Iron Crow Winter Counts," in Walker, *Lakota Society*, p. 139.

61. Hafen and Young, *Fort Laramie*, pp. 21, 66.

62. Hafen and Young, *Fort Laramie*, pp. 34–35, 63–64, 84; Sage, *Rocky Mountain Life*, pp. 121–22; Maj. Andrew Drips to Joseph V. Hamilton, 4 November 1843, in Robinson, "Journals and Letter Books," pp. 170–75, 177, and pp. 129, 135, 139, 147.

63. Hafen and Young, *Fort Laramie*, p. 74; McDermott, "James Bordeaux," p. 68, and "Joseph Bissonette," p. 50.

64. Hyde, *Red Cloud's Folk*, p. 40; Olson, *Red Cloud and the Sioux Problem*, p. 9.

65. In Walker, *Lakota Society*, p. 140; see also pp. 21, 88–89; Hyde, *Red Cloud's Folk*, pp. 53–54; Olson, *Red Cloud and the Sioux Problem*, p. 20. Addison Sheldon relied on Charles W. Allen's 1890 interviews with Red Cloud as a major source for his manuscript, "Red Cloud, Chief of the Sioux." Olson, in turn, based his account, cited above, on the Addison manuscript.

66. William Garnett to McGillycuddy, ca. 1920, Herman Materials. Both Hyde and Olson claim that Bull Bear died instantly; see Hyde, *Red Cloud's Folk*, p. 54, and Olson, *Red Cloud and the Sioux Problem*, p. 20.
67. Hafen and Young, *Fort Laramie*, p. 77.
68. Hinman, "Life of Crazy Horse," pp. 17–18.
69. Hyde, *Red Cloud's Folk*, pp. 86–87.
70. Olson, *Red Cloud and the Sioux Problem*, p. 21; Hyde, *Red Cloud's Folk*, p. 55; Ricker, interview with Philip F. Wells, roll 1, Ricker Manuscripts.
71. Ricker, interview with Wells; DeMallie, in Walker, *Lakota Society*, p. 177 n.31.
72. Sandoz, *Crazy Horse*, p. 234; Olson, *Red Cloud and the Sioux Problem*, p. 19.
73. Ricker, interview with William F. Girton, roll 3, Ricker Manuscripts.

2 AMERICAN EMISSARIES AMONG THE LAKOTAS: ENDEAVORS TO MODIFY POLITICAL CUSTOMS

1. Richardson, *Papers of the Presidents*, 3:172–73.
2. Hafen and Young, *Fort Laramie*, pp. 27, 34, 54.
3. Stevenson, "Expeditions into Dakota," pp. 356, 360; *Report of a Summer Campaign to the Rocky Mountains, etc. in 1845*, U.S. Senate, Executive Document no. 1, 29th Cong., 1st sess., p. 212.
4. McDermott, *The Frontier Re-Examined*, p. 38; Hafen and Young, *Fort Laramie*, p. 164.
5. Hafen and Young, *Fort Laramie*, p. 201; Unruh, *The Plains Across*, p. 169.
6. H. Rep. 197, 36th Cong., 1st sess., p. 1; Unruh, *The Plains Across*, pp. 175–77, 180, 186–88, 193–95, 197.
7. Hafen, "First Indian Agency," p. 379; Hoopes, "Thomas S. Twiss," p. 353.
8. For the Treaty of Fort Laramie, 17 September 1851, see Kappler, *Indian Affairs*, 2:594–96.
9. Hafen and Young, *Fort Laramie*, pp. 22, 33, 44.
10. Kappler, *Indian Affairs*, 2:594–96; S. Ex. Doc. 452, 57th Cong., 1st sess. At Fort Laramie on 15 September 1853 the Brulés Conquering Bear, Yellow Ears, Standing Bear, Burnt Man, and Eagle Body; and the Oglalas Smoke, Bad Wound, Medicine Eagle, Man Afraid of His Horse, and Big Crow signed a document approving this amendment. Blue Earth of the Brulés, who signed the 1851 treaty, was listed as deceased. See Anderson, "The Controversial Sioux Amendment," pp. 204–5.

11. The following description of the Horse Creek treaty council is based on typescript copies of B. Gratz Brown's reports published in the *Missouri Republican*, 6, 17, 22, 24, and 26 October and 2, 9, and 23 November 1851. These copies are found in folder 5, "Grand Council of the Plains, 1851—Report of the Treaty near Fort Laramie, 1851 from the *Missouri Republican* of St. Louis," box 110, Campbell Collection. Other interesting firsthand accounts may be found in DeSmet, *Life, Letters, and Travels*, 2:675–92, and Lowe, *Five Years a Dragoon*, pp. 77–90.

12. Between 1804 and 1806, members of the Lewis and Clark expedition encountered several Sioux bands. In August 1804, Capt. John Ordway visited a Brulé *tiyospaye*. Although he and his associates did not attempt to appoint a "head chief" for the Sioux, they did "make chiefs" among this band by presenting medals to the Brulé spokesmen. See Quaife, *Journals*, p. 120; Jackson, *Letters*, 1:310.

13. See for example Jackson and Spence, *Travels from 1838 to 1844*, p. 225; Bradbury, *Travels*, pp. 110–16; Springer, *Soldiering in Sioux Country*, p. 49; Pike, *Journals*, 1:38; Dodge, *Our Wild Indians*, pp. 68–70, 73–74, 76; Shaw, *Across the Plains*, p. 31.

14. Hyde states erroneously that not one Oglala signed the 1851 treaty; see Hyde, *Red Cloud's Folk*, p. 66.

15. Interestingly, after all the pomp and circumstance surrounding the great council, and Congress's decision to honor it for fifteen years, the 1851 treaty was never formally ratified by the Senate or proclaimed by the president. See E. B. Meritt, memorandum to the assistant secretary of the interior, 17 May 1928, file no. LC20262-28, Records Relating to Indian Treaties, RG 123, Documents Relating to the Negotiation of Ratified and Unratified Treaties with Various Indian Tribes, Microfilm T494, roll 4, NARS; and Frank B. Kellogg, memorandum to the secretary of the interior, 19 April 1928, in the same file.

16. Pike, *Journals*, 1:38. For an informative discussion on Indian and American concepts of treaty making, see DeMallie, "American Indian Treaty Making," pp. 5–8, "Touching the Pen," pp. 40–42.

17. DeMallie, "American Indian Treaty Making," pp. 5–8, and "Touching the Pen," pp. 40–42.

18. DeMallie, "American Indian Treaty Making," pp. 5–8, and "Touching the Pen," pp. 40–42.

19. Ricker, interview with Frank Salaway, roll 3, Ricker Manuscripts.

20. E. Johnson to William Hoffman, 11 October 1855, file no. 216 R 1856,

roll 546, AGO1; Hafen and Young, *Fort Laramie*, pp. 209–11; Ricker, interview with Salaway.

21. Hoopes, "Thomas S. Twiss," p. 354; Sandoz, *Crazy Horse*, p. 14; McDermott, "James Bordeaux," pp. 73–74; Johnson to Hoffman, AGO1. Frank Salaway, an Oglala mixed-blood who lived around Fort Laramie in the 1850s, claims he and other men stood on a knoll about a quarter of a mile from the Brulé village. Someone in his party had brought a spyglass, affording them a good view of the proceedings. For Salaway's account of the incident along with diagrams and maps of the Brulé village, see Ricker, interview with Salaway. For army commentary, see file no. 216 R1856, AGO1; and ARSW 1856, pp. 1–27.

22. Ricker, interview with Salaway.

23. Johnson to Hoffman; Hafen and Young, *Fort Laramie*, p. 231.

24. Ricker, interview with Salaway.

25. Hoopes, "Thomas S. Twiss," p. 356; S. Ex. Doc. 1, 34th Cong., 1st sess., part 1, p. 50; Mattison, "The Harney Expedition," pp. 111–14. For an official report on the Battle of Ash Hollow (Blue Water), see ARSW 1855, pp. 49–51.

26. H. Ex. Doc. 1, pt. 1, 34th Cong., 1st sess., pp. 400–401; Hoopes, "Thomas S. Twiss," p. 357.

27. For minutes of the Fort Pierre councils, 1–5 March 1856, see S. Ex. Doc. 94, 34th Cong., 1st sess.

28. Clow, "Mad Bear," p. 147.

29. Harney listed the following men as "principal chiefs" of the Sioux: Little Thunder (Platte River Brulés), One Horn (Miniconjous), Crow Feather (Sans Arcs), Fire Heart (Blackfeet Sioux), Bear's Rib (Hunkpapas), Two Bears (Yanktonais), Black Catfish (Yanktonais), Long Mandan (Two Kettles), and Struck by the Ree (Yanktons, replaced by Medicine Cow). See S. Ex. Doc. 94, pp. 11, 39.

30. S. Ex. Doc. 94, pp. 5, 29; H. Rep. Ex. Doc. 130, 34th Cong., 1st sess., p. 3.

31. H. Ex. Doc. 130, p. 3; Hoopes, "Thomas S. Twiss," p. 358; Hyde, *Red Cloud's Folk*, pp. 30, 85.

32. Acting Commissioner of Indian Affairs to Jacob Thompson, 5 June 1858, in H. Ex. Doc. 136, 35th Cong., 1st sess., pp. 4–5; Kvasnicka and Viola, *The Commissioners of Indian Affairs*, p. 60.

33. Olson, *Red Cloud and the Sioux Problem*, p. 9; Richard White, "The Winning of the West," p. 339.

34. Hyde, *Red Cloud's Folk*, p. 86; Ricker, interview with Wells.

### 3 STRATEGIES OF THE OGLALA LEADERS

1. Utley, *Indian Frontier*, p. 72; Smith, "The Bozeman," p. 35.
2. Hafen and Hafen, *Powder River Campaigns*, pp. 219, 221–23; Murray, *Military Posts*, p. 7.
3. Utley, *Indian Frontier*, p. 229.
4. Twiss to A. B. Greenwood, 16 August 1859, in ARCIA 1860, p. 497; Twiss, "Letter," p. 149.
5. DeMallie, "Touching the Pen," p. 50.
6. DeMallie, "Touching the Pen," p. 50.
7. Special report of Thomas S. Twiss, S. Ex. Doc. 35, 36th Cong., 1st sess., pp. 7–8, 11–13.
8. Anderson, "The Letters of Peter Wilson," pp. 261–62; Lottinville, *Paul Wilhelm*, pp. 362, 367; Riggs, "Journal," pp. 336–38; Frémont, *Narrative*, pp. 26, 83; Jackson and Spence, *Travels from 1838 to 1844*, pp. 23, 240; Denig, *Five Indian Tribes*, pp. 22, 25; Mattison, "The Harney Expedition," pp. 99–101; McDermott, "James Bordeaux," p. 78.
9. DeMallie and Parks, *Sioux Indian Religion*, p. 32.
10. Edward B. Taylor to R. B. Van Valkenburgh, 15 September 1865, H. Ex. Doc. 1, vol. 2, 39th Cong., 1st sess., p. 583.
11. Feather Tied to His Hair et al. to Agent, 25 July 1862, in ARSI 1862, pp. 516–17; Samuel N. Latta to William P. Dole, 27 August 1862, ARCIA 1862, pp. 336–37. See also Latta to Dole, 7 March 1863, ARSI 1863, pp. 284–85.
12. Latta to Dole, 27 August 1862.
13. Newton Edmunds to D. N. Cooley, 11 August 1865, ARSI 1865, p. 397.
14. Fritz, "The Board of Indian Commissioners," p. 65.
15. Whipple and Nesmith, quoted in Nichols, *Lincoln and the Indians*, p. 7.
16. Edmunds to Dole, 11 March 1865, ARCIA 1865, p. 378; Vital Jarrot to Dole, 15 July 1865, ARCIA 1865, p. 617; Unrau, "The Civilian as Indian Agent," p. 416.
17. Beeson, quoted in Fritz, *The Movement for Indian Assimilation*, p. 37; ARCIA 1858, pp. 354–59; James Harlan to Maj. Gen. John Pope, 6 July 1865, ARCIA 1865, p. 385; Prucha, *American Indian Policy in Crisis*, pp. 38–43, 45–46, 48–49.
18. Utley, *Indian Frontier*, pp. 94–96.
19. *The Condition of the Indian Tribes: Report of the Joint Special Committee Appointed under Joint Resolution of March 3, 1865*, S. Rep. 156, 39th Cong., 2nd sess., p. 3.

20. Doolittle to L. F. S. Foster, 7 March 1881, correspondence published in the *New Mexico Historical Review* 26 (April 1951): 156–57.
21. Report of Edmunds to Dole, 20 September 1864, ARCIA 1864, p. 404; Edmunds to Cooley, 14 October 1865, ARCIA 1865, pp. 368–69.
22. For the Treaty of Fort Sully negotiated with the Oglalas, 28 October 1865, see Kappler, *Indian Affairs*, 2:906–8; see also ARCIA 1866, pp. 4–5. John Pope to Ulysses S. Grant, 14 June 1865, ARCIA 1865, pp. 380–81.
23. Maynadier to Cooley, 25 January 1866, and 9 March 1866, ARCIA 1866, pp. 204–6.
24. Maynadier to Cooley, 25 January 1866, and 9 March 1866, ARCIA 1866, pp. 204–6; Ricker, interview with Colhoff, roll 4, Ricker Manuscripts; Sawyer to James A. Harlan, 19 January 1866, H. Ex. Doc. 58, vol. 8, 39th Cong., 1st sess., pp. 22–23.
25. Johnson to Sister Abi, 10 March 1866, in Unrau, *Tending the Talking Wire*, pp. 322–23; Maynadier to Cooley, 9 March 1866, ARCIA 1866, p. 207.
26. Maynadier to Cooley, 9 March 1866, ARCIA 1866, p. 207. See also Black Elk, *Sixth Grandfather*, pp. 319–20.
27. DeMallie, "Sioux Social Organization."
28. Chandler to Denman, 13 January 1867, S. Ex. Doc. 13, 40th Cong., 1st sess., p. 12; Powell, *People of the Sacred Mountain*, 2:422.
29. Nathaniel G. Taylor to W. T. Otto, 12 July 1867, S. Ex. Doc. 13, p. 3. See also N. B. Buford to E. M. Stanton, 6 June 1867, file no. M102-1867, roll 560, AGO2.
30. General Order No. 7, Headquarters, Department of the Platte, 23 June 1866, S. Ex. Doc. 13, pp. 62–63. The Oglala *tiyospaye* were led by Man Who Walks under the Ground, Big Head, Black War Bonnet, Standing Cloud; the Loafers, by Big Mouth and his brother, Blue Horse; and the Brulé bands were under Two Strike, Dog Hawk, Thunder Hawk, Standing Elk, Tall Mandan, Brave Heart, Spotted Tail, and Swift Bear.
31. Taylor to Cooley, 1 October 1866, ARCIA 1866, p. 211; *Report of the Commission Appointed by the President of the United States to Treat with the Indians at Fort Laramie, October, 1866*, in Records Relating to Indian Treaties, RG 123, Documents Relating to the Negotiation of Ratified and Unratified Treaties with Various Indian Tribes, 1801–1869, Microfilm T494, roll 9, NARS.
32. Chandler to Denman, 13 January 1867, S. Ex. Doc. 13, p. 11; M. T. Pat-

rick to Commissioner of Indian Affairs, 20 September 1866, folder, "Office of Indian Affairs Reports," box 110, Campbell Collection.

33. Sandoz, *Crazy Horse*, p. 210.

34. Chandler to Denman, 13 January 1867, pp. 12–13.

35. For federal government reports of the Fort Philip Kearny tragedy, see S. Ex. Doc. 13; S. Ex. Doc. 16, vol. 2, 39th Cong., 2nd sess.; H. Ex. Doc. 71, vol. 11, 39th Cong., 2nd sess.

36. C. M. Hines to John Hines, 1 January 1867, S. Ex. Doc. 13, p. 15.

37. Sergeant to clerk, 28 December 1866, received by Sherman, 28 January 1867, and forwarded to Grant, 2 February 1867, S. Ex. Doc. 15, vol. 2, 39th Cong., 2nd sess., p. 13.

38. Report of the Special Commissioner, 8 July 1867, S. Ex. Doc. 13, p. 62.

39. *Report of the Indian Peace Commission*, 14 January 1868, H. Ex. Doc. 97, vol. 11, 40th Cong., 2nd sess., p. 13; Powell, *People of the Sacred Mountain*, 2:424.

40. Sherman to W. S. Hancock, 26 January 1867, S. Ex. Doc. 13, p. 41.

41. Circular from the Commissioner of Indian Affairs to superintendents of Indian affairs and Indian agents, 27 July 1868, file no. 1145–65, AGO2, roll 367; General Order no. 10, 31 July 1866, DP; Bogy to Orville H. Browning, 4 February 1867, S. Ex. Doc. 13, pp. 8–9.

42. Bogy to Browning, 23 January 1867, S. Ex. Doc. 13, pp. 18–20.

43. Sibley to Samuel R. Curtis, 18 August 1867, quoted in Hoopes, *Road to the Little Big Horn*, p. 51.

44. See Walker, *Lakota Society*, p. 29, 59, 60–61, 86–87; Black Elk, *Sixth Grandfather*, p. 320.

45. Chandler to Denman, 13 January 1867, S. Ex. Doc. 13, p. 13.

46. Hyde, *Red Cloud's Folk*, p. 34; Ruby, *Oglala Sioux*, pp. 89–90.

47. Powers, *Yuwipi*, p. 8.

48. Ricker, interview with Colhoff and Three Stars, Ricker Manuscripts.

49. McGillycuddy to Campbell, 30 March 1929, box 107, Campbell Collection; Bogy to Browning, 4 February 1867, S. Ex. Doc. 13, p. 9; Powell, *People of the Sacred Mountain*, 2:418.

50. Bogy to Browning, 4 February 1867, S. Ex. Doc. 13, p. 9; Buford to Stanton, 6 June 1867, S. Ex. Doc. 13, p. 59.

51. S. Ex. Doc. 13, pp. 55–56; Armstrong, *Warrior in Two Camps*, p. 124.

52. Sandoz, *Crazy Horse*, p. 243.

53. Buford to Stanton, 6 June 1867, S. Ex. Doc. 13, p. 59; Alfred Sully to N. G. Taylor, 22 April 1867, roll 4, DS.

54. Sully to Taylor, 22 April 1867; Armstrong, *Warrior in Two Camps*, p. 125.
55. Sully to Taylor, 28 April 1867, S. Ex. Doc. 13, p. 93; Taylor to Otto, 12 July 1867, S. Ex. Doc. 13, p. 6.
56. Taylor to Otto, 12 July 1867, S. Ex. Doc. 13, p. 6; Buford to Stanton, 6 June 1867, S. Ex. Doc. 13, p. 59.
57. Buford to Stanton, 6 June 1867, S. Ex. Doc. 13, p. 60.
58. *Report of the Commission to the President of the U.S.*, 7 January 1868, H. Ex. Doc. 97; H. Ex. Doc. 1, 40th Cong., 3rd sess. See also Bailey, *Pacifying the Plains*, pp. 45–49.
59. Taylor to Otto, 12 July 1867, S. Ex. Doc. 13, p. 5.; Mattingly, "The Great Plains Peace Commission of 1867," p. 27.
60. H. Ex. Doc. 97, pp. 1–4.
61. The principal source used for the councils with the Oglalas and Brulés, 19–20 September 1867, is *Proceedings of the Great Peace Commission*, pp. 57–65.
62. H. Ex. Doc. 97, pp. 4–5.
63. A. F. Chamberlin to J. B. Sanborn, 4 April 1868, in *Proceedings of the Great Peace Commission*, p. 102.
64. Examination by the Indian Peace Commission into the Charges of Misappropriation of Indian Goods against M. T. Chamblin, 15–16 April 1868, file no. J40272, L D R; hereafter cited as L D R J40272.
65. For the councils with the Oglalas and Brulés, 28–29 April, see *Proceedings of the Great Peace Commission*, pp. 105–18.
66. L D R J40272.
67. Sherman to Grant, 8 May 1868, H. Ex. Doc. 239, vol. 15, 40th Cong., 2nd sess., pp. 1–3.
68. For an account of the 24–25 May 1868 councils with the Oglalas and Brulés, see *Proceedings of the Great Peace Commission*, pp. 105–18; L D R J40272.
69. For the 1868 Treaty of Fort Laramie with the Oglalas, signed 25 May 1868, ratified 16 February 1869, and proclaimed 24 February 1869, see Kappler, *Indian Affairs*, 2:998–1007. Touching the pen for the Oglalas were American Horse, Bad Hand, Bad Wound, Bear Hide, Bear with Yellow Ears, Bear's Back, Big Mouth, Big Wolf Foot, Black Bull, Black Hawk, Black Tiger, Blue Horse, Blue War Club, Brave, Carries the Lance, Crow, Cuts Off, Fire Thunder, Fool Hawk, Four Bears, Ghost Heart, Grass, High Wolf, Kills in a Hard Place, Kills the Bear, Little Crow, Mad Shade, Man Who Walks under the Ground, Medicine Eagle,

Poor Bull, Poor Elk, Presents the Pipe, Quick Eagle, Red Thunder, Sitting Bull, Whirlwind Dog, Whirlwind Hawk, and White Hawk. Little Wound's mark does not appear on the document. Man Afraid's does; however, much confusion persists over whether he signed the treaty in May, in the following November, or both. Perhaps one of his signatures is actually that of his son, Young Man Afraid.

70. Garrou to Taylor, ARCIA 1868, p. 713; J. P. Cooper to H. B. Denman, 27 August 1868, ARCIA 1868, pp. 711–13.

71. Sherman to Grant, 8 May 1868, H. Rep. Ex. Doc. 239, pp. 1–3.

72. Garrou to Taylor, 1 July 1868, ARCIA 1868, pp. 712–13; Cooper to Denman, 27 August 1868, ARCIA 1868, p. 712.

73. Ricker, interview with Baptiste Pourier, roll 3, Ricker Manuscripts.

74. Sandoz, *Crazy Horse*, pp. 223–24.

75. Fort Laramie Commandant to Sherman, 20 November 1868, in *Proceedings of the Great Peace Commission*, p. 173.

76. Fort Laramie Commandant to Sherman, 20 November 1868, in *Proceedings of the Great Peace Commission*, p. 175; Denman to Taylor, 6 November, ARCIA 1868, pp. 690–91.

77. For a list of goods along with their costs distributed during the Fort Laramie councils of 1867 and 1868, see Murray, "Treaty Presents at Fort Laramie"; *Proceedings of the Great Peace Commission*, p. 175.

78. Sandoz, *Crazy Horse*, pp. 233–34.

### 4 THE STRUGGLE TO ESTABLISH AN AGENCY

1. Utley, *Indian Frontier*, p. 103.

2. ARCIA 1869, pp. 47–48. See Prucha, *American Indian Policy in Crisis*, pp. 40, 46.

3. H. Ex. Doc. 1, 41st Cong., 2nd sess., pp. vii–viii; Utley, *Indian Frontier*, pp. 130–32.

4. Fritz, *The Movement for Indian Assimilation*, pp. 74, 76; Rahill, *Catholic Indian Missions*, p. 34.

5. Rahill, *Catholic Indian Missions*, pp. 32–33; Tatum, *Our Red Brothers*, p. ix.

6. Richardson, *Papers of the Presidents*, 9:4063–64; Prucha, *American Indian Policy in Crisis*, p. 50.

7. Olson, *Red Cloud and the Sioux Problem*, p. 83.

8. Welsh, *Visit to the Sioux*, p. 30.

9. Welsh, *Visit to the Sioux*, p. 30; Poole, *Among the Sioux*, pp. 29–31.

10. Clow, "The Brulé Indian Agencies, p. 150.

11. Poole to Burbank, 4 March 1870, roll 9, DS.
12. It is understandable how the Lakota words for "dog" (*sunka*) and "horse" (*sunka wakan* or *tasunka*) could be confused in translation. Red Horse is undoubtedly Red Dog, the Oyuhpe Oglala *itancan*.
13. Alex Chambers to Sherman, 28 April 1870, file no. W847-70, roll 896, UPA.
14. Sherman to Sheridan, 29 April 1870, transmitted by telegram from Sheridan to Christopher C. Augur, 29 April 1870, file no. W847-70, roll 896, UPA.
15. Augur to E. D. Townsend, 28 May 1870, DP.
16. *New York Times,* 2 June 1870, p. 4. Representing mostly the Bad Face, Oyuhpe, and Oglala Proper *tiyospaye* (northern Oglalas) were Brave Bear and his head shirtwearer-son Sword, Red Cloud, Red Dog, Yellow Bear, High Wolf, Sitting Bear, Little Bear, Long Wolf, Bear Skin, Brave, Afraid, Red Fly, Black Hawk, Rocky Bear, Swing Bear, and the One That Runs Through. The last named delegate, along with Black Hawk, Yellow Bear, and Sword, refused to leave on this potentially hazardous mission without their wives.
17. These data have been obtained from my preliminary computer analyses of hundreds of disparate primary sources, such as reservation censuses, beef ration rolls, special censuses and lists, and various other records of the Office of Indian Affairs and the Department of War. The ultimate goal of this computer project is to identify, examine, and analyze any patterns in the formation and dissolution of bands from the 1870s to the 1880s, and in the creation of reservation districts by the 1890s; the various members of Oglala families in the early reservation period; the band or district affiliation of these families; and where families went when they left their former bands or districts.
18. Olson, *Red Cloud and the Sioux Problem,* p. 97; Powell, *People of the Sacred Mountain,* 2:780.
19. See the following 1870 *New York Times* articles: 31 May, p. 4; 2 June, pp. 4–5; 4 June, p. 3; 7 June, p. 5; 8 June, p. 1; 9 June, p. 4; 10 June, p. 1; 11 June, p. 1; 12 June, p. 1; 15 June, p. 2; 16 June, pp. 1–4; and 17 June, pp. 1–2. For a full account of the Lakotas' visit to Washington, see Transcript of Interviews with Red Cloud, 3, 7, 11, and 13 June 1870, file no. C1416-70, roll 895, UPA.
20. *New York Times,* 1 June 1870, p. 5.
21. *New York Times,* 8 June 1870, p. 1; 12 June 1870, p. 1.
22. *New York Times,* 11 June 1870, p. 1.

23. Brunot to Parker, 10 November 1870, file no. B1053-70, roll 895, UPA; *New York Times*, 12 June 1870, p. 1.
24. See Transcript of Interviews with Red Cloud, 1870, file no. C1416-70, roll 895, UPA.
25. Telegram, Flint to George D. Ruggles, 1 August 1870, file nos. A1230-70 and M1047-70, roll 895, UPA; and Flint to Ruggles, 15 July 1870, file nos. A1145-70 and A1170-70, roll 895, UPA; Flint to Parker, 29 August 1870, file no. E505-70, roll 896, UPA.
26. Brunot to Cox, 29 October 1870, file no. B1050-70, roll 895, UPA.
27. Brunot to Cox, 29 October 1870, file no. B1050-70, roll 895, UPA.
28. For the following council reports and conversations, see *Report of United States Special Indian Commission*, 22 August–10 October 1870, file no. B1050-70, roll 895, UPA; and Brunot to Jacob D. Cox, 29 October 1870, UPA.
29. Brunot to Cox, 29 October 1870, roll 895, UPA; see also Flint to Augur, 27 January 1871, file no. 113 AGO 1871, roll 2, AGO3.
30. The military report lists Little Wound as an Arapaho chief with a forty-lodge following, but this man was surely the Kiyuksa Oglala chief of the same name. Joining the Oglalas at Fort Laramie between March and May were the following bands: Red Leaf and Swift Bear of the Brulés with sixty and twenty lodges, respectively, Plenty Bears of the Northern Arapahoes with thirty-four, and Medicine Man and Full Bear of the Northern Cheyennes with twenty-six and seventy-six lodges, respectively. See John E. Smith to Ruggles, 22 March 1871, file no. A210-71, roll 715, RCA.
31. J. Smith to Ruggles, 22 March 1871, file no. A210-71, roll 715, RCA.
32. Hyde, *Spotted Tail's Folk*, pp. 159–60; Sandoz, *Crazy Horse*, p. 249.
33. Telegram, Wham to Ely S. Parker, 28 March 1871, file no. W206-71, roll 715, RCA. See also H. R. Clum to Parker, 3 April 1871, file no. C224-71; Secretary of War to Secretary of the Interior, 12 April 1871, file no. W257-71, roll 715, RCA.
34. J. Smith to Ruggles, 22 March 1871, file no. A210-71, roll 715, RCA; and Smith and Wham to Parker, 24 March 1871, file no. W208-71, roll 715, RCA; Flint to Augur, 27 January 1871, file no. 114 AGO 1871, roll 2, AGO3.
35. Wham to Parker, 24 March 1871, file no. W229-71, roll 715, RCA; Clum to Parker, 3 April 1871, file no. C224-71; and Parker to Clum, 4 April 1871, file no. C224-71, roll 715, RCA.
36. Wham to Parker, April 12, 1871, file no. W279-71, roll 715, RCA.

37. Wham to Parker, 12 May 1871, file no. W375-71; telegram, Wham to Parker, 26 May 1871, file no. W406-71; J. Smith to Parker, 19 May 1871, file no. 1220-71; and Brunot to Secretary of the Interior, 22 May 1871, file no. B273-71, roll 715, RCA.

38. Unless otherwise indicated, the following account of the Fort Laramie councils and other conversations of 12–14 June 1871 is based on the report of Thomas K. Cree, general file no. B349-71, roll 715, RCA. Also present in the lodge were the following headmen, *blotahunka* (war leaders), and *wicasa yatapika* (prominent warriors): Sitting Bear, Fire Thunder, and Bear Robe (future followers of American Horse); Two Buffalos, Little Crow, and Rocky Bear (associated with Red Dog); White Eyes and Big Crow (kinsmen of Little Wound and Three Bears respectively); Corn Man and Spotted Horse (who would someday call White Bird their *itancan*); as well as Long Wolf, Cold Face, Full Wolf, Red Plume, Little Cloud, Spider (Red Cloud's brother), Pretty Crow, Big Foot, Quick Eagle, Milk, Buffalo Sheds His Hair, Pumpkin Seed, and Red Buffalo.

39. Brunot to Columbus Delano, 14 June 1871, file no. B349-71, roll 715, RCA.

40. Brunot to Columbus Delano, 14 June 1871, file no. B349-71, roll 715, RCA.

41. Brunot to Columbus Delano, 14 June 1871, file no. B349-71, roll 715, RCA; telegram, Brunot to Delano, 15 June 1871, file no. B330-71, roll 715, RCA.

42. Telegram, Brunot to Delano, 14 June 1871, file no. B349-71, roll 715, RCA.

43. Telegram, Wham to Parker, 2 July 1871, file no. W532-71, roll 715, RCA; telegram, J. Smith to Parker, 30 June 1871, roll 715, RCA.

44. Telegram, Wham to Parker, 7 July 1871, file no. W551-71, roll 715, RCA; telegram, Parker to Clum, 7 July 1871, file no. C427-71, roll 715, RCA; telegram, William D. Whipple to Sheridan, 8 July 1871, file nos. A428-71 and A434-71, roll 715, RCA.

45. Campbell to Parker, 17 July 1871, file no. A601-71, roll 715, RCA; J. Smith to Clum, 21 November 1871, file no. 1544-71, and Brunot to Secretary of the Interior, 21 October 1871, file no. 1939-71, roll 715, RCA; Delano to acting Commissioner of Indian Affairs, 31 October 1871, file nos. 1950-71 and 1954-71, roll 715, RCA.

46. Ricker, interview with Colhoff.

## 5 THE POLITICAL INFLUENCE OF THE WARRIORS

1. J. E. Smith to Clum, 21 November 1871, file no. 1544-71, roll 715, RCA.
2. J. Smith to Clum, 21 November 1871, file no. 1544-71.
3. J. W. Daniels to F. A. Walker, 1 February 1872, file no. D348-72, roll 716, RCA.
4. J. Smith to Clum, 21 November 1871; report of Smith, 16 December 1871, roll 715, RCA.
5. Daniels to Walker, 29 February 1872, file no. D374-72; J. Smith to Adjutant General, 21 March 1872, file no. 11319-72, roll 716, RCA; Hyde, *Red Cloud's Folk*, p. 194.
6. J. Smith to Adjutant General, 21 March 1872, roll 716, RCA.
7. J. Smith to Adjutant General, 21 March 1872, roll 716, RCA. See also Daniels to Walker, 29 February 1872; Daniels to Walker, 1 May 1872, file no. D456-72, roll 716, RCA.
8. J. Smith to Adjutant General, 21 March 1872; Daniels to Walker, 21 March 1872, file no. D398-72; 25 March 1872, roll 716, RCA.
9. Daniels to Walker, 30 March 1872, file no. D414-72, roll 716, RCA.
10. Daniels to Walker, 30 March 1872, file no. D414-72, roll 716, RCA.
11. For information on the council of 10 April, see Daniels to Walker, 11 April 1872, file no. D423-72; J. E. Smith to E. D. Townsend, 13 April 1872; Daniels to Walker, 14 April 1872, file no. D440-72; Daniels to Walker, 20 April 1872, file no. D436-72, roll 716, RCA.
12. Daniels to Walker, 14 April 1872, file no. D440-72, roll 716, RCA.
13. Young Man Afraid of His Horse was a member of the Oglala Crooked Lance Society and also the Northern Cheyenne Elk–Kit Fox Society; see folder, "The Cheyenne Dog Soldiers," box 61, Campbell Collection; Powell, *Sweet Medicine*, 1:97.
14. Walker, *Lakota Society*, pp. 7–8, 29, 31, 60–61, 71, 79, 84, 86–87, 94. Roles overlapped more often than this example would indicate. It was possible for a man to be both *wakiconza* and *blotahunka*, although the camp council customarily expected a *wakiconza* to set aside any other duties once empowered. Similarly, a *blotahunka* might choose an incumbent *akicita* to join the war party responsible for repulsing any threats to the village while on the march.
15. Daniels to Walker, 25 March 1872, file no. D404-72, roll 716, RCA; Saville to E. P. Smith, 31 December 1873, in *Report of the Special Commission*, pp. 447–48.
16. Daniels to Walker, 14 April 1872, roll 716, RCA; George Bent to Professor Holmes, January 1907, copy of letter obtained by W. S. Campbell,

folder 11, "Handwritten Notes, Research Materials, and Manuscripts of Warpath and Council Fire," box 85, Campbell Collection.

17. Daniels to Walker, 14 April 1872, roll 716, RCA.

18. Daniels to Walker, 14 April 1872, roll 716, RCA. See also Daniels to Walker, 11 April 1872, roll 716, RCA.

19. ARCIA, 1872, p. 268; Daniels to Walker, 14 April 1872, roll 716, RCA.

20. ARCIA 1872, p. 268; Daniels to Walker, 1 May 1872, roll 716, RCA.

21. Daniels to Walker, 11 April 1872, file no. D429-72, roll 716, RCA.

22. Telegram, Daniels to Walker, 17 May 1872, file no. D467-72, roll 716, RCA; Olson, *Red Cloud and the Sioux Problem*, pp. 151–52.

23. Olson, *Red Cloud and the Sioux Problem*, pp. 151–52.

24. For multiple interpretations of the Lakota word *akicita*, see Walker, *Lakota Society*, p. 29.

25. Daniels to Walker, 6 July 1872, file no. D14-72, roll 716, RCA.

26. Daniels to Walker, 6 July 1872, file no. D14-72, roll 716, RCA; B. R. Cowen, N. J. Turney, and J. W. Wham, "Reporting on the (August) councils at Fort Peck, Montana Territory, October 1872," in H. Ex. Doc. 96, 42nd Cong., 3rd sess., pp. 4–16.

27. Cowen et al., "Reporting on the (August) councils," pp. 4–16; Daniels to Walker, 6 July 1872 and 4 September 1872, roll 716, RCA.

28. Daniels to Walker, 11 September 1872, roll 716, RCA.

29. Telegram, Daniels to J. Smith, 22 September 1872, roll 716, RCA.

30. Telegram, J. Smith to Walker, 22 September 1872, file no. S201-72; telegram, Walker to J. Smith, 26 September 1872; J. Smith to Assistant Adjutant General, 27 September 1872, roll 716, RCA.

31. Telegram, J. Smith to Assistant Adjutant General, 27 September 1872; Daniels to Walker, 24 October 1872, file no. D141-72; Secretary of the Interior to E. D. Townsend, 9 November 1872, file no. A274-72, roll 716, RCA.

32. Daniels to Walker, 24 October 1872; 12 December 1872, file no. D183-72, roll 716, RCA.

33. Daniels to Walker, 24, 25 October 1872, file no. D144-72; telegram, J. Smith to Assistant Adjutant General, 1 November 1872; Daniels to Walker, 11 November, 12 December 1872, file no. D163-72, roll 716, RCA.

34. Daniels to Walker, 11 November 1872, roll 716, RCA.

35. Daniels to Walker, 12 December 1872, file no. D183-72, roll 716, RCA.

36. Daniels to Walker, 12 December 1872, file no. D183-72, roll 716, RCA; Daniels to Walker, 28 February 1873, file no. D331-73, roll 717, RCA.

37. Daniels to Commissioner of Indian Affairs, 23 March 1873, file no. D382-73, roll 717, RCA; Ricker, interview with Alexander Baxter, roll 6, Ricker Manuscripts.

38. Brunot to E. P. Smith, 11 April 1873, file no. B74-73, roll 716, RCA.

39. Kemble to E. P. Smith, 2 June 1873, file no. K35-73, roll 717, RCA.

40. J. E. Smith to Assistant Adjutant General, 7 March 1873, file no. W125-73, DP; Daniels to E. P. Smith, 15 April 1873, file no. D46-73; and John F. Coad to E. P. Smith, 27 May 1873, file no. C160-73; Kemble to E. P. Smith, 2 June 1873, roll 717, RCA; H. Westermann to Saville, 26 May 1874, box 24, BIAM.

41. Kemble to E. P. Smith, 2 June 1873, file no. K35-73, roll 717, RCA.

42. Kemble to E. P. Smith, 2 June 1873, file no. K35-73, roll 717, RCA. Pawnee Killer, with forty-five lodges, did not start out for the Red Cloud Agency until 3 April 1874, see Maj. N. A. M. Dudley to Saville, 3 April 1874, box 24, BIAM.

43. J. J. Reynolds to Assistant Adjutant General, 2 April 1873, box 24, BIAM; Kemble to E. P. Smith, 2 June 1873, roll 717, RCA.

44. Kemble to E. P. Smith, 2 June 1873, roll 717, RCA.

45. Saville to E. P. Smith, 29 December 1873, file no. S277-73, roll 718, RCA; Saville to E. P. Smith, 31 December 1873, in *Report of the Special Commission*, pp. 447–48.

46. For an account of the council of 20 June, see Brunot to E. P. Smith, 28 June 1873, roll 717, RCA.

47. Telegram, Henry E. Alvord to E. P. Smith, 23 June 1873, file no. A230-73; telegram, Daniels to Smith, 14 July 1873, file no. D278-73; Daniels to Smith, 23 August 1873, file no. D468-73, roll 717, RCA.

48. Telegram, Daniels to Commissioner of Indian Affairs, 25 July 1873, file no. D329-73; telegram, D. J. McCann to E. P. Smith, 26 July 1873; Daniels to Smith, 1 August 1873, file no. D393-73; J. A. Campbell to Columbus Delano, 9 August 1873, file no. 1591-73, roll 717, RCA; ARCIA 1873, pp. 244, 612.

49. Daniels to E. P. Smith, 23 August 1873, file no. D468-73, roll 717, RCA; ARCIA 1873, pp. 243–44.

50. Daniels to E. P. Smith, 23 August 1873, roll 717, RCA; ARCIA 1874, pp. 559–60.

51. Saville to E. P. Smith, 14 August 1873, file no. S343-73; Daniels to Smith, 23 August 1873, roll 717, RCA.

52. Saville to E. P. Smith, 22 September 1873, file no. S477-73, roll 717, RCA; ARCIA 1874, p. 251; Hyde, *Spotted Tail's Folk*, pp. 206–8.

53. Saville to E. P. Smith, 22 September 1873.
54. Saville to E. P. Smith, 22, 27 September 1873, file no. S511-73; Alvord to Commissioner of Indian Affairs, 25 June 1873, file no. A249-73, roll 717, RCA; Barclay White to Saville, 3 March 1874, box 24, BIAM.
55. ARCIA 1874, pp. 251–52.
56. Saville to E. P. Smith, in *Report of the Special Commission*, p. 446.
57. Saville to E. P. Smith, in *Report of the Special Commission*, p. 446.
58. Messages of Red Cloud, Red Dog, and Blue Horse to the president of the United States, 26 October 1873, transmitted through Saville, 18 November 1873, file no. P495-73, roll 717, RCA; Saville to Smith, 29 September 1873, file no. S505-73, roll 717, RCA.
59. Messages of Red Cloud et al., 26 October 1873.
60. Saville to E. P. Smith, 14 November 1873, file no. S692-73, roll 717, RCA.
61. E. P. Smith to Secretary of the Interior, 14, 15 November 1873, file no. 1810-73, roll 717, RCA.
62. Saville to E. P. Smith, 18 November 1873, file no. S733-73, roll 717, RCA.
63. Saville to E. P. Smith, 27 September 1873, file no. S509-73, roll 717, RCA.
64. Saville to E. P. Smith, 29 December 1873, roll 718, RCA.
65. See for example the affidavit of John H. Moore, enclosed in F. A. Walker to Delano, 20 November 1871, file no. 1999-71, roll 715, RCA; Rufus E. Taysey to Thomas H. Talbot, 7 January 1872, roll 716, RCA.
66. Fritz, *The Movement for Indian Assimilation*, pp. 158–60.
67. Saville to E. P. Smith, 27 September 1873, file no. S509-73, roll 717, RCA.
68. Saville to E. P. Smith, 11 December 1873, file no. S775-73, roll 717, RCA.
69. Saville to E. P. Smith, 18 November 1873, file no. S673-73, roll 717, RCA; Saville to Smith, 29 December 1873, file no. S277-73, roll 718, RCA.
70. Saville to E. P. Smith, 29 December 1873, file no. S277-73, roll 718, RCA.
71. Saville to E. P. Smith, 29 December 1873, file no. S277-73, roll 718, RCA.
72. Saville to E. P. Smith, 29 December 1873, file no. S277-73, roll 718, RCA.

73. Telegrams, Moore to E. P. Smith, 5 January 1874, file no. M18-74, 9 January 1874, file no. M43-74, roll 718, RCA; Saville to Smith, 2 February 1874, file no. S195-74, roll 719, RCA.

74. Saville to E. P. Smith, 14 February 1874, file no. S250-74, roll 719, RCA.

75. Telegram, Saville to Smith, 7 February 1874, file no. S212-74; Saville to Smith, 14 February 1874, roll 719, RCA; ARCIA 1874, pp. 355–56. In Saville's report to the commissioner of Indian affairs, he identified the assassin as a Hunkpapa, although most accounts of the murder list him as a Miniconjou. In his interview with Judge Eli Ricker, William Garnett recalled that the man's name was Kicking Bear, not High Foretop, although Lakotas frequently had more than one name (see Ricker, interview with Garnett).

76. Saville to E. P. Smith, 14 February 1874, file no. S236-74/S252-74, roll 719, RCA; Saville to Smith, 14 February 1874, file no. S250-74; Saville to Smith, 16 February 1874, file no. S251-74, roll 718, RCA. See also Capt. H. M. Lazelle to J. E. Smith, 3 April 1874, Field Records, Sioux Expedition, 1874, DP.

77. Saville to E. P. Smith, 14, 16 February 1874, roll 718 RCA. See also Saville to Smith, 2 February 1874, file no. S195-74, roll 719, RCA.

78. Saville to E. P. Smith, 14, 16, 22 February 1874, roll 718, RCA.

79. Saville to E. P. Smith, 22 February 1874, roll 718, RCA.

80. Saville to E. P. Smith, 16, 22, 23 February 1874, file no. S258-74, roll 718, RCA.

81. Saville to Commissioner of Indian Affairs, 23 February 1874, file no. S276-74, roll 718, RCA.

82. Saville to E. P. Smith, 5 March 1874, file no. S311-74, roll 718, RCA.

83. Telegrams, Sheridan to Sherman, 2, 7 March 1874; Saville to E. P. Smith, 5 March 1874, file no. S261-74, roll 718, RCA.

84. Saville to E. P. Smith, 24 March 1874, file no. S352-74; Saville to Smith, 3 August 1874, file no. S1057, roll 718, RCA. For the roll of Indians registered at the Red Cloud Agency during the second quarter of 1874, see Saville to Smith, 13 July 1874, file no. S877-74, roll 718, RCA.

85. Saville to E. P. Smith, 14 February 1874, file no. S250-74; Saville to B. F. Walters, 13 April 1874, roll 718, RCA; ARCIA 1874, p. 46. The guard included American Horse (probably not the head shirtwearer, but the Kiyuksa warrior of the same name), Bear Killer, Bear Shield, Beef Gall, Black Spotted Horse, Blue Shield, Bolting Bear, Face, Goes and Comes, Pumpkin Seed, Standing Soldier, Spotted Cow, and Water Crow.

86. Saville to E. P. Smith, 20 July 1874, file no. S959-74; Saville to Smith, 27 July 1874, file no. S994-74; Saville to Smith, 3 August 1874, file no. S1057-74; Saville to Smith, 7 August 1874, file no. S1056-74; Saville to Smith, 15 August 1874, file no. S1119-74; Saville to Smith, 31 August 1874, file nos. S1230-74, S1184-74, roll 718, RCA.

## 6 OGLALA WARRIORS AND AGENCY AFFAIRS

1. George A. Custer to Assistant Adjutant General, Department of Dakota, August 1874, in S. Ex. Doc. 32, 43rd Cong., 2nd sess., pp. 1–8. See also "Message of the President of the United States in Answer to a Senate Resolution of March 15, 1875, Information in Relation to the Black Hills," S. Ex. Doc. 2, vol. 1, 44th Cong., special sess., pp. 1–15.

2. Excerpts from the *Sioux City Daily Journal,* 4 September 1874; F. Marcy Lynde and Alfred H. Terry to Assistant Adjutant General, 3 September 1874, DM: Citizenship Expeditions to the Black Hills, roll 2.

3. For Professor Jenney's report of his expedition to the Black Hills, see ARCIA 1875, pp. 181–83.

4. See E. A. Howard to Commissioner of Indian Affairs, 14 August 1875, roll 841, STA; Bourke, quoted in Porter, *Paper Medicine Man,* p. 26.

5. Saville to E. P. Smith, 7 August 1874, file no. S1056-74, roll 718, RCA; Saville to Smith, 15, 24 August 1874, file no. S1119-74; Saville to Smith, 31 August 1874, file no. S1184-74, roll 718, RCA.

6. Saville to E. P. Smith, 28 September 1874, file no. S1376-74, roll 718, RCA.

7. Saville to E. P. Smith, 28 September 1874, file no. S1376-74; Saville to Smith, 13 November 1874, file no. S1630-74, roll 718, RCA; ARCIA 1874, pp. 441–42. Three Bears often affiliated with the *tiyospaye* of Fire Lightning and Two Lance. During the previous summer, Three Bears had come into the agency with nine lodges, accompanied by Two Lance with thirteen tipis. Fire Lightning's twenty-lodge band had separated from them, however. See N. A. Dudley to Saville, 26 June 1874, box 24, BIAM.

8. Saville to E. P. Smith, 5 October 1874, file no. S1407-774, roll 718, RCA; William H. Jordan to Assistant Adjutant General, 4 August 1874, DP: Sioux Expedition, 1874.

9. Except where noted, the account of the October incident is derived from Ricker, interview with Garnett.

10. Jordan to Assistant Adjutant General, 23 October 1874, roll 718, RCA;

testimony of Jordan, 10 August 1875, in *Report of the Special Commission,* p. 311.

11. Saville to E. P. Smith, 24 October 1875, in *Report of the Special Commission,* pp. 441–42.

12. Ricker, interview with Benjamin Tibbitts, roll 1, Ricker Manuscripts.

13. Ricker, interview with Garnett.

14. Jordan to Assistant Adjutant General, 13 October 1874, roll 718, RCA.

15. Ricker, interview with Tibbitts; testimony of Jordan, and Emmet Crawford, 25 August 1875, in *Report of the Special Commission,* pp. 310–11, 569; Jordan to Ruggles, 29 October 1874, file no. W1843-74, roll 718, RCA.

16. Telegram, Bradley to Adjutant General, 25 October 1874, file no. W1793-74, roll 718, RCA; testimony of O. C. Marsh, in *Report of the Special Commission,* p. 67.

17. Jordan to Ruggles, 29 October 1874, file no. W1843-74, roll 718, RCA; testimonies of Jordan and J. M. Lee, in *Report of the Special Commission,* pp. 311, 316–19; Ricker, interview with Tibbitts.

18. Sheridan to Sherman, 25 November 1874, file no. W1951-74, roll 718, RCA.

19. By late 1874, weekly rations per adult person consisted of three pounds of beef, one pound of flour, and a quarter pound of corn; one pound of bacon four times a month, in lieu of beef; and four pounds of coffee and eight pounds of sugar per hundred rations. See H. Ex. Doc. 43, 18 December 1874, 43rd Cong., 2nd sess.

20. Saville to C. C. Cox, 16 December 1874, file no. C1072-74, roll 718, RCA.

21. Saville to E. P. Smith, 30 November 1874, file no. S1804-74; Saville to Cox, 16 December 1874, file no. C1072-74, roll 718, RCA.

22. Saville to Cox, 16 December 1874; Saville to E. P. Smith, 8 January 1875, file no. S48-75, roll 719, RCA.

23. Saville to Cox, 16 December 1874; Jordan, copy of a report, 11 February 1875, file no. W531-75, roll 719, RCA.

24. Proceedings of a Council with the Indians at Red Cloud Agency, convened by James S. Collins, 29 March 1875, file no. 533-75, roll 719, RCA.

25. Proceedings of a Council; Black Elk, *Sixth Grandfather,* p. 170.

26. Collins to Grant, 4 April 1875, roll 841, STA.

27. Saville to E. P. Smith, 8 April 1875, file no. S597-75, roll 719, RCA.

28. Saville to E. P. Smith, 8 April 1875, file no. s597-75; telegram, Saville to Commissioner of Indian Affairs, 24 April 1875, file no. s642-75; telegram, Saville to Smith, 7 May 1875, file no. s745-75, roll 719, RCA.

29. Ricker, interview with Garnett. The thirteen spokesmen were the band *itancan* of the two major Oglala divisions, Red Cloud of the agency Bad Faces and Little Wound of the Kiyuksas; the headmen Black Bear and White Tail; and prominent Oglala and Wazaza warriors Scalp Face, American Horse, Fast Thunder, Young Bad Wound, Iron Horse, High Lance, Sitting Bull, Shoulder, and Conquering Bear.

30. Saville to E. P. Smith, 30 November 1874, file no. s1804-74, roll 718, RCA.

31. Saville to E. P. Smith, 5 June 1875, file no. s1022-75, roll 719, RCA; Marsh, *Affairs at Red Cloud Agency*, pp. 14–15.

32. For the *New York Times* coverage of the 1875 Washington trip, see the editions of 6, 10, 14, 19–20, 22, 24–28 May; 1–6, 10 June; and 19 July.

33. *New York Times*, 20 May 1875, p. 1.

34. *New York Times*, 24 May 1875, p. 1; 4 June 1875, p. 4.

35. Council with the Sioux Delegation, 27 May 1875, copy, box 779, PR.

36. Talk with Red Cloud in Washington DC, 28 May 1875, in *Report of the Special Commission*, pp. 832–35.

37. *New York Times*, 2 June 1875, p. 1.

38. Talk with Little Wound and Sitting Bull, Washington DC, 5 June 1875, in *Report of the Special Commission*, pp. 838–39. See also Saville to E. P. Smith, 14 February 1874, file no. s250-74; Saville to B. F. Walters, 13 April 1874, roll 718, RCA.

39. Luther Standing Bear recalled the time when his father, a delegate to Washington, had received a silk hat as a gift from federal officials. "Whenever a man returned from Washington and attended a council," Standing Bear wrote, "he was expected to come dressed up. This was a sort of 'badge,' to prove that he had really been to Washington" (Standing Bear, *My People the Sioux*, p. 70; see also Viola, *Diplomats in Buckskins*, p. 104).

40. Touching the pen for the Oglalas and Wazazas were the *tiyospaye itancan* Blue Horse, Day, High Wolf, Little Wound, Red Dog, Red Leaf, Slow Bull, along with Turkey Legs of the Northern Cheyennes. Other signers included Black Bear, Pawnee Killer, White Tail, and headmen Yellow Hair and Quick Bear; the war leaders Conquering Bear and White Crane Walking; and the young men Bear's Robe, Iron Horse, Red Top, and Tall Lance.

41. ARCIA 1875, pp. 179–80; E. P. Smith to Thomas C. Fletcher et al., 1 July 1875, file no. 1823-75, roll 719, RCA. In Marsh's official report he asserted that Saville was "unfit for the position" of agent, and "guilty of fraud." See Marsh, *Affairs at Red Cloud Agency*, p. 20. Other members of the commission were C. J. Faulkner, A. H. Bullock, George H. Lance, and B. W. Harris.

42. Testimony of Jules Ecoffey, 4 August 1875, *Report of the Special Commission*, pp. 216–17.

43. Informal council with Sitting Bull and Man Afraid of His Horse, 9 August 1875, *Report of the Special Commission*, pp. 216–17; 294–95.

44. Testimony of F. D. Yates, 10 August 1875, *Report of the Special Commission*, pp. 331–32; testimony of Jordan, 10 August 1875, *Report of the Special Commission*, p. 315; testimony of Leon Palladay, 11 August 1875, *Report of the Special Commission*, pp. 336–37.

45. *Report of the Special Commission*, p. 298. Representing the Oglalas and Wazazas were Red Cloud, Little Wound, Conquering Bear, Red Leaf, Tall Lance, High Wolf, Man Afraid of His Horse, Sword, and Sitting Bull; Leon Palladay and Nick Janis translated for the southern and northern Oglalas, respectively.

46. Hyde, *Red Cloud's Folk*, p. 238.

47. *Report of the Special Commission*, pp. 299–301.

48. Informal talk with a party of Oglalas, 10 August 1875, *Report of the Special Commission*, pp. 302–3. See also the talk with Red Cloud, 11 August 1875, in *Report of the Special Commission*, p. 308.

49. *Report of the Special Commission*, pp. xvii, lv–lix.

50. For a report of the Allison commission, see ARSI 1875, pp. 184–201. Assisting Allison were Bishop E. R. Ames, Judge F. W. Palmer, Brig. Gen. Alfred Terry, A. Comingo, Rev. Samuel Hinman, W. H. Ashley, A. G. Lawrence, and former trader F. P. Beauvais. John Collins undertook the duties of secretary, and Hinman, Comingo, and Ashby were directed to notify the various Lakotas agencies of the impending talks.

51. Saville to E. P. Smith, 16 August 1875, file no. S1368-75, roll 719, RCA.

52. Unless otherwise noted, the account of the Allison commission's visit to the Lakotas is derived from ARSI 1875, pp. 186–91, 509. In addition to the Oglalas and Brulés, bands of Miniconjous, Hunkpapas, Sihasapas, Two Kettles, Sans Arcs, Lower Brulés, Yanktons, Santees, Northern Cheyennes, and Arapahos had also sent delegates to the great council.

53. Ricker, interview with Charles Turning Hawk, roll 3, Ricker Manuscripts.

54. Little Big Man, quoted in Porter, *Paper Medicine Man*, p. 27.
55. ARSW 1875, p. 175.
56. Saville to E. P. Smith, 11 October 1875, file no. S1637-75; Saville to Smith, 25 October 1875, file no. S1707-75, roll 719, RCA. Two weeks later, Saville issued the results of the census: at the agency were 9,136 Lakotas, 2,172 Northern Cheyennes, and 1,565 northern Arapahos, for a total population of 12,873 (see Saville to Smith, 25 October 1875, file no. S1707-75, roll 719, RCA.
57. H. Ex. Doc. 184, 44th Cong., 1st sess., pp. 8–9.
58. Hastings to J. Q. Smith, 24 January 1876, file no. H167-76, roll 720, RCA.
59. Hastings to J. Q. Smith, 28 January 1876, file no. H204-76; telegram, Hastings to Smith, 24 February 1876, file no. H262-76, roll 720, RCA.
60. McGillycuddy to Hiram Price, 5 April 1882, file no. 6786-82, BIA, RG 75, Office of Indian Affairs, Letters Received 1881–1907, NARS; George Crook to Sheridan, 29 May 1876, file no. 3211-76; Townsend to Sheridan, 30 May 1876, file no. 3155-76; Jordan to Townsend, 2 June 1876, file no. 3539-76; telegram, W. Merritt to Sheridan, 7 June 1876, file no. 3439-76, Sioux War, roll 2, DM. See also Stewart, *Custer's Luck*, pp. 307–12.

7 GOING HOME TO PINE RIDGE

1. See for example Ambrose, *Crazy Horse and Custer*; Connell, *Son of the Morning Star*; Dippie, *Custer's Last Stand*; Graham, *The Custer Myth* and *The Story of the Little Big Horn*; Gray, *Custer's Last Campaign*; Hutton, *The Custer Reader*; and Stewart, *Custer's Luck*.
2. For a report of the Manypenny commission of 1876, see S. Ex. Doc. 9, 44th Cong., 2nd sess., pp. 5–18. Serving on the commission with Manypenny were Henry Bullis, Newton Edmunds, Bishop Henry Whipple, A. G. Boone, A. S. Gaylord, Gen. H. H. Sibley, and Samuel Hinman. Sibley declined to serve and was subsequently replaced by former Red Cloud agent, J. W. Daniels.
3. Unless otherwise stated, the account of the 1876 council is derived from S. Ex. Doc. 9, p. 7.
4. Ricker, interview with Garnett. Shortly after this incident, Sitting Bull returned to the north, where he was later killed at Fort Keogh by several Crow scouts working for the U.S. Army.
5. The following councilors signed the agreement: Red Cloud, Man Afraid of His Horse, Young Man Afraid of His Horse, Red Dog, American

Horse, Afraid of the Bear, Three Bears, Fire Thunder, Fast Bear, Good Voice Crow, Turning Bear, Weasel Eagle, Red Leaf, Fire Eyes (also known as White Bull), White Cow Man, Big Crow, Good Bull, Sorrel Horse, Weasel Bear, Two Lance, Bad Wound, High Bear, He Takes the Enemy, Soldier, Slow Bull (also known as Stupid Face), High Wolf, Big Foot, White Thunder, and Blue Horse.

6. Telegram, O. Elting to J. Q. Smith, 21 August 1876, file no. E116-76, roll 720, RCA; Olson, *Red Cloud and the Sioux Problem*, p. 227.

7. Ricker, interview with Garnett; Crook to Terry, 25 August 1876, Big Horn and Yellowstone Expedition, 1876, DDL.

8. S. Ex. Doc. 9, p. 19.

9. S. Ex. Doc. 9, p. 19; telegram, Crook to Sheridan, 24 October 1876, file no. 7719-76, Sioux War, 1876–1877, roll 4, DM.

10. Crook, Commission Given to Spotted Tail, 23 October 1876, Big Horn and Yellowstone Expedition, 1876, DDL. See also Crook's report to the *New York Herald*, 25 October 1876, in Anderson, "Indian Peace-Talkers," p. 240n; Ricker, interview with Garnett; Joseph Bissonette to A. S. Gaylord, STA.

11. Anderson, "Indian Peace-Talkers," pp. 235–36.

12. Ricker, interview with Garnett.

13. ARSW 1877, pp. 239, 494–96, 524–25.

14. ARSW 1877, pp. 240–45, 250.

15. Ricker, interview with Garnett; William Garnett's account of Crazy Horse's death relayed to Gen. H. L. Scott and Maj. James McLaughlin, in Hugh L. Scott Papers.

16. Ricker, interview with Garnett; C. A. Johnson to J. Q. Smith, 6 May 1877, file no. R151-77; Johnson to Smith, 4 June 1877, file no. R185-77, roll 721, RCA.

17. Benjamin R. Shopp to J. Q. Smith, 15 August 1877, file no. S822-77, roll 721, RCA.

18. Johnson to J. Q. Smith, 4 June 1877, file no. R185-77, roll 721, RCA; Clark to Commissioner of Indian Affairs, 10 September 1877, roll 841, STA.

19. Irwin to J. Q. Smith, 31 August 1877, file no. R337-77, roll 721, RCA; Irwin to Commissioner of Indian Affairs, 7 September 1877, roll 1, PRM.

20. James Irwin to Commissioner of Indian Affairs, 26 July 1877, file no. R277-77, roll 721, RCA.

21. Irwin to Commissioner of Indian Affairs, 1 September 1877, file no. R335-77, roll 721, RCA; Clark to Commissioner of Indian Affairs, 10 September 1877; telegram, Bradley to Sheridan, 6 September 1877, file no. 5363-77, Sioux War, 1876–77, roll 4, DM. Interpreter William Garnett claimed that this tension between the Crazy Horse camp and the agency Oglalas was played out during a sun dance held about three miles northwest of the agency. After counting coup on the sacred sun dance pole, the young men engaged in a mock battle. That year, the sun dance *wakiconza* decided that the "fight" should symbolize the destruction of Custer's forces, with Crazy Horse's warriors representing the victorious Lakotas, and the agency Oglalas, Custer's troops. The former were supposed to strike the agency warriors gently, but instead "began delivering hard blows with war clubs." Garnett, who was participating on the "Custer" side, recalled that he and several of his comrades soon became enraged. They fired their revolvers, driving the Crazy Horse people out of the campground and compelling Lt. W. P. Clark to intervene, thus violating the sacredness of the sun dance (see Ricker, interview with Garnett).

22. Telegram, Irwin to J. Q. Smith, 5 September 1877, roll 721, RCA; Clark to Commissioner of Indian Affairs, 10 September 1877; Bradley to Adjutant General, 7 September 1877, file no. 5491-77, Sioux War, roll 4, DM.

23. Bradley to Adjutant General, 7 September 1877; Irwin to J. Q. Smith, 6 September 1877, roll 1, PRM; copy of telegram, Sheridan to Townsend, 6 September 1877, file no. W847-77, roll 721, RCA. See also Ricker, interview with Chipps (Encouraging Bear), roll 3, Ricker Manuscripts; Garnett's account in Scott Papers.

24. Porter, *Paper Medicine Man,* p. 67; telegram, Irwin to Commissioner of Indian Affairs, 6 September 1877, file no. R338-77, roll 721, RCA. For conflicting accounts of Crazy Horse's death, see Ricker, interviews with Garnett, John Shangrau, Richard C. Stirk, Chipps, Salaway, American Horse, rolls 2–3, 6, Ricker Manuscripts. See also Bradley to Adjutant General, 7 September 1877; and the Jeanne Smith Collection, August 1991, files 27–30, 36–39, 42, 47, 49, Oglala Lakota College Archives, Pine Ridge Reservation.

25. For an account of the 1877 trip to Washington, see copy of a report of the council, 26 September 1877, sent by Commissioner of Indian Affairs to Charles G. Penney, 19 April 1894, file no. 13199-94, box 779, PR; and the *New York Times,* 26–29 September and 2–6 October 1877.

26. Telegram, Irwin to Commissioner of Indian Affairs, 10 October 1877,

file no. R407-77, roll 721, RCA; ARCIA 1877, p. 18; Ricker, interview with Tibbitts et al., roll 1.

27. Irwin to E. A. Hayt, 27 October 1877, file no. R447-77, roll 721, RCA.

28. Irwin to Hayt, 5 November 1877, file no. 501-77; Irwin to Hayt, 10 January 1878, roll 722, RCS.

29. At this time the agency bands were under the *itancan* American Horse, Black Bear, White Bird, Young Man Afraid, Red Cloud, Red Dog, Slow Bull, High Wolf, Little Wound, Blue Horse, Day, and Three Bears. There were approximately three hundred lodges of northern Lakotas traveling with the main caravan. During the trip, about one hundred returned north along with thirty lodges of agency Oglalas. See Clark to Carl Schurz, 7 November 1877, roll 841, STA; telegram, Irwin to Commissioner of Indian Affairs, 26 November 1877, roll 721, RCA; telegram, Clark to Adjutant General, 30 November 1877, file no. 771, DDT; Ricker, interview with Garnett.

30. Copy of plats of trail to and post of the New Red Cloud Agency, prepared by McGillycuddy, 13 December 1877, file no. W45-78, roll 723, RCA; copy of a telegram, Sheridan to Terry, 3 December 1877, file no. W1204-77, roll 721, RCA; Ricker, interview with Garnett.

31. Telegram, Irwin to Commissioner of Indian Affairs, 13 December 1877, file no. R509-77, roll 721, RCA.

32. Telegram, Irwin to Commissioner of Indian Affairs, 12 January 1878 and 11 February 1878, file no. 1212-78, roll 722, RCA.

33. Bartlett, 29 January 1878, file no. 1409-78, copy of letter sent to Irwin and subsequently forwarded to Commissioner of Indian Affairs; Irwin to Hayt, 4 March 1878, file no. 1409-78, roll 722, RCA.

34. Telegram, Irwin to Commissioner of Indian Affairs, 11 February 1878.

35. Irwin to Hayt, 27 January 1878, file no. 1141-78; telegram, Irwin to Hayt, 17 February 1878, file no. 1236-78, roll 722, RCA.

36. Telegram, Hayt to W. M. Leeds, 18 February 1878, file no. 1235-78, roll 722, RCA; telegram, Hammond to Commissioner of Indian Affairs, 2 March 1878, roll 13, DS 1861–70.

37. Red Dog to Daniels, 11 March 1878, file no. D202-78, forwarded by Daniels to the president, 7 April 1878; Irwin to Hayt, 18 March 1878, file no. 1500-78, roll 722, RCA; Red Cloud to P. D. Vroom, 14 March 1878, file no. W558-7; see also George McCrary to Secretary of the Interior, 5 April 1878, file no. W558-78, roll 723, RCA.

38. Hammond to Commissioner of Indian Affairs, letter from James Irwin enclosed, 3 April 1878, file no. H704-78; telegram, Irwin to Commis-

enclosed, 3 April 1878, file no. H704-78; telegram, Irwin to Commissioner of Indian Affairs, 2 May 1878, file no. 1738-78; Irwin to Commissioner of Indian Affairs, 7 May 1878, file no. 1826-78; telegram, 14 May 1878, file no. 1881-78; telegram, 9 June 1878, file no. 1991-78; telegram, Irwin to Secretary of the Interior, 25 June 1878, file no. 11526-78; Irwin to Hayt, 5 July 1878, file no. 11212-78; Hayt to William M. Leeds, 15 August 1878, file no. 11544-78, roll 722, RCA.

39. The members of this special commission included Col. D. H. Stanley, J. M. Haworth, and Rev. A. L. Riggs (official interpreter). Commissioner Hayt also joined the commission for a brief period before returning to headquarters. For a report of the Stanley commission's visit to the Oglalas and Brulés, see ARCIA 1878, pp. 156–61; James O'Beirne to Hayt, 27 August 1878, file no. 042-78, enclosed in a copy of the letter Little Big Man dictated to the president, 1 August 1878, roll 723, RCA.

40. O'Beirne to Hayt, 27 August 1878, file no. 042-78, roll 723, RCA; Secretary of War to Secretary of the Interior, 26 September 1878, file no. W13-79, roll 725, RCA.

41. O'Beirne to Hayt, 7 March 1879, file no. 092-79; telegram, Hayt to O'Beirne, 26 March 1879, file no. 0121-79, roll 725, RCA. Big Road finally surrendered with two hundred lodges at Fort Keogh, Montana Territory, in early fall 1880; see McGillycuddy to Commissioner of Indian Affairs, 1 October 1880, file no. M2058-80, roll 726, RCA.

42. Telegram, Irwin to Commissioner of Indian Affairs, 30 August 1878, file no. 11702-78, roll 722, RCA.

43. Irwin to Schurz, 5 September 1878, file no. 11118-78, roll 722, RCA.

44. Irwin to Schurz, 5 September 1878, file no. 11118-78, roll 722, RCA.

45. Irwin to Schurz, 5 September 1878, file no. 11118-78, roll 722, RCA.

46. Telegram, Irwin to Commissioner of Indian Affairs, 25 September 1878, file no. 11932-78, roll 722, RCA; telegram, Hayt to Irwin, 27 September 1878, box 723, PRT.

47. Telegram, O'Beirne to Commissioner of Indian Affairs, 8 October 1878, file no. 069-78, roll 722; telegram, 9 October 1878, file no. 058-78, roll 723, RCA.

48. Irwin to Commissioner of Indian Affairs, 11 November 1878, file no. 12255-78, roll 723; Telegram, 24 November 1878, roll 724, RCA.

49. Inspector J. H. Hammond deemed the new name Pine Ridge inappropriate, there being "no ridge country here." He suggested "Oglala," but most officials thought that few would be able to spell this word cor-

rectly (see Hammond to Commissioner of Indian Affairs, 9 December 1878, file no. H1996-78, roll 722, RCA.

50. O'Beirne to Hayt, 12 February 1879, file no. 056-79, roll 725, RCA.

**AFTERWORD**

1. For a good overview of the changes in Oglala political organization between the 1890s and 1930s, see Biolsi, *Organizing the Lakota.*

# Bibliography

DOCUMENTS AND MANUSCRIPTS

Campbell, Walter Stanley. Collection. Western History Archives. University of Oklahoma, Norman.

Dorsey, James Owen. Papers. MS 4800. National Anthropological Archives. Washington DC.

Herman, Eddie, and Vera Herman. Materials on the Dakotas, 1922–50. MS 4685. National Anthropological Archives, Washington DC.

McGillycuddy, Valentine T. Correspondence with Col. Garrick Mallery, Pine Ridge, 17 August 1884. MS 2372, box 11. National Anthropological Archives. Washington DC.

Ricker, Eli S. Manuscripts, Series Two. Microfilm. Nebraska State Historical Society, Lincoln.

Riggs, Stephen R., and Thomas L. Notes on Dakota Culture. MS 925. National Anthropological Archives. Washington DC.

Scott, Hugh L. Papers. Box 2, manuscript 2932. National Anthropological Archives. Washington DC.

Siouan Census Rolls of the Several Reservations (Pine Ridge). MS 2610. National Anthropological Archives. Washington DC.

Smith, Jeanne. Collection. August 1991. (Several photocopied pages of the killing of Crazy Horse.) Oglala Lakota College Archives, Pine Ridge Reservation, South Dakota.

U.S. Army. Adjutant General's Office. Records of the Adjutant General's Office, 1780s–1917. Record Group 94. Letters Received by the Office of the Adjutant General (Main Series), 1822–1860. Microfilm M567, roll 546. NARS.

———. Letters Received by the Office of the Adjutant General (Main Series), 1861–70. Microfilm M619, rolls 367, 560, 563, 722, 812. NARS.

———. Letters Received by the Office of the Adjutant General (Main Series), 1871–1880. Microfilm M666, rolls 2, 25, 58, 83, 108, 143, 181, 238, 259, 271, 273, 277–92, 294, 322–23, 381. NARS.

———. Letters Received by the Office of the Adjutant General (Main Series) 1881–89. Microfilm M689, rolls 224, 279, 446, 537–38, 634, 676. NARS.

U.S. Army. Continental Commands. Records of the Continental Commands, 1821–1920. Record Group 393. Department of Dakota, 1866–1911, Headquarters Records, General Records, and Correspondence: Letters Received Relating to the Sioux Indians, 1863–1866; Telegrams Received, 1877. NARS.

———. Department of Dakota, 1866–1911. Big Horn and Yellowstone Expedition, 1876: Letters, Telegrams, and Endorsements Sent, May–October 1876. NARS.

———. Department of Dakota, 1866–1911. Field Records, Yellowstone Expedition, 1872–73: Letters Received and Telegrams Received, 1872–73. NARS.

———. Military Division of the Missouri, 1865: Letters Received, 1865. NARS.

———. Military Division of the Missouri, 1866–91, General Records and Correspondence. Special Files of Letters Received, 1863–85: Citizen Expeditions to the Black Hills, 1874–75; Indian Scouts, 1874–77; Sioux War, 1876–77. Microfilm 1495, rolls 2–4, 15. NARS.

———. Department of the Platte, 1858–59: LS, July 1858 to June 1859. NARS.

———. Department of the Platte, 1866–98. Headquarters Records, General Records, and Correspondence. Field Records, Sioux Expedition, 1874: Letters Received, 1874. NARS.

———. Department of the Platte, 1866–98. Powder River Expedition, 1876: Letters Received, 1876; LS, November–December 1876. Records Relating to Indian Treaties. Record Group 123. Documents Relating to the Negotiation of Ratified and Unratified Treaties with Various Indian Tribes, 1801–69. Microfilm T494, rolls 4, 9. NARS.

U.S. Department of the Interior. The Secretary of the Interior. Annual Reports, 1863–80.

U.S. Department of War. The Secretary of War. Annual Reports, 1849–80.

U.S. Office of Indian Affairs. The Commissioner of Indian Affairs. Annual Reports, 1840–80.

———. Records of the Office of Indian Affairs. Record Group 75. Censuses (Indian Service Records). Censuses: General Reservation Censuses, Undated Censuses, 1874; Special Censuses and Lists, 1877–89. NARS-KC.

———. General Records. General Correspondence: Copies of Miscellaneous Letters Sent, 1876–80; Miscellaneous Correspondence Received, 1871–89; Telegrams Received, and Copies of Telegrams Sent, 1876–80. NARS-KC.

———. Legal and Legislative Records. Legal Records: Council Proceedings, 1875–80; Petitions, 1875–80; Records of Controversies, 1867–80. NARS-KC.

———. Letters Received 1824–81. Microfilm M234: Red Cloud Agency, 1871–80, rolls 715–25; Spotted Tail Agency, 1875–80, rolls 840–45; Upper Platte Agency, 1846–70, rolls 893–96. NARS.

———. Letters Received 1881–1907. NARS.

———. Miscellaneous Letters Sent by the Agents or Superintendents at the Pine Ridge Indian Agency, 1876–1914. Microfilm M1229, rolls 1–12. NARS.

———. Records of the Land Division. Irregularly Shaped Papers, 1849–1907: No. 68, The Great Peace Commission of 1868. NARS.

———. Records of the Statistics Division. Reports of Inspection of the Field Jurisdiction of the Office of Indian Affairs, 1873–1900. Microfilm M1070, rolls 37, 43, 57. NARS.

———. Records of the Superintendencies and Agencies of the Office of Indian Affairs. Records of the Dakota Superintendency, 1861–70 and 1877–78; and the Wyoming Superintendency, 1870. Microfilm M1016: Dakota Superintendency, rolls 1–5, 7, 9–13. NARS.

———. Records Relating to Indian Census Rolls and Other Enrollments. Microfilm M595, rolls 362–63. NARS.

———. Reports of Inspection of the Field Jurisdiction of the Office of Indian Affairs, 1873–1900. Microfilm M1070, rolls 37, 43, 57. NARS.

———. Special Cases. No. 147: Conditions at Pine Ridge Agency. NARS.

———. Special Files, 1807–1904. Microfilm M574. No. 219: Red Cloud and Spotted Tail; No. 264: McGillycuddy. NARS.

———. Trust Responsibilities Records. Records of Annuity and Allotment Benefits: Notebooks Recording Issues and Stocks of Annuity Goods, 1878–89; Ration Tickets, ca. 1880–89; Vouchers and Abstracts of Articles Issued to Indians (Abstract D), 1879–89. NARS-KC.

Webb, H. G. "The Dakota Sun Dance." (Description of the Oglala Sun Dance of 1883.) MS 1394a. National Anthropological Archives. Washington DC.

Williamson, John P. Correspondence with Col. Garrick Mallery, 10 April 1877. MS 2372, box 11. National Anthropological Archives. Washington, DC.

OTHER SOURCES

Abel, Annie H., ed. *Tabeau's Narrative of Loisel's Expedition to the Upper Missouri.* Norman: University of Oklahoma Press, 1939; reprint, 1969.

## Bibliography

Adams, Donald K., ed. "The Journal of Ada A. Vogdes." *Montana* 13 (1963): 2–17.

Ahern, Wilbert H. "Assimilationist Racism: The Case of the 'Friends of the Indian.'" *Journal of Ethnic Studies* 4 (summer 1976): 23–32.

Albers, Patricia, and Beatrice Medicine, eds. *The Hidden Half: Studies of Plains Indian Women*. New York: University Press of America, 1983.

Allen, Charles W. "Red Cloud and the U.S. Flag." *Nebraska History* 21 (1940): 293–304.

Ambrose, Stephen E. *Crazy Horse and Custer: The Parallel Lives of Two American Heroes*. New York: Doubleday, 1975.

Amiotte, Arthur. "Lakota Sun Dance: Historical and Contemporary Perspectives." In *Sioux Indian Religion*, ed. Raymond J. DeMallie and Douglas R. Parks, pp. 79–89. Norman: University of Oklahoma Press, 1987.

Anderson, Gary Clayton. "Early Migration and Intertribal War: A Revision." *Western Historical Quarterly* 11 (January 1980): 17–36.

———. *Kinsmen of Another Kind: Dakota-White Relations in the Upper Mississippi Valley, 1650–1862*. Lincoln: University of Nebraska Press, 1984.

Anderson, Harry H. "The Controversial Sioux Amendment to the Fort Laramie Treaty of 1851." *Nebraska History* 37 (September 1956): 201–20.

———. "Fur Traders as Fathers: The Origins of the Mixed-Blooded Community among the Rosebud Sioux." *South Dakota History* 3 (summer 1973): 233–70.

———. "Indian Peace-Talkers and the Conclusion of the Sioux War of 1876." *Nebraska History* 40 (December 1963): 223–54.

Anderson, Harry H., ed. "The Letters of Peter Wilson, First Resident Agent Among the Teton Sioux." *Nebraska History* 42, no. 4 (December 1961): 237–64.

Armstrong, William H. *Warrior in Two Camps: Ely S. Parker, Union General and Seneca Chief*. Syracuse NY: Syracuse University Press, 1978.

Athearn, Robert G. *William Tecumseh Sherman and the Settlement of the West*. Norman: University of Oklahoma Press, 1956.

Bad Heart Bull, Amos. *A Pictographic History of the Oglala Sioux*. Lincoln: University of Nebraska Press, 1967.

Bailey, John W. *Pacifying the Plains: General Alfred Terry and the Decline of the Sioux, 1866–1890*. Westport CT: Greenwood Press, 1979.

Belden, George P. *Belden, the White Chief; or Twelve Years among the Wild Indians of the Plains*. Athens: Ohio University Press, 1974.

*Bibliography*

Berthrong, Donald J. *The Southern Cheyennes*. Norman: University of Oklahoma Press, 1963.

Biolsi, Thomas. *Organizing the Lakota: The Political Economy of the New Deal on the Pine Ridge and Rosebud Reservations*. Tucson: University of Arizona Press, 1992.

Black Elk. *Black Elk Speaks, Being the Life Story of a Holy Man of the Oglala Sioux*. New York: William Morrow, 1932.

———. *The Sixth Grandfather: Black Elk's Teachings to John G. Neihardt*. Ed. Raymond J. DeMallie. Lincoln: University of Nebraska Press, 1984.

Blish, Helen H. "Ethical Conceptions of the Oglala Dakota." *University of Nebraska Studies* 26, nos. 3–4 (1927): 79–123.

Bradbury, John B. *Travels in the Interior of America, 1809–1811*. Vol. 5 of *Early Western Travels, 1748–1846*, ed. Rueben Gold Thwaites. 32 vols. Cleveland: Arthur H. Clark, 1904–7.

Brininstool, E. A. *Crazy Horse: The Invincible Ogalalla Sioux Chief*. Los Angeles: Wentzel, 1949.

———. *Fighting Red Cloud's Warriors*. Columbus OH: Hunter-Trader-Trapper, 1926.

Brown, Joseph Epes. "Becoming Part of It." In *I Become Part of It: Sacred Dimensions in Native American Life*, ed. D. M. Dooling and Paul Jordan-Smith, pp. 9–20. New York: Parabola Books, 1989.

Burpee, Lawrence J., ed. *Journals and Letters of Pierre Gaultier de Varennes de la Verendrye and His Sons*. Toronto: Champlain Society, 1927.

Clow, Richmond L. "The Brulé Indian Agencies, 1868–1878." *South Dakota Department of Historical Report and Historical Collections* 36 (1972): 143–204.

———. "Mad Bear: William S. Harney and the Sioux Expedition of 1855–1856." *Nebraska History* 61 (summer 1980): 133–51.

Connell, Evan S. *Son of the Morning Star: Custer and the Little Bighorn*. New York: Harper and Row, 1984.

Culbertson, Thaddeus A. *Journal of an Expedition to the Mauvaises Terres and the Upper Missouri in 1850*. Ed. John Francis McDermott. Smithsonian Institution, Bureau of American Ethnology Bulletin 147. Washington DC, 1952.

Danziger, Edmund J., Jr. "The Indian Office during the Civil War: Impotence in Indian Affairs." *South Dakota History* 5 (1974): 52–72.

———. *Indians and Bureaucrats: Administering the Reservation Policy During the Civil War*. Urbana: University of Illinois Press, 1974.

Deloria, Ella C. *Speaking of Indians*. New York: Friendship Press, 1944.

———. "The Sun Dance of the Oglala Sioux." *Journal of American Folklore* 42 (1929): 354–413.

DeMallie, Rayond J. "American Indian Treaty Making." *American Indian Journal* 3 (January 1977): 2–10.

———. "Change in American Indian Kinship Systems: The Dakota." In *Currents in Anthropology: Essays in Honor of Sol Tax,* ed. Robert Hinshaw, pp. 221–41. The Hague: Mouton, 1979.

———. "Lakota Ghost Dance: An Ethnohistorical Account." *Pacific Historical Review* 51 (November 1982): 385–405.

———. "Male and Female in Traditional Lakota Culture." In *The Hidden Half: Studies of Plains Indian Women,* ed. Patricia Albers and Beatrice Medicine, pp. 237–65. New York: University Press of America, 1983.

———. "Pine Ridge Economy: Cultural and Historical Perspectives." In *American Indian Economic Development,* ed. Sam Stanley, pp. 237–312. The Hague: Mouton, 1978.

———. "Sioux Ethnohistory: A Methodological Critique." *Journal of Ethnic Studies* 4 (fall 1976): 77–84.

———. "Sioux Social Organization: Some Ethnohistorical Considerations." Paper presented at the D'Arcy McNickle Center for the History of the American Indian, Newberry Library, Chicago, 6 March 1986. Manuscript supplied courtesy of the author.

———. "Touching the Pen: Plains Indian Treaty Councils in Ethnohistorical Perspective." In *Ethnicity on the Great Plains,* ed. Frederick C. Luebke, pp. 38–53. Lincoln: University of Nebraska Press, 1980.

DeMallie, Rayond J., ed. "Nicollet's Notes on the Dakota." In *Joseph N. Nicollet on the Plains and Prairies,* ed. Edmund C. Bray and Martha Coleman Bray, pp. 250–81. St. Paul: Minnesota Historical Society, 1976.

DeMallie, Raymond J., and Douglas R. Parks, eds. *Sioux Indian Religion.* Norman: University of Oklahoma Press, 1987.

Denig, Edwin T. *Five Indian Tribes of the Upper Missouri: Sioux, Arickaras, Assiniboines, Crees, Crows.* Norman: University of Oklahoma Press, 1930.

DeSmet, Pierre Jean. *Life, Letters, and Travels of Father Pierre Jean De Smet.* 4 vols. Ed. Hiram M. Chittenden and A. T. Richardson. New York: Francis P. Harper, 1905.

———. *Oregon Missions and Travels over the Rocky Mountains in 1845–46.* New York: Edward Dunigan, 1847.

Dippie, Brian W. *Custer's Last Stand: The Anatomy of an American Myth.* Missoula: University of Montana Press, 1976.

———. "'What Will Congress Do about It?' The Congressional Reaction to the Little Big Horn Disaster." *North Dakota History* 37 (1970): 161–89.

Dodge, Richard Irving. *Our Wild Indians: Thirty Three Years' Personal Experience among the Red Men of the Great West.* 1882. Reprint. Freeport NY: Books for Libraries, 1970.

Dooling, D. M., and Paul Jordan-Smith, eds. *I Become Part of It: Sacred Dimensions in Native American Life.* New York: Parabola Books, 1989.

Dorsey, James Owen. *Siouan Sociology: A Posthumous Paper.* Smithsonian Institution, Bureau of American Ethnology Annual Report 15, pp. 207–44. Washington DC, 1897.

———. "The Social Organization of the Siouan Tribes." *Journal of American Folklore* 4 (1891): 257–63.

Eastman, Mary. *Dahcotah; or, Life and Legends of the Sioux Around Fort Snelling.* New York: John Wesley, 1849.

Eggan, Fred, ed. *Social Anthropology of North American Tribes.* Chicago: University of Chicago Press, 1955.

Ellis, Richard N. *General Pope and U.S. Indian Policy.* Albuquerque: University of New Mexico Press, 1970.

Etienne, Mona, and Eleanor Leacock, eds. *Women and Colonization: Anthropological Perspectives.* New York: Praeger, 1980.

Ewers, John C. *Indian Life on the Upper Missouri.* Norman: University of Oklahoma Press, 1968.

Fay, George E., ed. *Treaties and Land Cessions between the Bands of Sioux and the USA, 1805–1906.* University of Northern Colorado Museum of Anthropology, Occasional Publications in Anthropology, Ethnology, Series 24. Greeley CO, 1872.

Feraca, Stephen E. "The Political Status of the Early Bands and Modern Communities of the Oglala Dakota." *W. H. Over Museum News* 27 (1966): 11–26.

Fowler, Loretta. *Arapahoe Politics: Symbols in Crises of Authority, 1851–1978.* Lincoln: University of Nebraska Press, 1982.

Fritz, Henry E. "The Board of Indian Commissioners and Ethnocentric Reform, 1878–1893." In *Indian-White Relations: A Persistent Paradox,* ed. Jane F. Smith and Robert M. Kvasnicka, pp. 57–78. Washington DC: Howard University Press, 1976.

———. *The Movement for Indian Assimilation, 1860–1890.* Philadelphia: University of Pennsylvania Press, 1963.

Frémont, John C. *Narrative of the Exploring Expedition to the Rocky Mountains in the Year 1842 and to Oregon and North California in the Years 1843–44.* New York: D. Appleton, 1846.

Goetzmann, William H. *Exploration and Empire: The Explorer and the Scientist in the Winning of the American West.* New York: Alfred A. Knopf, 1966.

Goldfrank, Esther S. "Historic Change and Social Character: A Study of the Teton Dakota." *American Anthropologist* 45 (1943): 67–83.

Graham, W. A. *The Custer Myth: A Source Book of Custeriana.* Lincoln: University of Nebraska Press, 1986.

———. *The Story of the Little Big Horn: Custer's Last Fight.* Lincoln: University of Nebraska Press, 1988.

Grange, Roger T., Jr. "Fort Robinson, Outpost on the Plains." *Nebraska History* 39 (September 1958): 191–240.

———. "The Garnier Oglala Winter Count." *Plains Anthropologist* 8, no. 20 (May 1963): 74–79.

Gray, John S. *Custer's Last Campaign: Mitch Boyer and the Little Bighorn Reconstructed.* Lincoln: University of Nebraska Press, 1991.

Green, Rayna. "The Pocahontas Perplex: The Image of Indian Women in American Culture." *Massachusetts Review* 16 (1975): 698–714.

Gregg, Josiah. *Commerce of the Prairies; or, The Journal of a Santa Fe Trader during Eight Expeditions across the Great Western Prairies, and a Residence of Nearly Nine Years in Northern Mexico.* 2 vols. New York: Henry G. Langley, 1844. Reprint, Ann Arbor MI: University Microfilms, 1966.

Grumet, Robert Steven. "Sunksquaws, Shamans, and Tradeswomen: Middle Atlantic Coastal Algonkian Women during the Seventeenth and Eighteenth Centuries." In *Women and Colonization: Anthropological Perspectives,* eds. Mona Etienne and Eleanor Leacock, pp. 43–62. New York: Praeger, 1980.

Hafen, LeRoy R. "Thomas Fitzpatrick and the First Indian Agency of the Upper Platte and Arkansas." *Mississippi Valley Historical Review* 15 (December 1928): 374–84.

Hafen, LeRoy R., ed. *The Mountain Men and the Fur Trade of the Far West: Biographical Sketches of the Participants by Scholars of the Subject.* 10 volumes. Glendale CA: Arthur H. Clark, 1966.

Hafen, LeRoy R., and Ann Hafen, eds. *Powder River Campaigns; Sawyer's Expedition of 1865: A Documentary Account Comprising Official Reports, Diaries, Contemporary Newspaper Accounts and Personal Narratives.* Vol. 12 of *The Far West and the Rockies Historical Series, 1820–1875.* Glendale CA: Arthur H. Clark, 1961.

———. *Relations with the Indians of the Plains, 1857–1861: A Documentary Account of the Military Campaigns, and Negotiations of Indian Agents, etc.* Glendale CA: Arthur H. Clark, 1959.

Hafen, LeRoy R., and Francis Marion Young. *Fort Laramie and the Pageant of the West, 1834–1890.* Glendale CA: Arthur H. Clark, 1938. Reprint, Lincoln: University of Nebraska Press, 1984.

Hardoff, Richard G., ed. *Lakota Recollections of the Custer Fight: New Sources of Indian-Military History.* Spokane WA: Arthur H. Clark, 1991.

Hassrick, Royal B. *The Sioux: Life and Customs of a Warrior Society.* Norman: University of Oklahoma Press, 1964.

———. "Teton Sioux Kinship System." *American Anthropologist* 46 (1944): 336–47.

Hebard, Grace Raymond, and E. A. Brininstool. *The Bozeman Trail: Historical Accounts of the Blazing of the Overland Routes into the Northwest and the Fights with Red Cloud's Warriors.* 2 vols. Cleveland: Arthur H. Clark, 1922.

Hennepin, Louis. *A Description of Louisiana, Translated from the Edition of 1683 and Compared with the "Nouvelle Decouverte," the La Salle Documents, and Other Contemporary Papers.* Trans. John Gilmary Shea. New York: John G. Shea, 1880.

———. *A New Discovery of a Vast Country in America.* Ed. Reuben Gold Thwaites. 2 vols. Chicago: A. C. McClurg, 1903.

Hinman, Eleanor H. "Oglala Sources on the Life of Crazy Horse." *Nebraska History* 57 (winter 1976): 1–51.

Hoebel, E. Adamson. *The Cheyennes; Indians of the Great Plains.* New York: Holt, Rinehart, and Winston, 1978.

Hoig, Stan. *The Sand Creek Massacre.* Norman: University of Oklahoma Press, 1962.

Hoopes, Alban W. *The Road to the Little Big Horn—and Beyond.* New York: Vantage Press, 1975.

———. "Thomas S. Twiss: Indian Agent on the Upper Platte, 1855–1861," *Mississippi Valley Historical Review* 20 (December 1933): 353–64.

Howe, M. A. DeWolfe. *Life and Labors of Bishop Hare, Apostle to the Sioux.* New York: Sturgis and Walton, 1912.

Hoxie, Frederick E., ed. *Indians in American History.* Arlington Heights IL: Harlan Davidson, 1988.

Hutton, Andrew Paul, ed. *The Custer Reader.* Lincoln: University of Nebraska Press, 1992.

Hyde, George E. *Red Cloud's Folk: A History of the Oglala Sioux*. 1937. Norman: University of Oklahoma Press, 1957.

———. *A Sioux Chronicle*. Norman: University of Oklahoma Press, 1956.

———. *Spotted Tail's Folk: A History of the Brulé Sioux*. Norman: University of Oklahoma Press, 1961.

Jackson, Donald, ed. *Letters of the Lewis and Clark Expedition with Related Documents, 1783–1854*. 2nd (enlarged) ed. 2 vols. Urbana: University of Illinois Press, 1978.

Jackson, Donald, and Mary Lee Spence, eds. *Travels from 1838 to 1844*. Vol. 1 of *The Expeditions of John Charles Frémont*. Urbana: University of Illinois Press, 1970.

Jahner, Elaine A. "The Spiritual Landscape." In *I Become Part of It: Sacred Dimensions in Native American Life,* ed. D. M. Dooling and Paul Jordan-Smith, pp. 193–203. New York: Parabola Books, 1989.

James, Edwin. *James's Account of Stephen H. Long's Expedition, Part IV, 1819–1820*. Vol. 17 of *Early Western Travels, 1748–1846*, ed. Reuben Gold Thwaites. 32 vols. Cleveland: Arthur H. Clark, 1904–7.

Johnson, Elden, ed. *Aspects of Upper Great Lakes Anthropology: Papers in Honor of Lloyd A. Wilford*. St. Paul: Minnesota Historical Society Press, 1974.

Kappler, Charles J. *Indian Affairs: Laws and Treaties*. 5 vols. Washington DC: Government Printing Office, 1904.

Keating, William H. *Narrative of an Expedition to the Source of the St. Peter's River*. 2 vols. 1824. Minneapolis: Ross and Haines, 1959.

Kehoe, Alice "The Shackles of Tradition." In *The Hidden Half: Studies of Plains Indian Women,* ed. Patricia Albers and Beatrice Medicine, pp. 53–70. New York: University Press of America, 1983.

Kelsey, Harry. "The Doolittle Report of 1867: Its Preparation and Shortcomings." *Arizona and the West* 17 (summer 1975): 107–20.

Kvasnicka, Robert M., and Herman H. Viola, eds. *The Commissioners of Indian Affairs, 1824–1977*. Lincoln: University of Nebraska Press, 1979.

Larpenteur, Charles. *Forty Years a Fur Trader on the Upper Missouri: The Personal Narrative of Charles Larpenteur*. Ed. Elliott Coues. 2 vols. New York: Francis P. Harper, 1898.

Lewis, Meriwether, and William Clark. *The Original Journals of the Lewis and Clark Expedition, 1804–1806*. Ed. Reuben Gold Thwaites. 8 vols. New York: Antiquarian, 1904–5.

Lottinville, Savoie, ed., *Paul Wilhelm, Duke of Württemberg: Travels in North America, 1822–1824*. Norman: University of Oklahoma Press, 1973.

## Bibliography

Lowe, Percival G. *Five Years a Dragoon ('49 to '54) and Other Adventures on the Great Plains.* Ed. Donald Russell. Kansas City MO, 1906. Reprint, Norman: University of Oklahoma Press, 1965.

Lowie, Robert H. "Plains Indian Age-Societies: Historical and Comparative Summary." American Museum of Natural History, Anthropological Papers 11, part 13, pp. 877–992. Washington DC, 1916.

———. "Some Aspects of Political Organization among the American Aborigines." *Journal of the Royal Anthropological Institute* 78, nos. 1–2 (1948): 11–24.

Luebke, Frederick C. *Ethnicity on the Great Plains.* Lincoln: University of Nebraska Press, 1980.

Mardock, Richard. *The Reformers and the American Indians.* Columbia: University of Missouri Press, 1971.

Marsh, Othniel Charles. *A Statement of Affairs at Red Cloud Agency, Made to the President of the United States.* N.p., 1875.

Mattingly, Arthur P. "The Great Plains Peace Commission of 1867." *Journal of the West* 15 (July 1976): 23–37.

Mattison, Ray H. "The Harney Expedition against the Sioux: The Journal of Captain John B. S. Todd." *Nebraska History* 43, no. 2 (June 1962): 89–130.

Maximilian, Prince of Wied. *Travels in the Interior of North America, 1832–1834.* Vol. 22 of *Early Western Travels, 1748–1846,* ed. Reuben Gold Thwaites. Cleveland: Arthur H. Clark, 1904–7.

McDermott, Francis, ed. *The Frontier Re-Examined.* Urbana: University of Illinois Press, 1967.

McDermott, John D. "James Bordeaux." In vol. 5 of *The Mountain Men and the Fur Trade of the Far West: Biographical Sketches of the Participants by Scholars of the Subject,* ed. LeRoy R. Hafen, pp. 65–80. Glendale CA: Arthur H. Clark, 1966.

———. "Joseph Bissonette." In vol. 4 of *The Mountain Men and the Fur Trade of the Far West: Biographical Sketches of the Participants by Scholars of the Subject,* ed. LeRoy R. Hafen, pp. 49–60. Glendale CA: Arthur H. Clark, 1966.

McFarling, Lloyd, ed. *Exploring the Northern Plains, 1804–1876.* Caldwell ID: Caxton, 1955.

McGillycuddy, Julia. *McGillycuddy, Agent: A Biography of Dr. Valentine T. McGillycuddy.* Stanford: Stanford University Press, 1940.

Mead, Margaret, ed. *Cooperation and Competition among Primitive Peoples.* Boston: Beacon, 1937.

Mirsky, Jeanette. "The Dakota." In *Cooperation and Competition among Primitive Peoples,* ed. Margaret Mead, pp. 382–427. Boston: Beacon, 1937.

Moorehead, Warren K. "The Passing of Red Cloud." *Kansas State Historical Society Transactions* 10 (1907–8): 295–311.

Munkres, Robert L. "Indian-White Contact before 1870: Cultural Factors in Conflict." *Journal of the West* 10 (July 1971): 439–73.

Murray, Robert A. *Military Posts in the Powder River Country of Wyoming, 1865–1894.* Lincoln: University of Nebraska Press, 1968.

———. "Treaty Presents at Fort Laramie, 1867–68: Prices and Quantities from the Seth E. Ward Ledger," *Museum of the Fur Trade Quarterly* 13, no. 3 (fall 1977): 1–5.

Nadeau, Remi. *Fort Laramie and the Sioux Indians.* Englewood Cliffs NJ: Prentice-Hall, 1967.

Nasatir, A. P., ed. *Before Lewis and Clark: Documents Illustrating the History of the Missouri, 1785–1804.* 2 vols. St. Louis: St. Louis Historical Documents Foundation, 1952.

Nichols, David A. *Lincoln and the Indians: Civil War Policy and Politics.* Columbia: University of Missouri Press, 1978.

Olson, James C. *Red Cloud and the Sioux Problem.* Lincoln: University of Nebraska Press, 1965.

Ortiz, Alfonso. "Indian-White Relations: A View from the Other Side of the 'Frontier.'" In *Indians in American History,* ed. Frederick E. Hoxie, pp. 1–16. Arlington Heights IL: Harlan Davidson, 1988.

Parker, John, ed. *The Journals of Jonathan Carver and Related Documents, 1766–1770.* St. Paul: Minnesota Historical Society Press, 1976.

Parkman, Francis. "The Oglala Sioux." In *Exploring the Northern Plains, 1804–1876,* ed. Lloyd McFarling, pp. 129–40. Caldwell ID: Caxton, 1955.

Pennington, Robert. "An Analysis of the Political Structure of the Teton Dakota Tribe of North America." *North Dakota History* 20 (July 1953): 146–66.

Pike, Zebulon Montgomery. *The Journals of Zebulon Montgomery Pike with Letters and Related Documents.* Ed. Donald Jackson. 2 vols. Norman: University of Oklahoma Press, 1966.

Pilcher, Joshua. "The Indian Tribes of the Upper Missouri." In *Exploring the Northern Plains, 1804–1876,* ed. Lloyd McFarling, pp. 67–76. Caldwell ID: Caxton, 1955.

Pond, Samuel W. "The Dakotas or Sioux in Minnesota As They Were in 1834." *Minnesota Historical Society Collections* 12 (1908): 319–501.

Poole, DeWitt Clinton. *Among the Sioux of Dakota; Eighteen Months' Experience As an Indian Agent.* New York: D. Van Nostrand, 1881.

Porter, Joseph C. *Paper Medicine Man: John Gregory Bourke and His American West.* Norman: University of Oklahoma Press, 1986.

Powell, Peter J. *People of the Sacred Mountain.* 2 vols. New York: Harper and Row, 1981.

———. *Sweet Medicine: The Continuing Role of the Sacred Arrows, the Sun Dance, and the Sacred Buffalo Hat in Northern Cheyenne History.* 2 vols. Norman: University of Oklahoma Press, 1969.

Powers, William K. *Oglala Religion.* Lincoln: University of Nebraska Press, 1977.

———. *Yuwipi: Vision and Experience in Oglala Religion.* Lincoln: University of Nebraska Press, 1982.

Priest, Loring B. *Uncle Sam's Stepchildren: The Reformation of U.S. Indian Policy, 1865–1887.* New Brunswick NJ: Rutgers University Press, 1942.

*Proceedings of the Great Peace Commission of 1867–1868.* Washington DC: Institute for the Development of Indian Law, 1975.

Prucha, Francis Paul. *American Indian Policy in Crisis: Christian Reformers and the Indian, 1865–1900.* Norman: University of Oklahoma Press, 1976.

———. *The Churches and the Indian Schools, 1888–1912.* Lincoln: University of Nebraska Press, 1979.

Prucha, Francis Paul, comp. *Documents of U.S. Indian Policy.* Lincoln: University of Nebraska Press, 1975.

Quaife, Milo M., ed. *The Journals of Captain Meriwether Lewis and Sergeant John Ordway Kept on the Expedition of Western Exploration, 1803–1806.* Madison WI: State Historical Society, 1916.

Radisson, Pierre Esprit. *Voyages of Pierre E. Radisson: Being an Account of His Travels and Experiences among the North American Indians from 1652–1684.* Ed. Gideon D. Scull. New York: B. Franklin, 1943.

Rahill, Peter J. *Catholic Indian Missions and Grant's Peace Policy, 1870–1884.* Washington DC: Catholic University Press, 1953.

*Report of the Special Commission Appointed to Investigate the Affairs of the Red Cloud Indian Agency, July 1875.* Washington DC: Government Printing Office, 1875.

Richardson, James D., comp. *A Compilation of the Messages and Papers of the Presidents, 1789–1897.* 10 vols. Washington DC: Government Printing Office, 1896–99.

Riggs, Stephan R. "Journal of a Tour from Lac-Qui-Parle to the Missouri

Bibliography

River." *Collections of the South Dakota Department of History* 13 (1926): 330–44.

Ripich, Carol A. "Joseph W. Wham and the Red Cloud Agency, 1871." *Arizona and the West* 12 (1970): 325–38.

Robinson, Doane. "The Education of Red Cloud." *Collections of the South Dakota Department of History* 12 (1924): 156–78.

———. *A History of the Dakota or Sioux Indians*. Minneapolis: Ross and Haines, 1956.

Robinson, Doane, ed. "Fort Tecumseh and Fort Pierre Journals and Letter Books." *Collections of the South Dakota Department of History* 9 (1918): 69–239.

Ruby, Robert H. *The Oglala Sioux: Warriors in Transition*. New York: Vantage Press, 1955.

Sage, Rufus B. *Rocky Mountain Life; or, Startling Scenes and Perilous Adventures in the Far West, during an Expedition of Three Years*. Boston: Wentworth, 1857.

Sandoz, Mari. *Crazy Horse: The Strange Man of the Oglalas*. New York: Alfred A. Knopf, 1942. Reprint, Lincoln: University of Nebraska Press, 1961.

Shaw, Reuben Cole. *Across the Plains in Forty Nine*. Ed. Milo M. Quaife. Chicago: Lakeside Press, 1948.

Smith, Jane F., and Robert M. Kvasnicka, eds. *Indian-White Relations: A Persistent Paradox*. Washington DC: Howard University Press, 1976.

Smith, Martin Greer. "Political Organization of the Plains Indians." *Nebraska University Studies* 24 (1925): 1–84.

Smith, Sherry. "The Bozeman: Trail to Death and Glory." *Annals of Wyoming* 55 (spring 1983): 32–50.

Sneider, Mary Jane. "Women's Work: An Examination of Women's Roles in Plains Indian Arts and Crafts." In *The Hidden Half: Studies of Plains Indian Women*, ed. Patricia Albers and Beatrice Medicine, pp. 101–21. New York: University Press of America, 1983.

Springer, Charles H. *Soldiering in Sioux Country, 1865*. Ed. Benjamin Franklin Cooling III. San Diego: Frontier Heritage Press, 1971.

Standing Bear, Luther. *Land of the Spotted Eagle*. Lincoln: University of Nebraska Press, 1978.

———. *My People the Sioux*. Lincoln: University of Nebraska Press, 1975.

Stedman, Raymond William. *Shadows of the Indian: Stereotypes in American Culture*. Norman: University of Oklahoma Press, 1982.

Stevenson, C. Stanley, ed. "Expeditions into Dakota, 1844–45." *Collections of the South Dakota Department of History* 9 (1918): 47–375.

Stewart, Edgar L. *Custer's Luck*. Norman: University of Oklahoma Press, 1955.

Strayer, Brian. "Fur Trappers' Attitudes toward the Upper Missouri Sioux, 1820–1860." *Indian Historian* 12, no. 4 (1979): 34–40.

Tatum, Lawrie. *Our Red Brothers and the Peace Policy of U.S. Grant*. Lincoln: University of Nebraska Press, 1970.

Thwaites, Reuben Gold, ed. *Early Western Travels, 1748–1846: A Series of Annotated Reprints of Some of the Best and Rarest Contemporary Volumes of Travel, Descriptive of the Aborigines and Social and Economic Conditions in the Middle and Far West, during the Period of Early American Settlement*. 32 vols. Cleveland: Arthur H. Clark, 1904–7.

———. *The Jesuit Relations and Allied Documents: Travels and Explorations of the Jesuit Missionaries in New France, 1610–1791*. 73 vols. Cleveland: Burrows Brothers, 1896–1901.

Trennert, Robert A. *Alternative to Extinction: Federal Indian Policy and the Beginnings of the Reservation System, 1846–1851*. Philadelphia: Temple University Press, 1975.

Twiss, Thomas S. "Letter of Thomas S. Twiss, Indian Agent at Deer Creek." *Annals of Wyoming* 17 (July 1945): 148–52.

Unrau, William E. "The Civilian as Indian Agent: Villain or Victim?" *Western Historical Quarterly* 3 (October 1972): 405–20.

Unrau, William E., ed. *Tending the Talking Wire: A Buck Soldier's View of Indian Country, 1863–1866*. Salt Lake City: University of Utah Press, 1979.

Unruh, John D., Jr. *The Plains Across: The Overland Emigrants and the Trans-Mississippi West, 1840–1860*. Urbana: University of Illinois Press, 1979.

Utley, Robert M. "The Celebrated Peace Policy of General Grant." *North Dakota History* 20 (July 1953): 121–42.

———. *Frontier Regulars: The U.S. Army and the Indian, 1866–1891*. New York: Macmillan, 1973.

———. *Frontiersmen in Blue: The U.S. Army and the Indian, 1848–1865*. New York: Macmillan, 1967.

———. *The Indian Frontier of the American West, 1846–1890*. Albuquerque: University of New Mexico Press, 1984.

———. *The Last Days of the Sioux Nation*. New Haven CT: Yale University Press, 1963.

Viola, Herman J. *Diplomats in Buckskins: A History of Indian Delegations in Washington City*. Washington DC: Smithsonian Institution Press, 1981.

## Bibliography

Walker, James R. *Lakota Belief and Ritual.* Ed. Raymond J. DeMallie and Elaine A. Jahner. Lincoln: University of Nebraska Press, 1980.

———. *Lakota Myth.* Ed. Elaine A. Jahner. Lincoln: University of Nebraska Press, 1983.

———. *Lakota Society.* Ed. Raymond J. DeMallie. Lincoln: University of Nebraska Press, 1982.

———. "Oglala Kinship Terms." *American Anthropologist* 16 (1914): 96–109.

———. "The Sun Dance and Other Ceremonies of the Oglala Division of the Teton Dakota." American Museum of Natural History, Anthropological Papers 16, part 2, pp. 50–221. Washington DC, 1917.

Washburn, Wilcomb E., ed. *The American Indian and the U.S.: A Documentary History.* 4 vols. New York: Random House, 1973.

Wedel, Mildred Mott. "Le Sueur and the Dakota Sioux." In *Aspects of Upper Great Lakes Anthropology: Essays in Honor of Lloyd A. Wilford,* ed. Elden Johnson, pp. 157–71. St. Paul: Minnesota Historical Society Press, 1974.

Weist, Katherine M. "Beasts of Burden and Menial Slaves." In *The Hidden Half: Studies of Plains Indian Women,* ed. Patricia Albers and Beatrice Medicine, pp. 29–52. New York: University Press of America, 1983.

Wells, Robin F. "Plains Indian Political Structure: A Comparative Study." Kroeber Anthropological Society, Papers 24 (1961): 1–16.

Welsh, Herbert. *Civilization among the Sioux Indians; Report of a Visit to Some of the Sioux Reservations of South Dakota and Nebraska.* Philadelphia: Office of the Indian Rights Association, 1893.

———. *Four Weeks among Some of the Sioux Tribes of Dakota and Nebraska.* Philadelphia: Office of the Indian Rights Association, 1882.

Welsh, William. *Report of a Visit to Spotted Tail's Tribe of Brulé Sioux Indians, the Yankton and Santee Sioux, Ponkas and the Chippewas of Minnesota in September, 1870.* Philadelphia: McCalla and Stavely, 1870.

———. *Report of a Visit to the Sioux and Ponca on the Missouri River.* Washington DC: Government Printing Office, 1872.

White, Richard. "The Winning of the West: The Expansion of the Western Sioux in the Eighteenth and Nineteenth Centuries." *Journal of American History* 65 (September 1978): 319–43.

Wissler, Clark. "Societies and Ceremonial Associations in the Oglala Division of the Teton-Dakota." American Museum of Natural History, Anthropological Papers 11, part 1, pp. 1–99. Washington DC, 1912.

# Index

Fort Philip Kearny, 61, 64–66, 69, 79, 81, 82
Fort Pierre, xii, 48–50; council of 1856 at, 41–43
Fort Platte, 10
Fort Randall, 79, 80
Fort Recovery, 48
Fort Reno, 61, 64, 79, 81–82
Fort Rice, 77, 80
Fort Riley, 62
Fort Sedgwick, 61, 70
Fort Sidney, 121
Fort Sully, 73, 80; council of 1865 at, 57–58
Fort Tecumseh, 22
Fort Thompson, 73
Fort Wallace, 62
Four Bears, 189n
Frémont, John C., 10, 48–49
Full Wolf, 193n

Gadsden Purchase, 28
Garnett, Richard (Lt.), 37
Garnett, William, 23, 136, 142, 157, 160, 205n
Garnier, John, 21
Garrou, Charles, 77, 80–81
Ghost Heart, 189n
Girton, William, 26
giveaway, 3
Goes and Comes, 198n
Good Bull, 204n
Good Voice Crow, 204n
Gopher (Oglala band), 25
Gordon, George (Maj.), 158
Grant, Ulysses S., 69, 85–86, 88, 91, 104, 110, 140–41
Grass, 93–94, 189n
Grattan, John (Lt.), 38–40
Gray Bear, 93
Gray Eyes, 137

Gray Goose (Thomas Tyon), xi, 6–7
Great Sioux Reservation, 80, 86–87, 91, 101–2, 106–7, 114, 132, 175
Greenwood, A. B., 47
Guadalupe Hidalgo, Treaty of, 28
Guernsey, Orrin, 57

Hammond, J. H., 166–67
Hancock, William (Gen.), 65
Harney, William (Gen.), 40–42, 44, 50, 72, 76, 79, 87, 135; meeting with Lakotas, 42–43
Harvey, Thomas, 31
Hastings, James, 153
Hat Creek, 114
Hayes, Rutherford B., 163, 166
Hayt, Ezra, 163, 166, 168–69, 171
headmen, 11, 67
head shirtwearer, 17, 96
He Dog, 67–68, 158, 163
Hennepin, Louis, xii, 5
He Takes the Enemy, 204n
High Bear, 204n
High Eagle, 82–83
High Eagle, Robert, 9, 11
High Forehead (Straight Foretop), 37, 39, 41
High Foretop, 128
High Lance, 201n
High Wolf, 98, 110, 116, 125–26, 189n, 191n, 201n, 204n, 206n; as delegate to Washington DC, 89–90, 109; as public spokesman, 80
Hines, C. M., 64
Hoffman, William (Col.), 42
Holy Bald Eagle. *See* Black Twin
holy man (*wicasa wakan*), 2, 11
Horse Creek Council (1851). *See* Fort Laramie: council of 1851 at
Howard, E. A., 128
*hunka*, 4–5, 13

9 780803 287587